CW00816248

THE ART OF
BATTING

THE ART OF BATTING

THE CRAFT OF CRICKET'S GREATEST RUN SCORERS

JARROD KIMBER

BLOOMSBURY SPORT

LONDON · OXFORD · NEW YORK · NEW DELHI · SYDNEY

BLOOMSBURY SPORT
Bloomsbury Publishing Plc
50 Bedford Square, London, WC1B 3DP, UK
Bloomsbury Publishing Ireland Limited
29 Earlsfort Terrace, Dublin 2, D02 AY28, Ireland

BLOOMSBURY, BLOOMSBURY SPORT and the Diana logo are trademarks of Bloomsbury
Publishing Plc

First published in Great Britain 2025

A catalogue record for this book is available from the British Library

Library of Congress Cataloguing-in-Publication data has been applied for

ISBN: HB: 978-1-3994-1654-2; TPB: 978-1-3994-1652-8; eBook: 978-1-3994-1656-6

2 4 6 8 10 9 7 5 3 1

Typeset in Bembo Std by Deanta Global Publishing Services, Chennai, India
Printed and bound in Great Britain by Clays Ltd, Elcograf S.p.A.

For PK and Lynn.

My favourite No. 11 and the scorer he never bothered.

CONTENTS

INTRODUCTION

The man who built modern batting

'This guy was just born to bat.' – Rahul Dravid

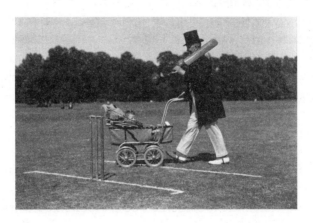

An enormous doctor with a blood-soaked gown covering his dad bod stands in the doorway to greet you. His impressive beard contains flecks of bone, and he holds a rusty trephine that still has little chunks of skull from his last patient. This is a man who believes that pus is a natural part of the healing process, who doesn't wash up during procedures and thinks 'bad air' is responsible for infections around surgical wounds.

During the late 1800s, doctors still used leeches, amputations were common and the use of carbolic acid to clean wounds was normal. Yet, despite all that, this was groundbreaking medical science. It would not have looked that way to us, so judging it by what we know today is unfair. All those mistakes led to the medical science that now saves millions of lives.

One of those medical practitioners was W.G. Grace, who in the winter months of the 1880s was a doctor in Bristol. When the

Englishman wasn't doing that, he was the greatest batter of the entire 1800s. The thought of seeing someone who only practised for a couple of months a year (and wasn't the sort to listen to others) is horrifying, but his patients were too star-struck or infected to worry. If someone was to unnecessarily remove your leg without antiseptic or anaesthesia, it might as well be the greatest batter that ever lived.

If you have a look at Grace batting – from the rare footage that exists – he may not look that special. From a batting perspective, he's a little like a man using a bloodletting fleam to cut open your veins in the hope it will cure your headache.

There are caveats here. W.G. was 47 years old when the Lumière brothers invented moving pictures in 1895. He was well and truly past his best when a camera picked up his batting. There is footage from 1905 via British Movietone showing him going through some warm-ups. By this stage, W.G. was averaging only 19 for the year; his lowest total in 41 English summers and one in Australia. Of course, by then he was ancient – 56 years old – and it's remarkable that he was still playing first-class cricket at all. Until that year, he was still doing more than well enough to keep his place.

While not at the top of his form, he could still bat at a decent level.

When you watch the footage, he doesn't look like a batting genius. His feet are too close together, almost next to each other. His open stance, with the left foot out of the way of the right, is upright and tall. And his bat face is open, with a bottom-hand-heavy grip. Everything about him looks like he wants to hit to the off side, and when he plays to the leg, he almost does so inside out. The off-side shots have power and certainty. The ones to the leg are a little more jittery, almost polite in comparison.

If I showed you this footage and told you he was the greatest batter of all time, there is no way you would believe me (unless the beard gave it away). Grace played in a way that looks to modern eyes more like an uncle at a family barbecue than an all-time great.

Like those early doctors, Grace was laying down the early science of batting, and so much of this came from a stroke of luck. His family's material wealth and status, and the coaching and facilities that came with it all, were an advantage. But Grace also lived in an era when over- and under-arm bowling coexisted.

He was a kid learning to play both. They each had their challenges: over-arm bowling was superior but was in its early development stage in the 1850s, and under-arm had the advantage of terrible pitches.

But the real key here is the length. For about 70 years, there had been front-foot and back-foot players. What there hadn't been is players who made that decision based on where the ball pitched. They were premeditating. And this was easier when most bowlers delivered under-arm. Once that arm went out to round – shoulder height – and then jumped up again to nearer the ear, deciding beforehand what you were going to do became a nightmare.

Grace simply did what eight-year-olds can now do around the world. When the ball was full, he'd come forward. When it was short – which was happening more frequently – he'd go back. If it seems simple now, it was revolutionary then. Until that point, cricket was a bowlers' game.

Great batters before Grace existed. For instance, the greatest batters before him were Fuller Pilch, Nicholas Felix and Alfred Mynn. They all dominated England cricket in the first half of the 19th century. In first-class cricket, they averaged 18.6, 18.1 and 13.4. Grace averaged 39.4, despite playing for over 44 years and making 54,000 runs.

Grace was as dominant over other players of his era as the Australian legend Don Bradman was of his, putting him on the level of a man who averaged 99.94 in Tests.

His breakout year, 1866, was his second. Grace played eight games, scoring over 500 runs and averaging 52. No one else made that many runs while averaging over 33. He was 17 years old. A decade later, in 1876, he made twice as many runs as the next best player; only one other batter averaged 42 from over 500 runs. In eight days he scored 839 runs: 344 (a world record), 177 and 318 not out. In 1895 he made the most runs again, in his 30th first-class season. Of those making over 500 runs, he was one of two with more than a 50-run average. England player Archie MacLaren averaged 0.2 runs more than Grace that year. And to beat the big man, MacLaren had to score 424 in one first-class innings, the world record.

From 1868 to 1880, he topped the first-class averages 10 times. Between 1868 and 1876, he scored 54 first-class hundreds; the next highest didn't even manage 10. His peak was Everest.

All this proves Grace was the best batter for three straight decades by a huge margin, and it is not even close. But here is my favourite stat ever. In 1871, 52 first-class matches were played in England. That includes County cricket, university, Gentlemen v Players and other nonsense games that had a first-class status that summer. All the other batters combined made seven hundreds. Grace made 10.

He didn't just outscore other players, he outscored all of cricket.

Grace's Test record does not instantly jump out. He played his last Test in 1899 after making his debut in 1880. England had played 66 matches by then, but he didn't see Test cricket as the ultimate, so he appeared in only 22. Think of him more like a great early-2000s batter who thought T20 was beneath them. He also just starts playing after his peak; 1880, for instance, is the period he starts his surgery. He is also older at this point. He still makes a hundred in his first Test, and until 1889 he is still the best batter in Tests – by a distance – with an average of 36.

From 1890 until 1900, he plays another 11 matches. In those he averaged 29, so not that much less. But what changes is cricket: this is the decade where it transforms from a bowlers' game into one dominated by batters. Of players with 300 Test runs in this period, Grace's average is only the 22nd best. So, all his career in Tests was spread out in his 30s, as he was building his practice, and in his 40s, when the guys who grew up watching him were at their peak.

Batting exists as we know it today because of W.G. Grace; a man of privilege, from sex to skin colour to social standing. He was born into a family of great cricketing talent and his skill, athleticism and intellect are beyond doubt. Sure, he was a misogynist, a cheat, a shamateur. Had he been a poor woman and just as talented, chances are we wouldn't even know his game.

But when you are looking at Root's sweep, Tendulkar going straight, Miandad's cover drive, Sobers' slashing square or Bradman's late cut, that's Grace. He built the shots you love.

This is a book about the art of batting, told through the stories of the greatest batters. It started with a simple aim, to find the

50 greatest Test batters, and it ended up as an autopsy of how batting works, with the eyes, mind, head and so much more. Each chapter looks at what batting is, how it works and maybe even how to replicate it. Our metrics involved watching films, reading contemporary reports, talking to experts, comparing batters with others from their era in the same matches, but also looking where they made their runs, when they made them, what position they came in and how long they were good for. If we could find a rock to look under, we did.

The last point is perhaps the most interesting, when Indian No.3 Rahul Dravid was talking about passing on knowledge through coaching (something he did well enough to win a World Cup) he stopped at one point and sighed when talking about his teammate Sachin Tendulkar:

This guy was just born to bat. He hit a lot of balls as a youngster, and he practised a lot and all that. But I've seen a lot of other people also do that. He's not the only one. But there was something.

That's the hard part about batting, right? You can't explain why somebody picks up length quicker than somebody else. It's hard to bottle some of that, some of those gifts. How is A.B. de Villiers able to move into position as the ball just seems to land?

The conversation about talents not translating made me think about the sons of great batters. In 2021 Arjun Tendulkar – Sachin's son – was picked up by the Mumbai Indians in what was a controversial choice, as clearly his talent wasn't quite at that level. But the junior Tendulkar was still at worst a fringe professional cricketer, having spent a lot of time with his father and all his friends, not to mention having access to Lord's training sessions.

One of the greatest batters of all time worked on his son's career as much as he could, and Arjun Tendulkar turned out a bowler. All that knowledge that Sachin had, and he had to watch his son become a left-arm swing bowler.

He isn't alone, there really hasn't been two great batters in terms of father-son. Perhaps the closest are Hanif Mohammad and his son Shoaib or Vijay Manjrekar and Sanjay. With all due respect to both sons, neither are considered greats. Don Bradman's son, John, who at the age of 18 – instead of being fast-tracked through Adelaide's cricket scene – was contemplating changing his name. Ultimately, he would, in his 30s.

W.G. Grace had three sons and a daughter. Charlie and William Gilbert Junior (known as Bertie) both played professionally in first-class cricket. The former only ever played four games, but the latter would play in 40, and W.G. often said Bertie would become a good cricketer. While he had some talent, he wasn't a top player.

Often W.G. would choose Bertie for one of his matches and the two sometimes opened together. Regularly, Bertie would fail, and his father would make a huge score. Like the time he was playing for Gloucestershire and made just one run, then watched his father smash 301. In 57 matches, Bertie would average 15.1 and never make a hundred.

W.G. was the man on whom batting was built, but the son of God was mortal.

1

EVOLUTION

Batting skills change in every generation

'The game changes, and the very best evolve with it.' – Jarrod Kimber

Pat Cummins is bowling around the wicket. Australia need one wicket and England require 45 more to win a Test at Headingley in 2019. The Australian quick delivers the ball towards the top of off stump. England's all-rounder Ben Stokes runs across the crease, and his front foot (if you can still call it that) is in front of leg stump. His back foot is out where the wide line would be in limited overs cricket. With a straight bat, he laps the ball over his shoulder, and it flies off to the boundary on his way to beating Australia in one of the best innings anyone has ever played.

But that ball didn't go to just any boundary, it was just to the legside of the keeper. That rope hasn't been protected since the 1800s.

The first cricket bats look something like a hockey stick, not at all like modern bats. They look that way because the ball was rolled along the ground. As the game developed, the ball lifted off the surface, and with that came the style of bat we have now.

The next big change was the debate over how high the arm should go. At first, bowlers raised their arm to shoulder level, which is called 'round-arm bowling'. But after people kept lifting it, it became over-arm bowling. This caused huge problems right across cricket because the wickets were not tended to correctly. They were backyard pitches with hard balls that would keep low or fly off sideways. That was harder because most batters still didn't use pads or gloves. There were also no boundaries. If you wanted a run, you had to leg it. Cricket was a low-scoring, hard-to-survive game.

From that, greats like Fuller Pilch, Nicholas Felix and Alfred Mynn emerged. Many believe Pilch was the greatest early batter. He averaged 18.6 with 7147 runs and only three hundreds. Felix averaged 18.1, while Mynn was back on 13.4. They were the greatest trio of batters in the early part of the game, yet look at those numbers. Imagine what the strugglers would have been going at.

But wickets improved, batters put on protective equipment and there was a cataclysmic change in batting, largely because of a man called W.G. Grace. His privileged upbringing – in a hugely talented family – meant he had a lot of time to perfect batting. But over the period he was growing up, he played against all three kinds of bowling – over-, round- and under-arm. To combat that, Grace played on the front foot when it was full, and the back foot when it was short. That changed everything.

Externally, the biggest change to cricket had nothing to do with the sport, but agriculture. In 1850, wickets in first-class cricket fell every 12 runs. By 1900 it was 24. What happened was an invention called a muck spreader; before this, manure was distributed by hand. Because of that, it was thrown in little chunks. So the ball would be bowled into the pitch and could hit little bits of dung – a whole new meaning to the term 'shit bowling'. This meant it could do all sorts of weird things.

When the manure was liquified and spread properly, the pitches got a lot better, but so did the batters. Arthur Shrewsbury of England was an incredible player from the late 1800s and a great of early batting. On top of averaging 35.5 in Tests, he was also a master at pad play. What he did then will sound silly now, but he ensured his pads were a second line of defence if he missed the ball. Bats did not get wider, but to bowlers it would have felt that way.

So you had three things happening at once in the late 1800s – pads as a line of defence, the muck spreader and the professionalisation of curating wickets.

The next change was Colonel H. H. Shri Sir Ranjitsinhji Vibhaji, Jam Sahib of Nawanagar, GCSI, GBE, but more famously known as Ranji. Neville Cardus called him 'the *Midsummer Night's Dream* of cricket'. He only played 15 Test matches, and he did not cross 1000 runs, but he averaged 45 in those. His first-class average was 56.4 with 24,692 runs. If you dive deeper, some of this is incredible. Against the three biggest counties – Yorkshire, Lancashire and Surrey – he made 6234 runs while averaging over 70 against the latter two and 50 against the first. This was a batter of incredible skill and talent.

But, not at first. In fact, Ranji was afraid of the ball when he was young. So his coach Dan Hayward (brother of Tom Hayward, one of the best batters of his time) trained Ranji by tying his right leg to the ground. This one coaching technique changed cricket forever. It meant that Ranji had to develop another skill for the ball coming straight at him, and that is the leg glance. Before this, batters only hit the ball to the legside when there was no other option, or the delivery was heading that way. It was seen as almost impolite and uncouth to hit to leg. Ranji opened that up.

An Australian opener of the early 1900s, Victor Trumper, thumped that legside door down. His Test average of 39 is hard to handle for modern fans. Unlike Grace, he played Tests when he was in his prime – 38 of them. That record today would be seen as ordinary, but he wasn't that. One of his claims to greatness is his impact on other players.

Images of Trumper show him taking the ball from outside off stump and dragging it to leg. It does not sound that incredible, but this was a revolutionary act.

Players did play across the line, but it wasn't part of their overall plan, and they didn't do it like Trumper. His ability to repeat this act meant that you had to think about where you put fielders; this wasn't something that happened before. Teams started bowling outside off, which was seen as defensive but eventually would become the modern line. Until Trumper attacked the straight ball, attacking the stumps was the smart move, but with him and Ranji turning those balls to leg while the pitches got better, bowlers started leaking runs.

The bowlers fought back at this point. Fred 'The Demon' Spofforth mastered swing, and many other bowlers worked that out in the decades that followed. Bernard Bosanquet, a bored Etonian who was playing professional cricket as a batter, accidentally invented cricket's new ball: the googly (or, as it was known then, the Bosie). After changing the future of cricket by inspiring a bunch of South Africans to take up the art, the ball was so dominant that Bosanquet was forced to defend his delivery from accusations that it was ruining cricket because no one could pick it.

That was laughable by the late 1920s, when batting had become incredibly easy. It was a decade that saw the debuts of England legends Wally Hammond, Herbert Sutcliffe and the continuation of Jack Hobbs. Not to mention Don Bradman. Batting and pitch curation had evolved so much that batters had started to clock the game, completely taking over from bowlers.

The Marylebone Cricket Club (MCC) formalised cricket's laws at their base in Lord's and still write them today. They argued about how to make cricket a fairer sport to bowlers after years of bat domination. They reduced the size of the ball in 1927 and made the stumps bigger in 1931, but neither had much of an impact. But the leg before wicket (lbw) dismissal had been contentious since Shrewsbury had started kicking the ball away when it was not pitched in line. So, in 1935, an experimental law allowed for batters to be dismissed even if the ball pitched outside off stump. There were 560 lbw dismissals in first-class matches in England in 1935; 483 were assumed to be given under the amended law. By 1937, the Laws of Cricket had changed. The Second World War followed, so the impact was hard to tell.

This was cricket nerd stuff, but the other change was that fast bowlers used the middle of the pitch more often. Bodyline (the hugely controversial Ashes series of 1932/33) was the crescendo of what had been brewing since the early 1920s. If you couldn't dismiss these great batters, maybe you could rattle them. It was a natural reaction to the amount of runs that were being scored. Because of the 'private men's club'-style administration of cricket at the time, it made people feel awkward. So it went away.

4

Bowlers found another way to take wickets after the war. Inswing and off-spin bowlers started to dominate. Seamers also bowled more off-cutters to right-handers. The idea was simple; pitch it on the stumps and jag it back into the pads. It meant that cricket became similar everywhere. But the MCC countered that with a change to the laws in 1957 that stopped fielding teams from having more than two players behind square on the legside (many people believe this law changed because of Bodyline).

The 1950s was probably cricket's dead-ball era. It had the second-slowest scoring ever in a Test decade (after the 1880s) and was the only decade after the First World War where the average was under 30 (28.4).

Since Ranji, there hadn't been any pioneering cricket shots. There was the draw shot – where you try to hit the ball between your body and the stumps – which probably failed due to how unrepeatable and dangerous it was. Most cricket shots were from the 1800s, and many are not even chronicled as they were so common. William Yardley and Walter Read both played something akin to switch hits in the 1800s, but neither caught on.

It's possible that Duleepsinhji, Ranji's nephew, played something that may have been one as well. But the main inventors were the Mohammad brothers of Pakistan – both Hanif and Mushtaq have been credited at times – in the 1960s with the reverse sweep.

Hanif was a great. This was demonstrated in Bridgetown in 1958 when Pakistan collapsed badly in their first innings and West Indies made them follow on almost 500 runs behind. At stumps on day three (of a six-day match), Pakistan had recovered to 160/1. Hanif Mohammad was 61 not out. That night he received a note from his captain, Abdul Hafeez Kardar, saying, 'You are our only hope.'

A day later he was 161 not out; that night, the note said, 'You can do it.'

Another 24 hours later he was 270 not out; that night, the note said, 'If you can bat until tea tomorrow, the match will be saved.' The match was drawn, Hanif had batted for 907 minutes for his 337 runs, more than half of Pakistan's 657.

Despite that knock, Hanif averaged 44 in Tests. Fine for mortals (especially as an opener), but he was godlike. He never went at over 50 against any Test nation other than the West Indies, 38.8 in New Zealand and 26.6 over 12 matches in England. So, he has the record of a fine Test player and two innings of a great. The second one was in first-class cricket, where Hanif made 499.

While many – even today – are not happy with the reverse sweep, it is a simple attempt at changing the field setting. A standard spin field does not have a man at deep backward point on the boundary.

The important thing for cricket was not the field manipulation part, but this was the first shot that had to be committed to before you knew the delivery. Sure, you could decide to slog, run down to whack, or defend before the ball was delivered, however, those shots did not require you to decide before the bowler released the ball. The reverse sweep would open up the options for batters willing to try something new.

There were a bunch of changes that all moved the game towards fast bowlers. They didn't happen straight away, but over a long period of time. South Africa and Pakistan both had matting wickets in home Tests. A part of the wrong 'un-obsessed victory that South Africa had was because of the matting wickets. They spun as much on day one as they did at the end of the game. South Africa naturally moved on to grass wickets, but it took Pakistan longer, and some embarrassment.

In 1959, Australia were touring Pakistan. On day four of the third Test in Karachi between those two teams, former US President Dwight Eisenhower came to meet the players and watch the game. It was a turgid day of cricket, with Pakistan scoring 104 runs for the loss of five wickets. The Australians mentioned that playing on turf was better than matting in front of Eisenhower, who had also commented about the lack of a turf wicket. Ayub Khan, the then Pakistan president, subsequently decided that Pakistan's Tests would only be played on turf pitches, so the Karachi Test was the last to be played on a matting wicket.

When people complain about day/night Tests ruining players' records, no one worried about the fact games were played on matting. But there was a far bigger change that also finished in 1960. That was the last time a wicket was uncovered for a Test match in England.

According to the *Old Ebor* blog, it is even more confusing than that:

Tests in other countries were a different question, and various rules applied. For example, the pitches for the 1929–30 series between the West Indies and England employed full covering throughout, something which had not been agreed beforehand and for which the West Indies board later apologised. The same happened in the third Test of the 1934–35 series in British Guiana. But the MCC generally did not want covering to be used for Tests involving England. A request from Australia to use full covering during the 1936–37 Ashes series was denied, but several rain-affected pitches in that series — which had a bearing on the outcome of the series — persuaded the English captain Gubby Allen that full covering might be necessary in Australia. The MCC also declined a request from the South African authorities to have full covering for the 1938–39 series.

Having covered wickets in hotter countries made more sense because the wickets became even more dangerous following rain. The wet top of the wicket and the hard underbelly meant the ball could go vertical, at pace. So, Australia started covering the wickets. As *Old Ebor* writes:

> When the West Indies toured Australia in 1951–52, which fell outside the direct jurisdiction of the MCC, full covering was used for the first time in Test matches. This proved successful, as did South Africa's 1952–53 series in Australia; therefore when the Australian authorities proposed that the 1954–55 Ashes series should have full covering, the MCC reluctantly agreed although it was to remain "experimental". But this full covering endured afterwards in Australian Test matches, ending the prospect of a sticky wicket in Australia. In 1956–57, the MCC agreed for full covering for a series in South Africa.

It was not until 1979 that all England wickets were the same.

A sticky wicket is nothing like a normal pitch, and the best way of explaining this is through Don Bradman. In 2009, a commentator called Dave Wilson on CricketWeb.net worked out Bradman's average on wet pitches. A few years later, Indian sports writer Arunabha Sengupta came up with the same number – 20.3.

That is a long way short of his overall average of 99.94. The only real flaw in his record is playing on those wet wickets, which he did only 15 times. He passed 50 only once and made more ducks in those games than the rest of his career combined. There is no doubt that Bradman struggled a lot when the wicket was uneven.

But when an overall average is still that high, it must mean the normal wickets suited him. In the 65 times he played on dry pitches he made 29 hundreds, so almost half of his innings on them were hundreds. He averaged 119.9 in those knocks.

There are two ways of thinking about this. Bradman did have a weakness, but also his batting was the future. He was moving the game forward by merely existing. And he needed a solid wicket, because he was a player of the future, not the past.

But it meant that to be successful, you either needed to be great at both types of batting required or, like Bradman, great at one or the other.

In general, uncovered wickets get a very bad rap. Often, they were very friendly to batters, especially by the 1920s when the curation of wickets had taken so many steps forward. At that point, wickets had to be made to survive the elements for five days without the need for covering. It was just those few occasions, when the conditions changed them, that they were nearly impossible.

The wickets being covered really changed cricket. Finger spin was dominant in Asia or where wickets had rain. When Australia started covering their wickets for Sheffield Shield games in the 1920s, finger spin almost disappeared. England kept having it, as uncovered wickets helped them so much more.

As covered pitches came in, there was less help for the spinners and England stopped using them as much. From the 1920s to the 1950s, England used spinners for more than 40% of their overs. From the 1980s until now, it has been around 20% each decade. The 2020s started off with it under 20% for the first time ever. The same thing can be seen in Australia, South Africa, New Zealand and the West Indies. Cricket was very much a combination of seam and spin everywhere outside of Asia until the pitches were covered, and then pace bowling took over.

In Asia, cricket went to spin on turf wickets. It meant that, again, batting was split. There are many players good at facing spin outside Asia but who struggle there, and many who could handle pace on subcontinental wickets but struggle elsewhere. No matter the era, batting has always been different depending on the conditions. They have always changed.

Until 1963, Tests were dominated by finger spin, medium-paced seam bowlers and swing. The finger spinners and seamers struggled with the pitches as they got covered. But swing bowling took a hit from another change, when cricket went from the back foot no-ball to the front foot. It was a terrible change, based on an overreaction to bowlers learning how to slide closer to the batter and the idea that it helped taller bowlers. The change was made to the front foot, which has probably played a part in bowlers getting injured so much more, but it also directly helped taller bowlers. That change – along with the covered wickets – really disrupted cricket.

The front-foot bowling meant that bowlers stayed taller in the crease, so having tall quicks was the best option. The covered wickets meant they needed something outside of finger spin or the ability to get the ball to hit the seam – they needed extra pace. Those two changes started to happen around the 1950s and '60s. By 1976, the West Indians had tall, fast bowlers everywhere. The rest of the world took a while to catch up, but the game changed completely to where the dominant bowling style was faster and taller.

Now, cricket outside of Asia was a hit-the-deck sport. The West Indian bowlers pioneered this, so their two main deliveries were back of a length and bouncers.

That changed how you had to be a great batter; you could no longer be a technician alone. To handle bowling as it got faster and more around your throat, you needed an added level of athleticism. Taller batters came through the game because the ball no longer kept as low and batting was also changed by those players.

Taller bowlers with higher actions evolved. Their natural length was shorter, so they became seam rather than swing bowlers. It wasn't the seam bowling of before, where skilled medium pacers hit the string all day long. These were big fast bowlers smashing the ball into the wickets, and more than ever before, into players. That brought about the inventions of helmets (and other padding) which had been toyed with throughout history but never quite worked.

If you wanted to make runs after 1980, you needed a back foot game. It was hilarious that just as batters were working out how to handle more balls at their throats, cricket evolved differently in Pakistan and you had to worry about your toes. Suddenly, reverse swing was a major part of the game. This was a method that had already existed in the West Indies and Australia, but they'd never quite managed to harness it consistently. But Pakistan bowlers did, and what started as their domain spread to the rest of the bowling attacks. It meant that fast bowlers had their first old-ball weapon, keeping them relevant for longer into an innings.

A larger revolution happened at the exact same time that was far more noticeable to most cricket fans: limited overs cricket. Thanks to Kerry Packer and the Asian TV markets, 50-overs cricket became incredibly popular through the 1990s. With that, how batters saw their game altered. The Australian team changed running between wickets, and then started playing more aggressively with the bat. While the other countries were slower, the rest of the world found more boundaries too. The 2000s were the first decade ever with a scoring rate of more than three an over. Every decade since the millennium has been over that mark.

This is where cricket finally opened up the last part of the field, behind the wicketkeeper. The uppercut was one shot there, but you needed an obvious bouncer around off stump to play that shot.

Douglas Marillier was a middling Zimbabwe batter who saw that teams had started bringing their fine leg up and created a scoop of sorts. He would get low and flick the ball over his left shoulder for a boundary. At the same time, Australian Ryan Campbell went with another creation altogether, where he almost pulled the ball directly behind. Neither of those shots took over straight away, but players did start to play more versions of them. Then a few years later, Sri Lankan opener Tillakaratne Dilshan played his version in T20 cricket – a straight bat sweep over his head from seam bowlers, which became known as the Dilscoop. All these pioneers were trying things that led to the ramps and scoops cricket sees today.

Technology also changed a lot around this point. The middles of bats were larger, and with covered wickets being easier to trust, the ability to swing through the line meant that batting had its greatest period. Better training and fitness regimes meant players could hit the ball further as well. The ability to play day/night Tests (which are generally low scoring) is just another way batting has changed in modern times.

But the biggest technological change spreaders to cricket since muck was the Decision Review System (DRS), and Hawkeye ball tracking technology.

How Hawkeye was invented for cricket is unknown; Paul Hawkins, the founder, has not given the full story. But I believe it's highly possible that cricket (and many sports) changed on 5 June, 1996, in a Minor Counties Championship game.

Before becoming a doctor with a PhD in artificial intelligence, Hawkins was a cricketer trying to make it as a professional. In all the databases I found, there was only one Paul Martin Hawkins who played Minor Counties in the right age bracket. I can only assume this is him. He was run-out for a duck in the first innings. In the second innings, he was given out lbw for a second duck, meaning Hawkins played one semi-professional game and never made a run.

As a friend of mine suggested, could this be Paul Hawkins' origin story? He was a young batter, aged 22, perhaps trying to test if he could make the pro levels of cricket. And at his one big break, he failed massively, cruelly run-out in the first innings and then sawn-off lbw in the second.

Hawkeye is now used in football world cups, replaces the strike zone in minor league baseball, has been around in tennis forever and features in so many other sports worldwide. Hawkins has changed sport everywhere, but still can't get anyone to annul his lbw.

You can see the results of Hawkeye before cricket brought it into DRS. At first, spinners started taking a lot more lbw wickets and seamers stopped getting as many. But then the quicks worked this out, started pitching the ball up more and bowling straighter, leaving England's famed channel and the West Indies back of a length behind. Using your pads against spinners has completely changed, and umpires can no longer factor in 'should've used your bat' when a player leaves the ball.

The most recent change in cricket has been the wobble seam ball (Wobbleball). This is a delivery that hides what the bowler is trying to do. Instead of hitting the seam every time, it sometimes misses it, meaning most of these deliveries go dead straight, but occasionally they seam in or hold their line and go away. Because bowlers are not hitting the seam every ball, you can do this for longer into the innings.

From 1960 until the end of 2023, the average of pace bowling per wicket was 30.7. That dropped to 25.4 in 2018, the lowest in that period. It was 26.3 in 2019 and 27.1 in 2021. This was incredibly low, and it meant that batters had to work out a whole new way of batting. Modern legends like the Australian Steve Smith and India's Virat Kohli saw massive drops in their averages. There is always more than one reason why.

But most players with a 15-year career must overcome a change in batting at one point. That is part of the greatness – the fact that the game changes, and the very best evolve with it.

2

EYES

The role a 'good eye' plays in making runs

'You train every other muscle, why wouldn't you train your eyes?' — Nasser Hussain

Saeed Anwar can't see the ball properly. What is in front of him has never existed before, and even though the ball is coming slowly, something is blocking him from following it as it first comes out of the hand. The Pakistan batter has seen everything, but not this.

This is not a normal thing for a player of his quality. He would average more than 50 in Tests when opening the batting. It was a short career of only 55 matches from over 11 years, but he scored 4000 runs at 45.5. He would have played more, but he was dropped for three years after making a pair on his debut – despite averaging 68 in first-class cricket the season before he was picked and 48 between his debut and comeback. If Anwar had played the kind of matches his talent demanded, he'd be a great.

That meant Pakistan missed out on several Tests from the man with the second-best average of any opener in the 1990s with 2000 runs.

One way to see his quality – and that of all openers – is how they do when batting in England, New Zealand and South Africa. Those are the toughest conditions when you are facing the new ball. In those, he averaged 42 combined. From three matches in Australia, he had a hundred as well. He also averaged more away than home. This is an incredible record for an Asian opener.

In One Day International (ODI) cricket, he is often forgotten as one of the openers who changed the game. Before Sanath Jayasuriya opened for Sri Lanka in the 1990s, he struck at 85 when he scored his thousandth ODI run; the fastest in ODI cricket by a mile at this point.

In the 2020 article by Osman Samiuddin (author of *The Unquiet Ones*), 'Is Saeed Anwar Criminally Underrated?', it wasn't just the numbers he mentioned:

> No foot movement, no force, nothing – just a ball's fleeting acquaintance with the bat, face expertly twisted sideways at contact, as if a snub. And off she goes, teasing point to his right, giving eyes to third man to his left, eyes itself only for the boundary rope. It's as minimalist a boundary as you'll ever see and it's stunning.

Shane Warne said he was the best Pakistani batter he had bowled to and wrote, '[it's the] style you remember, not the figures.'

He was clearly one of the most talented batters, even if his career never quite looked incredible. Yet, there was one bowler he couldn't pick up: Sri Lankan wizard Muttiah Muralitharan.

Murali had 800 victims in Test cricket. Unless the future of the sport changes, no one will ever beat that mark. His run up was a jaunty jog that showed no real menace or fear. Even at the crease, it looked like a standard finger spin delivery would be bowled. But as Murali rolled his arm over, there was an action like no one else's.

Many people focus on the arm being bent and whether it is straightened enough to be a no-ball for throwing. But something else happened: an inversion.

Most seamers deliver the ball with the underside of their wrist facing the batter. Leg-spinners start with the right side of their wrist facing the batter before turning it over late. Off-spinners go the other way, though it's not as dramatic a movement.

By the time Saeed Anwar reached Test level, he would have seen these kinds of actions so often that his brain could pick them up subconsciously. He probably wouldn't even be able to talk someone through it, he just understood which delivery was coming and where to look for it.

Murali was an off-spinner, of sorts. His balls spun away from Saeed Anwar's outside edge as a left-hander. But off-spinners are finger spinners, twisting the ball out of their fingers with a huge rotation of their hips.

Murali bowled something much more like a wrong 'un or back-of-the-hand slower ball. Meaning as you were facing him, you were seeing the back of the wrist. There is no other kind of bowler who ever used this method, in part because they would have been called for chucking – rightly or wrongly – and also because Murali had an elbow deformity and a flexible wrist that made such a weird action possible.

The ball coming out the back of the hand, over his fingers, shielded it from sight in a way that no other bowler had mastered. If it took you a moment longer to pick it up, it meant you were facing one of the most accurate big-spinning deliveries ever on a time delay. That is what happened with Saeed Anwar. For a while, he was so worried about facing Murali that he saw a specialist eye trainer.

Had he played for Australia under their coach Darren Lehmann, he would have been given the South Australian's advice.

According to a Sam Perry article in the *Guardian* about Lehmann's coaching course when he was still in charge of Australian cricket, 'The first point of his opening slide simply said "WTBC" (translation: "Watch the ball, cunt"), going to show that even the most elementary aspect of Australian batting now requires aggression.'

The issue with this advice is that batters don't just watch the ball. It's a lot more complicated.

Dr Sherylle Calder has worked with many of the best athletes on the planet. Her job is simply to train athletes where to look, through her organisation EyeGym. After being a hockey player herself, her career has involved working with cricketers from Australia, Pakistan, England and South Africa, as well as many of the leading associate nations such as Scotland, Ireland, Canada, Kenya and Namibia. She has spent decades in Cape Town studying how athletes use their eyes.

Her earlier work was with Bob Woolmer and John Buchanan, two of cricket's maddest scientists. In working with Woolmer, the former coach of South Africa and Pakistan, she had access to his work on the game, best seen in perhaps the most important cricket book of all time, *Bob Woolmer's Art and Science of Cricket*.

By that stage, the South African guru was starting to understand cricket on a level that previous generations never had access to. One thing they worked out is that the ball moves too fast at international level for anyone to follow it. This isn't just a cricket thing – badminton, tennis and baseball are the same.

It is simply impossible for a top athlete to hit a ball, or shuttlecock, travelling at the speeds they're delivered at. Yet, many professionals do this every single day.

The simple reaction time of most people on the planet is 200ms (milliseconds), and it takes 150ms to execute a blink. Now imagine you are holding a bat facing an international fast bowler delivering the ball and you have 500ms from the time the ball leaves the hand until it reaches you. With speedsters like Australia's Mitchell Starc and England's Jofra Archer, it's even quicker.

How do any batters hit these balls?

All the movements a batter makes are based on what happens in the first 250–300ms of the delivery. The length of most Test match deliveries is between 4–8 metres from the stumps; most pro batters will already roughly know that the ball will be on that length before it has been released. More than that, they know the line will be off stump or just outside.

When the bowler does something different like pitching the ball up further or bowling wider, subtle signs will appear in their body and wrist position as the ball comes out. Not all batters see that, but in the first part of the ball's journey, the batter uses information from the release to guess what will happen. Then, their subconscious and brain elasticity kick in, and they repeat their normal movements for the ball.

Yes, they are playing cricket by prediction.

Professional cricketers have been tested in labs compared to amateurs, using an experiment tried often in sports. As the ball is released, they simply turn the lights out. An amateur, even a good one, will be completely lost and unsure of which shot is needed. A professional will be in roughly the right area, playing an appropriate shot.

We think batters have incredible eyesight and brilliant reflexes. But the truth is far more complicated, and there are actual cases where players have had worse than average eyesight.

Edgar Martínez is a Hall of Fame baseballer from the Seattle Mariners. Twice he led the league in batting average and hit 309 career home runs. He did all that while suffering from strabismus, an abnormality that prevents his eyes from working in tandem. So, while facing 105mph pitching, Martínez's eyes would lose their depth perception. This is bad when you are young and fit, but it's a condition that gets worse with age and fatigue. Martínez regularly played more than 150 games in a year and would end up with more than 2000 altogether. He was 41 when he retired.

If you want a less scientific case in cricket, how about Don Bradman? While serving as a physical fitness instructor during the Second World War, the army allegedly rated Bradman's eyesight poor. After the war he averaged 105 from 15 Tests. But we also know the Nawab of Pataudi played for India after a car crash damaged his right eye. Pataudi still remarkably made six Test centuries after the accident.

Not that eyesight doesn't matter.

West Indian Lawrence Rowe was perhaps as elegant as any batter in the world. During the 1970s, he would don the maroon cap of the West Indies, drag his Gray-Nicolls Scoop down the wicket, and then use the most beautiful technique. He barely seemed to hit the ball. A square drive from a spinner looks like a dab, but it races away to the point boundary. Against the quicks he would flick balls from off stump, and even outside, to the square leg boundary without any flourish or panic.

All the while, he would whistle tunes to himself as if lost in thought while walking around a pond in a park.

But he wasn't just about aesthetics. Rowe was the first man to score two hundreds on Test debut (only Pakistan's Yasir Hameed – against Bangladesh – has done it since). In fact, one of those was a double hundred. His match aggregate of 314 remains the most runs on debut. It was also the first double hundred and hundred on debut. He also made 300 opening the batting against England, and after 12 Tests he was averaging over 70.5.

It appeared that no bowler could stop him – and they didn't, what happened next was a shocking run of injuries. 'Rowe's life almost fatally attracted tragedy,' reported a blog on the *Repeating Islands* website, in which Rowe explains:

> The knee injury, that happened in 1973, was wrongly diagnosed by a doctor who thought it was just a mild strain and the cast was removed. That was a mistake. It was a ligament tear and took me a year to really recover. I suffered because of that during the England tour.

A knee injury for a batter changes two things: how you come down the pitch to spinners (something Rowe did gracefully and with lightning speed) and your bat path – instead of coming down straight, it often comes from an angle towards gully. Not an ideal situation for a player who whipped across the line like Rowe.

Another issue was discovered when he kept getting sick playing in matches. Signed as an overseas player for Derbyshire, he suffered recurring headaches during games and showed signs of heavy hay fever. When tested, it turned out that Rowe was allergic to grass – perhaps the worst thing for any cricketer.

The knee injury and allergy to the playing surface were both major issues, but another really changed everything. When having dinner with then-team manager Gerry Alexander (an attacking keeper batter who'd made a Test hundred), Rowe held the menu really close to his face so he could read it.

When he returned home, he went to see a doctor. Rowe did so well on the eye chart that he even read the manufacturer's name at the bottom. The doctor concluded that he had better than 20/20 vision.

Clearly, that test wasn't concluded on both eyes. Soon after, it was found that Rowe had pterygium, a growth in his left eye that blurred his sight. For a time, surgery helped, and he tried glasses (which he said made everything look 'oblong and hazy'). He went to contact lenses, but in the 1970s they were not advanced enough and made his eyes water.

By the end of the West Indian summer of 1974, Lawrence Rowe had averaged 47 in first-class cricket to go along with his 70 in Tests. For the rest of his career, he averaged 32.4 in the first-class game.

By the end, he was so broken that Michael Holding, the great fast bowler, tells a story of Rowe not wanting to go out and bat in a festive match because the pitch was damp and 'he could not be the Lawrence Rowe the people were expecting'. Holding also said that Rowe was the best batter he ever saw.

Rowe was a shadow of a man that people had once compared to Sobers, Headley and Bradman. Tony Cozier once said there was no one better than Rowe, but also added that by the end, 'The fear of failure gripped him.'

Rowe's career would end in disgrace when this hobbling, one-eyed man with headaches would take the money to play cricket in South Africa. His fellow Jamaicans turned on him, and he fled to the USA to hide.

Nobody knows how great Rowe would have been. He averaged nearly 60 at home but only 29 away, but all those touring Tests were with knee, grass and eye issues.

There are players at the highest level who see things differently. England captains and Essex batters Nasser Hussain and Graham Gooch found themselves going up against Pakistan's Wasim Akram and his reverse swing for Lancashire. Hussain couldn't work out which way it was going, which is a problem at 90mph.

Gooch told Hussain, 'As he runs in, before he starts hiding the ball in his hand, have a look. He gives you a few clues.'

Hussain looks up and realises he couldn't see what Gooch was looking at. It was not just about eyesight, but that played a part. 'I had laser eye surgery when I was playing. So I've always struggled with my left eye.'

But Hussain's real issue was focusing on where the ball was: 'His arms were so quick.' He was told what to look for, and he was obviously good enough to do it against most bowlers, but even someone good enough to score 14 Test hundreds and make 20,000 first-class runs could not consciously see any signs.

It wasn't the only case where Hussain couldn't see something his teammate did. 'Paul Collingwood used to pick Murali in white-ball cricket with the way the ball was spinning and the way the seam was going. And even that, I struggled to see. Some players can pick the seam and know where it's going.'

So how could Rowe continue to make runs at all, and Nasser Hussain live well enough without Graham Gooch's telescope eyes? To understand this, you need to understand what batters actually do.

A top batter is at first watching where the fielders are. If you have a lot of slips, chances are the bowler wants to move the ball away from you. If there is no mid-on or mid-off, the bowler probably doesn't pitch up often. A short leg might mean inswing, extra bounce or short balls. Two or even three fielders out on the legside means get ready for some bouncers. This is what can be learned on the first ball. But the fields are changing all the time, and the batter is lodging each one of these changes as they happen.

Then you have the run up, which also gives a lot of information. The bowler might have come from wider than usual or closer to the umpire, which could change the angle of the ball. There is also what they are doing with the ball; you may be able to see the seam and how it is angled or if they have their wrist cocked for a slower ball. For a spinner, a different grip might let you know what the next ball is. As they deliver, where they release the ball from lets you know the chances of the bounce and angle the ball will be travelling. It might mean an inswinger or wrong 'un if they really drop their front arm. At this point, the ball has not been delivered and the batter has already amassed so many clues.

The trick is how to learn all this so that it becomes subconscious. When most batters are asked, they can't tell you all these details, yet they are processing this information all the time.

The eyes still play their part and need to be trained, as Hussain notes:

Towards the latter part of my career, we met a specialist who gave us various eye drills with a screen and where lights used to flash on and off. To train the eyes really. He viewed the eyes as muscles, you train every other muscle, why wouldn't you train your eyes?

People talk about batters having a good eye, but it is a skill like anything else.

There is no point having perfect footwork or an understanding of wrist position if you cannot also look in the right places. England wicketkeeper Matt Prior calls this the TV, trying to blur out everything else and just look at the most important part: a small box around the ball.

This is not easy. In front of any batter is the bowler, pitch, stumps, the sightscreen; if you're a professional there is a stand; for an amateur there is a tree or row of houses. Oh, and the bowler is moving. Not just their body but their hand. It's moving up and down as they enter the crease. As they come to their delivery stride, some show the ball clearly, some accidentally obscure it, others do this on purpose. Then there is a flurry of action that results in the ball being so hard actually to focus on.

Often when a player loses form, it is simply a part of this that breaks down. They are not focusing their eyes on the right place.

That is where Dr Calder comes in; she trains athletes to look at the right thing. Calder trains batters to focus on tracking the ball. When working with batters, she focuses on two major parts: how to track the ball and how to jump (saccade) their eyes.

Calder believes these are trainable skills like learning to play a sweep shot:

Cricketers have all got strengths and weaknesses in their visual system. Skills they are really good at, and the skills they're really bad at, so what I do is identify the good ones, bad ones, and just make both of them better. Sportsmen are really famous for almost covering up their poor skills. So batters would more consistently use shots they are comfortable with, but it's that odd ball that gets you out. With technology and analysis nowadays, they know exactly what you're doing and they get you out, on that one shot that you're not good at playing.

That level of analysis happens in baseball and tennis, too, which require similar reactions. Baseball and tennis are fairly two-dimensional sports compared to cricket. In baseball, you're trying to hit the ball with the same shot consistently, basically in front of you. Tennis is a little different, but again there are fewer shots and options of where you can strike the ball.

Batting in cricket is 360 degrees. You can hit the ball anywhere, and there are many options to get the ball into each place. Of course, against the very fastest bowlers, top players often limit their shot choice. Instead of reacting to the ball, they are going in with perhaps as few as two or three scoring options that favour their best shots.

Again, that means they're premeditating what they will do.

To face a quick bowler in cricket, you must use information gleaned from before the ball – the 200ms – starts travelling towards you, make a predictive jump after delivery and to a certain extent premeditate your shot. That may not make it sound like as much of a batter's game.

Of course, batters have fought back. Better use of the crease, bigger bodies, stolen singles, and bat technology are in their favour. In the future, they'll have access to edgertronic cameras that shoot 882 frames per second and are pointed at the front of bowlers' hands to deliver incredible secrets.

Any small change from normal by a bowling action can create havoc.

This was seen in the form of Sri Lankan Lasith Malinga. The release point of most bowlers is around 2 metres high, and from either side of the umpire. There are many weird actions that cause issues, but Malinga was like no one else, and when he released the ball, it came from the chest of the umpire. This created problems not only with seeing the ball, but also because the trajectory was unlike any other bowler.

He had many weapons; he was fast, accurate and smart. Other bowlers would be compared to him unfavourably when it came to his yorker. But Malinga's action was made to bowl that ball because he was bowling low to low. When he missed his length, it was still nearly impossible to get under his half volleys, and his full tosses were better than most bowlers' length balls. That is because most bowlers try to beat you with lateral movement or bounce. Malinga beat players with a vertical drop. By the end of limited overs games when you were trying to slog, you had to adjust to a delivery coming out of the hand in front of the umpire (or off the pitch against left-handers), pace, a low-to-low action, and often the dip he got from the revolutions that came from under the ball.

The only way to get used to him was to face him loads and be a brilliant straight hitter. His average of 19.7 in T20s suggests that didn't happen a lot.

This is why an action of Brett Lee or Chris Woakes – despite their pace – can be easier to handle than that of South African Mike Procter who ran in with a hitch that made it look like he bowled from his wrong foot. Or India's Jasprit Bumrah who delivers the ball around 40 centimetres closer to the batter than normal. This is because he releases the ball leaning forward towards the batter, in a style cricket had rarely – if ever – seen before. The weirder the action, the fewer clues a batter will receive.

Because you only get 3 metres of the ball travelling to take in everything, any change is going to be harder. Whether you are facing a perfect action like Michael Holding, or something rogue like Shoaib Akhtar, the more you know the better, because you are about to perform a jump with your eyes – a saccadic eye movement by its scientific term. The batter moves their eyes to where they believe the bowler will deliver after their initial track. It is hard to focus on the ball as it comes in, and then when it comes down at the professional level, it's arriving so quickly that your reflexes aren't much use, but that jump helps you cheat.

It is easier to make a saccadic movement against the type of bowler you are used to playing, like South African quick Allan Donald who had a beautiful traditional action rather than Malinga who slings his arm sideways to jumble up his cues.

But it isn't just the quick bowlers, as Saeed Anwar found out. Another Sri Lankan mystery bowler, Ajantha Mendis, came along. He brought with him the carrom ball, a delivery that you flick from your fingernails, like you would a classmate's ear in primary school. Something like Australian mystery spinner Jack Iverson's from the 1950s, but it was a ball that even Sri Lankan spinner Rangana Herath had bowled. Mendis perfected this delivery that to a batter looked like an off-spinner but turned away.

In a 2008 Test he combined with Murali to bowl at India at Galle International Stadium. At 167 without loss, the tourists were flying in the first innings when Gautam Gambhir, a left-handed batter, faced a ball that pitched on off stump, and he thought would move away. It went the other way, and he was lbw. Rahul Dravid was out caught at short leg a few minutes later when he was tentative because he wasn't sure which way the ball would turn. VVS Laxman would be out after, when he went to pull a ball that behaved weirdly, and he spooned it.

Those last two victims are two of the greatest ever players of spin. Back in 2001, they shared the 376-run partnerships against Shane Warne in Kolkata to win a match for India after Australia had enforced the follow-on.

This innings – and many others – show what a player Laxman was. There was a point in this innings when Shane Warne gives up and bounces him, because the idea of bowling normally makes no sense. Even with Warne coming around the wicket and pitching the ball metres outside leg stump, Laxman manages to run inside the line of the leg break, but is standing only inches inside the return crease, yet from that position, he still manages to play a cover drive. The entire shot looks like someone made it with artificial intelligence.

That was the level of Laxman against spin while Rahul Dravid averaged 68.4 against spin in his career. These two players were incredible, but Mendis took both and six in total. Because of that India would only make 329, but at the other end was India's powerful opener Virender Sehwag, who played one of the greatest innings ever, scoring 61% of India's total and making 201 not out.

What did Sehwag do differently from the others? He didn't let Mendis settle into a line and length. He scored 70 runs from 77 balls, including three sixes and five fours, but it wasn't just the intent. New Zealand batter Ross Taylor says, 'Sehwag smashed anyone, he just looked at him as an off-spinner.'

In cricket circles, there is a theory that Taylor played a part in players working out Mendis, that he saw different fingers rising like antennae when the carrom ball was incoming. This spread through the players' Blackberry network of that era. 'There's definitely a little bit of tax added to that. I can't claim that.'

But Taylor did face Mendis a lot:

There was a lot of discussion about fingers and thumb and what to look out for. And as most batters at all levels know, watching the ball or watching the bowler and watching the ball is a big part.

But then when you start having to watch fingers, you can start confusing yourself a little bit. I think you almost had to play him as an off-spinner. And the one that went away, himself and Sunil Narine and all those guys, you just hoped that you played and missed and didn't nick it. Where first and foremost, if you could smother the ball coming into you. All the straight ones gave yourself a better chance to survive and succeed for longer periods of time obviously. But I think one of my best innings against him and I just didn't get out.

The innings Taylor is talking about was for the Royal Challengers Bangalore, now Bengaluru (RCB) at Centurion in 2009. Taylor was brutal, hitting 81 from 33 balls. But in the middle of it, Mendis went for one for 21 from his four overs. Taylor scored six from six against him, and 75 from 27 against the rest. 'It was more a survival than trying to smack him a lot of the time during that period.'

So Sehwag attacked, others defended, many played like he was an off-spinner, and there were some clues to which way the ball was turning.

But even a year later, it would have been difficult for Taylor to see Mendis and others. His eyesight started to change thanks to pterygium:

It's probably a batter's worst nightmare if your eyes are going.

I'm no optometrist or ophthalmologist, but it's a growth that starts on your nose and grows across to your eye, attaches to it and starts dragging it, so it's the shape of a rugby ball.

It's a gradual thing. I think I first noticed it probably in 2010, because from 2010 to 2011, a guy in our Central Districts team was talking about it, so I noticed I had it there.

You'd always turn up to breakfast and your eyes are red because everyone thinks you've had a big night on the turps, but you've been scratching your pterygium; it's all red. So I think for a couple of years I struggled at night time. I just didn't pick the ball up as well.

It wasn't just at night, when in Brisbane for a chase of 504, it got dark early:

A thunderstorm came in the afternoon at the Gabba almost every day, and I just couldn't pick up the ball. I'd got a duck in the first innings, and I don't know, I just knew there was something up. I got 26 in the second innings and we lost. I went to our physio, and I said, just for peace of mind, "Can I go and see an optometrist and get it seen to?"

I went and had an eye test, got it all done and the man said, your pterygium's not far away from your pupil. You're probably going to need an operation in the next six to 12 months. So, I think in my own mind, it was just nice to know that there was something wrong.

I went back the next day, did some more tests, got some eye drops, flew out to Perth, started using these eye drops a lot and then got 290.

So, was my highest-ever Test score because of the eye drops? A lot of people were saying that, but I think for me, it was just knowing that my eyes were getting better.

Also, how they explained it to me was that when it's dark, it gets bad, that's why I dislike batting at night time or fielding.

I was also lucky that it was 40 odd degrees, and the sun was out in Perth the whole time. So it wasn't dark and gloomy like Brisbane.

Taylor is right. In ODI cricket, he averaged 57 in day games. In day/night matches, it was 47 in the first innings and 40 at night. But if you just look until 2016, he averaged only 36.3 in night ODI innings, and after fixing his eyes it was 50.1. You check his T20 stats, and it's even more stark. In night games before 2016, it was 18.9, and after that, it more than doubled to 38.9.

There is no doubt that he was affected. Taylor could literally see the difference:

I ended up having an operation maybe a year or so later and I had throw downs with our trainer two weeks after the operation. I saw the ball actually swing from the hand and pick it up where you just see this thing moving at you which was a bit freaky.

But this is what it tells you the most about batters. In the two years before that eye test, Taylor averaged 51 across all international cricket. In the two years after seeking help, he also averaged 51.

Ross Taylor could score runs even with a rugby-shaped obstacle encroaching on his pupil. The best batters can see in the dark, even when they can't.

3

RAPID

Fast bowling is scary as hell

'Feel it go past you and hear the thing whizzing through the air, displacing the wind.' – Mark Butcher

Corey Richards is psyched up. The New South Wales (NSW) batter has been told he's being promoted to score fast, and he's got himself so worked up that he doesn't listen to what number he is supposed to go in. So when his NSW teammate Craig Simmons loses his castle, Richards runs out on the field past the man who was due to bat at No. 3.

When he gets into the middle he is buzzing, and he can't wait to attack the bowling. But he is stopped by Australian Test opener Phil Jaques. Jaques was picked late for Australia, but he averaged 47 over nine Tests before his back started giving him issues. He was clearly a quality player, averaging the same amount in first-class cricket. And when Richards came out to join him full of piss and vinegar, it was the Test player who had to let the domestic guy know something was different. Jaques stops Richards, stares into his eyes and says, 'This is quick.'

Richards doesn't listen, but a moment later, he works out what the warning was about. The ball is short and angled in. He leans back but realises he is too late. Luckily, the ball swings away. Later, he gets a straight ball and this first-class player looks almost afraid. Despite this being a one-day game, because South Australia were out so cheaply, the interval is taken during NSW's innings.

When Richards and Jaques come back out, the pace is still there. Richards swings hard at a length ball but is late on it and edges to slip. Next ball, Matthew Phelps comes out and plays a forward defence that feels like a second after it hits his pad. He is gone, and somehow Australian batter Brad Haddin survives the hat-trick and gets off strike. So Jaques is back on strike, and he gets a short ball that just wants to destroy him. It climbs right up until the only thing protecting him is the glove and the ball goes through to the keeper for the third wicket of the over.

'That was definitely the quickest spell of bowling I've faced. I've faced Shoaib Akhtar and Dale Steyn, but he was just a different level. That pace was different gravy,' is what Phil Jaques said to me when I was researching this spell a decade later. The bowler he was talking about was Shaun Tait, who was on the losing side that day, but he bowled 10 overs from five spells with no maidens, allowed 41 runs, delivered 14 wides and took 6 wickets.

That wasn't seam bowling, that was pace. Raw, violent and uncontrolled.

David 'Bumble' Lloyd, the former England batter, talks about facing quick bowling like it's a Western:

It's a shootout at the O.K. Corral, and he wants to take your head off. Then you need bravery. Particularly as an opener. But, even going down the order, that ball hurts. There's a thrill if you can succeed, so you need a hell of amount of skill, you need to be brave, you need an essence of luck, but you make your own luck by your preparation. But the thrill of the game is I know I can get hurt.

Former England batter Mark Butcher says:

> You can hear the ball. Feel it go past you and hear the thing whizzing through the air, displacing the wind, and it's like someone throwing one of those ninja stars at you.
>
> When it hits – if you hit it – it hits the top of the bat up near the splice and kind of jolts and smashes into your hand, it hurts, really stings. The sort of sensations that you just don't, you can't really appreciate unless you play at that sort of level against those types of balls.

Butcher is right. Most of us don't know what it is like to face real pace at over 90mph. But he is wrong in saying that amateur players don't understand. It's players like him – with incredible skills, reflexes and the ability to foretell what is happening – who usually don't have to worry about what it is like to face something that fast and confusing. Most terrible batters are used to facing balls that are too quick, that they can't see or hit, or that hurt them.

What 90mph bowling really does is turn great batters into the rest of us for a moment.

There are methods, as Ross Taylor explains:

> Not having exaggerated foot movements. You still stay with your batting stance, shoulder width apart but not trying to get out too far and not get too far back. If anything, use the crease a little bit, bat a little bit deeper in your crease and then you'd watch players like Graeme Smith. For instance, he used to bat so far back in his crease, just to give him that. And it's not even half a foot, there's almost a foot extra time to see the ball move.

The problem with fast bowling is that the only way to really practise it is to grow up in the West Indies, South Africa, Australia – during their glory years – or play Test cricket. There are plenty of batters who see the ball incredibly well until the bowling gets over 87mph. That is another level unlocked.

Rahul Dravid says:

> I feel you need to get used to playing fast bowling, the more you can get access to playing fast bowling. And that's why I think Indians play fast bowling better now.

28

Like when I see the way these guys can do today, they have four throw-down specialists travelling with them, bowling machines and endless net bowlers. I was facing Sachin Tendulkar bowl medium pace because our seam bowlers had got tired.

In an interaction with Bangladesh opening batter Tamim Iqbal on his YouTube channel in 2020, Virat Kohli explained the role of D. Raghavendra, the throw-down specialist:

I believe the improvement this team has shown while playing fast bowling since 2013 has been because of Raghu [Raghavendra].... After playing Raghu in nets, when you go into the match, you feel there is a lot of time.

India's history gives us a good idea of how hard it is to play fast bowling. When they toured England in 1952, they had to go up against Fred Trueman, the world's leading pace bowler at the time. He had skill, a repeatable action and pace. This is why he was the first to pass 300 wickets. This is where it all started.

Against him was Polly Umrigar, a star of Indian batting. His record was mostly based on scoring against Pakistan, New Zealand and the West Indies. Against England and Australia he averaged 26.9, compared to the 53.7 against the lesser attacks. A big part of his issue was pace. In four Tests, he batted seven times and managed 43 runs. The low scores were an issue, but it was the optics that really caused problems.

Umrigar backed away from Trueman, similar to a tail-ender, but really more like a kid facing a cricket ball for the first time. Tony Lock, who was fielding close on the legside, said, 'I say Polly, do you mind going back? I can't see the bowler.'

India was a cricket culture completely inspired by spin bowling. Post-Independence India had some seamers, but even then, they were largely skill-based swing bowlers. The pace and brutality of Trueman was just nothing they could get used to. In one part of that series, Trueman would take 10 wickets and nine of them were bowled. Not everyone struggled; one of India's great bats – Vijay Hazare – managed runs. But the stories of Indian batters all backing away, being soft and afraid, stayed with their team for years.

There was an overcorrection to the narrative when Indian opener Sunil Gavaskar ended up with an average of 70.2 in the Caribbean. Most of those runs come from eras when their wickets were slower and they still relied on spin bowling. When the West Indies became a great team, he played six Tests against that side in the Caribbean and averaged 30. But Gavaskar was an incredible player of seam bowling; this is clear from his average of over 40 in New Zealand and England.

The next generations kept finding incredible players of seam and importantly quick bowling. Rahul Dravid remembers:

Growing up as a young Indian batsman, especially in my era, we were constantly told that your test is against real pace. I think just that exposure to pace is important.

I grew up in Bangalore where we didn't play any cricket on turf. There was only one turf ground in those days in Bangalore. It was the main stadium where kids like me would never get access to. I practised on a mat.

While it's not ideal for certain kinds of techniques, it's certainly good for your back foot game because the ball bounces a lot more. I remember playing with people like Venkatesh Prasad or Javagal Srinath, you had to cut and you had to pull. So I grew up playing a little bit like that. I think I remember I played one first-class game on a mat. I think that was the year the BCCI [Board of Control for Cricket in India] said, no, every first-class game has to be on a turf wicket.

So we started playing on turf and then you quickly realise that to be successful in India in domestic cricket and to go up the ranks, you had to be a very good player of spin, because everywhere we went, every team had three or four good spinners, and the tracks turned a lot.

I got to England in '96 on my first trip and England played four fast bowlers and one spinner, 65th over or something like that, and it just literally gets through to 80, and then they're fast bowlers again. And I realised that Test cricket is about fast bowling.

It's actually a flip. It was 15 overs of pace and then 65 overs of spin in India when I was growing up playing domestic cricket, to suddenly being just the opposite in the first 80 overs when I was playing international cricket.

In 2014, I was there at Adelaide when Virat Kohli scored twin hundreds to almost win a Test in his first assignment as captain. He was dogmatic. He was dominant. He was floating above the crease like a supernatural being. It would be an understatement to just call it batting. Australian left-arm speedster Mitchell Johnson broke an entire team there a year before. In the space of two balls, Kohli had smashed him, smiled at him and then laughed as he bowled a wide. He would go on to score four centuries in four matches on that tour.

Virat Kohli batted at No. 4 for India in the first Test after Sachin Tendulkar's retirement. He nearly scored twin hundreds against a South African attack of Dale Steyn, Morné Morkel, Vernon Philander and Jacques Kallis in Johannesburg, scoring 119 in the first innings and 96 in the second. In March 2022, Rohit Sharma would call it his best memory of Kohli the batter ahead of his hundredth Test.

In an interview with Nagraj Gollapudi in *Cricket Monthly* in 2015, Kohli talked about his battle with Dale Steyn in that Test:

> In the Johannesburg Test, Dale was bowling a few bouncers when I was in my 30s. He kept urging me to pull. Then I saw that one ball for which I had visualised a proper pull shot, playing it down, and I beat deep square leg four feet to his left. I hit it that hard. That clean. So I felt: this is exactly what I had imagined and this is exactly what happened.

Kohli averages 54 in Australia and 49.5 in South Africa. Among Asian batters with at least 1000 runs in the two countries, he has the highest average – even more than Tendulkar and Sri Lankan No. 3 Kumar Sangakkara. Even then, raw averages do not tell us the full story. He averages 69% more than the top six batters in the matches he played in South Africa, and 40% more in Australia.

As of 21 February, 2024, he averages 63.6 against bowling of 87mph or more (outside India) according to the *CricViz* database – the highest by an Indian batter from the recorded data.

The West Indies really changed the number of bouncers. Not in the 1970s, but 50 years earlier. They tried this method at a few players, including Wally Hammond who struggled with it. The first issue for Hammond was that he stopped playing the hook shot. Like it was for the Indian players, there weren't really a lot of quicks around, so it wasn't a problem you had to constantly worry about.

The great blog *Old Ebor* has a lot on Hammond's issues with the fast short ball. England wicketkeeper Les Ames said, 'When we came up against the West Indians, I did detect on Wally's part a slight weakness against the really quick, short stuff. Yes, of course, [Manny] Martindale and [Learie] Constantine worried him a bit.' In fact, Constantine dismissed Hammond eight times in 10 Tests.

England batter Bob Wyatt told a story about how he opened the batting with Hammond in South Africa and the fast bowler Sandy Bell was making the new ball rise sharply; Wyatt was left to face the attack while Hammond largely made sure he was at the other end. He also recalled the Gentlemen v Players match in 1939 (by which time Hammond was an amateur and captained the Gentlemen) when Hammond 'virtually threw his wicket away' while Bill Bowes and Bill Copson were bowling fast and in intimidatory fashion. Even Reg Sinfield, a huge admirer of his old teammate, admitted in later years that Hammond, who occasionally opened the batting for Gloucestershire with him, 'preferred to leave him to face the bulk of the new ball'.

Hammond was clearly a great player, but he loved dominating classic seam and spin. Don Bradman was another player who had an issue with the short ball, which is what led to England using their leg theory (Bodyline) on him for the 1932/33 Ashes. This wasn't just short-pitched bowling from the tearaway quick Harold Larwood and left-armer Bill Voce. It was also the fields, which were set up with as many fielders behind square on the legside as they wanted, and with all that Bradman's average dropped to 56.6 – the only time in his career he went at less than 66.

Had Bradman and Hammond played in other eras, they would have worked out a way to play it better. But they were at the birth of the short ball as a consistent tactic with fields to back it up. The period when players really had to learn how to play the short ball was when the West Indians brought it back in the 1970s and '80s. Clive Lloyd didn't pick four fast bowlers straight away; it took a little while to assemble. But he certainly let his bowlers bowl short.

Compared to the Lord's Test of 2023, which had the most recorded bouncers, the West Indians bowled a lot fuller. Their bouncers were to set up for full balls. The Sabina Park game against India in 1976 changed their style, but in the first innings there were three bowled/lbws in there, and in the second, it was six. What the West Indians did was use the bouncer as a threat. But their best ball was more of the back of a length delivery that rose. At 90mph from a giant bowler, the designation means little. There was no rest, there was no weak link. If you couldn't handle pace, you had to wait for Carl Hooper or Viv Richards to bowl some off-spin late in the afternoon. The rest of the time it was high pace with incredible skill and overs that never seemed to end. For two decades you were rated as a batter on how you handled the four fast men.

Allan Border would have to be the most incredible player against this attack on their pitches, averaging 53 over 11 matches. For his trouble, he would be beaten up routinely by short balls, regularly getting struck on the body and head. Conversely, an equally talented player in Javed Miandad played in the Caribbean seven times in that period and averaged 33.7. Miandad showed his talent through his entire career, but a player from flatter Pakistani wickets was going to struggle with four quicks at his chest in that era.

The Asian stars worked it out over time, even if they were behind. One shot Asian batters play against high pace is the upper cut, or slash to the off side. But it wasn't just them, it was a shot Australian No. 4 Mark Waugh played as well. In part, because he felt the West Indians would target him as he had no pull or hook shot:

If you're not a natural hooker and puller against the West Indies, it does reduce your scoring options a great deal. I started to back away and I backed away in a Test in Melbourne on Boxing Day.

I gave myself room. And although it was risky, I was banking on the ball being short, even though I'd exposed my stump, so it just gave me the option to hit over the slips or over point to the short ball rather than hooking it.

I thought that was the safest shot for me, personally. It didn't look pretty, but I think it was a bit frustrating for the bowlers at times as well. There was a bit of premeditation, obviously, in that sort of style of batting. But to me, just standing there and getting hit from pillar to post and not being able to score any runs against the West Indies was pointless. I had to come up with some sort of other option.

You can tell the story of Sachin Tendulkar and high pace through two upper cuts to the fastest bowlers in the world. In the 2003 World Cup, he was facing the world's fastest bowler Shoaib Akhtar when the Pakistani speedster dropped short and wide. By this point, Sanath Jayasuriya had perfected the slash over third for six. But that isn't the shot Tendulkar played. That is a shot where you are using the pace and helping the ball away. Sachin's version was a normal cut, but he hit it high in the air, and the ball flew over backward point for a massive six.

Five years later, he is facing Australian Brett Lee on the world's fastest wicket, the Western Australian Cricket Association (WACA) in a Test. Lee bowls a very fast short ball at Tendulkar. The batter bends his back like he's at a beach limbo party and with a fairly straight bat, ramps the ball over the slips' head for six. Tendulkar was 34 at the time.

By the time Tendulkar perfected his version, it was quite a smooth, normal-looking shot, compared to the more frantic early versions by someone like Waugh. 'It looked like I was scared by backing away, but I was just trying to open up some scoring options,' Tendulkar explained.

Test batting against pace had changed so much now it was the Australian who was accused of being scared and the Indian in control.

But fear and fast bowling always go hand in hand. Most people see it as a test of courage to stand in front of the ball moving at that pace. That is certainly true; anyone who has stood at the crease when someone was bowling too fast for them will know that fear.

Rahul Dravid talked about it:

I cannot honestly ever say that I was never scared of fast bowling or I'm not scared of getting hit. I was certainly scared of getting hit. I didn't want to get hit, but I also wanted to be in the contest.

I love the fact that it was challenging and it just got me a bit nervous.

So, Dravid was both afraid of being hit and a great player of pace bowling. That means that courage is only one small part. Most players who struggle against real quick bowling do so because they do not have the hard and soft technical skills to handle real pace. Someone like Polly Umrigar is seen as soft, but in truth, he never worked out the skills needed for high pace. Maybe over time, if he was exposed to it early enough, he would have developed them, but not all batters do (the same way that not all players learn to handle the spinning or seaming ball).

When you are a batter who struggles with turn, people might think of you as a lumbering player or a bit one-dimensional. A batter who struggles with seam or swing might be seen as a little technically deficient. But if you struggle against high pace, you are yellow.

It doesn't make sense. If you think about it, the people with the greatest courage are the ones who are standing in front of quick bowling without any skill to face it. They are the ones most likely to be hit and embarrassed.

West Indian Viv Richards was as good a player of fast bowling as anyone, and he didn't wear a helmet because he saw the ball so much earlier than anyone else, with incredible skills to back that up. In modern cricket, there are still international players from Bermuda who bat without helmets on. They have the courage, but their talent is not like Viv's, and they often get themselves in awful tangles trying to play the short ball.

Many times people will talk about Richards hooking the ball off his nose for six. Yet when you go back to many of his greatest innings or collections of his best shots online, you will see something repeatedly – he is inside the line. His athleticism and anticipation mean that by the time the bouncer that was aimed at his face has arrived, it is now safely to the left of him. He will either smash it away, or it will go past him harmlessly. That is just not something a normal player can repeat.

Most players like the Waughs are stuck in a place where the fast short ball is just something to be survived. Richards took that option away from the bowlers and did it quickly. If you bowled two back of a length and one bouncer in an over, he could have

14 runs from pulls and hooks. What is your next option as a fast bowler? Richards took away one of their main threats and really turned it around at them.

Steve Waugh played high pace well, but he had to rope-a-dope bowlers by jumping up, taking balls on the body and riding each bouncer like an invisible rodeo bull. If you couldn't dismiss Waugh with the short one – many tried, few did – then at least you could slow him down.

The man who took over from him as Australian captain was Ricky Ponting. He played the short ball in a very different way. If it was short, he took it on. While Richards is the last player never to use a helmet, Ponting was still facing fast bowling into the late 1990s at times without one. By the time the Australian made his debut, even Richie Richardson, another incredible player of fast bowling, had exchanged his wide-brim maroon hat for a helmet.

So when Ponting was hit, it shook up the world.

England quick Steve Harmison was not only fast, but tall. On the first morning of the 2005 Ashes, he'd already hit Australian openers Justin Langer and Matthew Hayden. When Ponting came in, he was flying. The short ball at Ponting was 87mph, but it looked faster. Ponting went into his hook position, but the ball was through him so fast, smashing into the grille of his helmet.

None of this seemed to bother Ponting, who just readjusted the helmet, marked his guard and got ready for the following ball. But then he started bleeding from his face.

Getting hit like this can mess with how you play fast bowling. Another Australian legend was hit at Lord's and afterwards he was not the same.

Steve Smith once averaged 96.2 against seam bowling in Tests over a five-year period, making him the closest thing we've ever had to Bradman. The next best mark was Kane Williamson's 55.8; meaning Smith was nearly double the competition.

It was quite the turnaround from a player who was picked for his leg spin to bat No. 8 (though even then people thought batting was his stronger suit) who Ponting once said couldn't bat in the top six for Australia.

Then in 2019 Jofra Archer hit him on the neck at Lord's – less than five years after his friend Phil Hughes lost his life from a similar blow. Until that hit, Smith was averaging 63.2. After the blow, it dropped to 47.1.

There are other things worth remembering. From the middle of 2017, global averages dropped for around six years due to the Wobbleball taking over. Smith was batting lower down the order, and he also needed Tommy John surgery to repair a torn ligament inside the elbow.

A lot of his numbers were down in this period. But focusing in on the bouncer, before the hit by Archer, Smith was averaging 122 against them; after (until 29 May, 2024) it was 50.2. Back of a length against pace was 100.9, then it dropped to 27.5. How much of this was natural ageing curves, teams bowling to him straighter (before they would bowl outside off), his elbow or just general wear and tear? But getting hit by a spell of bowling that Steve Waugh described as one of the toughest he had seen did seem to change his batting.

According to *CricViz*, Steve Smith averages 65.1 against bowling 87mph and above (excluding BCCI matches, as of 21 February, 2024). So, before the Archer hit, he was clearly one of the best players of high pace ever.

This pattern has been seen before. South African Neil Adcock was one of the fastest bowlers in the world when New Zealand played him in a Test over Christmas in 1953. The wicket was also unsafe, with balls shooting straight up. Their openers, Geoff Rabone and Murray Chapple, were both hit before they were dismissed. That brought in Bert Sutcliffe (not to be confused with England's Herbert, who the Kiwi was named after) who would usually have opened. He was New Zealand's best Test bat, and on the way to greatness, with a 49.8 average after 11 matches when that Test started.

Adcock got his third ball to lift, striking Sutcliffe in the head; he lost consciousness and bled on the pitch. He was taken to hospital where he lost consciousness again. But he headed back out to bat, even though beating the follow-on was still a huge challenge. When he went back out to bat, they went through so many bandages that they had to try towels to stop the bleeding. He had also had a shot of whisky. So, out in the middle he was concussed, bleeding and a little tipsy. Yet he still attacked Adcock and the legendary off-spinner Hugh Tayfield to help pass the follow-on, and build an emotional partnership with the bowler Bob Blair, who had lost his fiancée in a train accident only hours before.

Sutcliffe was never the same batter after being hit. He was hunted by fast bowlers afterwards, who would almost always test him with bouncers. He still scored runs, but he was no longer a great. He retired as New Zealand's best Test bat, but was haunted by how good he could have been.

With Ponting, there was no lingering issue, like Viv Richards. Until the end of his career he was playing the short ball well. *CricViz* proves that, despite almost all of Ponting's peak coming after ball tracking became available with Hawkeye. From 2007 onwards Ponting averaged 40.1 in Tests, but *CricViz* tells us he went at 53.2 against 87mph and above. We can only imagine what he was like in his peak.

Like Richards, Ponting's main weapon against the quicks was the pull and hook. Rahul Dravid was obsessed with learning how he did it:

How's Ricky Ponting playing that pull so well? How's he hitting that shot so well? What is it about his technique that allows him to particularly do that?

Technically I think just a high backlift that allowed him to actually control that sort of, but a lot of people have had high backlifts.

He was exposed to quite a lot of fast bowling early on in his career. And he had to play a lot of pull shots and hook shots early on. So I think that certainly gave him a really good grounding on being able to do that.

The fact that he was so good at the pull and off the back foot meant that it reduces the fast bowlers options by quite a lot.

One of the key pace weapons actually gets lost because the ball will only swing and seam for that much. Then this becomes when people who have pace can push you on the back foot. Ponting, being exceptional at that, meant that people were then forced to pitch it up to him with an older ball, or when the ball was softer and he was good enough to capitalise on that as well.

Most players lose options against high pace; they rein in their backlifts, only use a couple of shots and go for survival. When you have a player like Ponting who plays all his shots against pace, it means he can use the speed of the ball against the bowler, and there is no place to bowl to slow him down. As Jimmy Adams says:

> Your range of scoring is larger than most people because there is a length that the mortals will try to get out of the way, to evade, whereas you might be clattering them to the boundary. That is immediate pressure. And if a bowler gets to the point where he realises that that's not a mistake, it wasn't a top edge, it's not something that is liable to get a wicket any time soon, then either he has to stop trying that, or he might be giving up runs at a rate that will see him taken out of the attack very shortly.

But Adams points out that Ponting gave himself another level against high pace. 'Most of these modern-day great artists will pull, which is an in front of square shot. Ricky, his range was from fine leg all the way around to wide mid-on. Which is what the great batters have, a wider range than the mortals.'

Think of the time and technical skills needed for Ponting to be able to pick the ball up early, play it safe and then still have time to pick where he wants to hit it. As Adams says:

> When I say fast bowling, let me define that a little bit because good fast bowling will find out any batsman. I'm talking about sharpish bowling that he was very good against. He was better than Lara and Tendulkar facing body line bowling, fast bowling, in terms of how he could handle it, and how he could take that kind of bowling and put the pressure back on the bowler, where your Laras and your Tendulkars would survive.

Dravid is still wondering where it all came from:

> Ponting was playing the pull shots as a young kid, maybe there's some constraint there or something. It's up against a really fast bowler, or it is indoors or something. He just got a fascination for it, and someone had the courage to put him out there in those days, pulling without a helmet, and so he had to get good at it.
>
> Maybe that was the thing that I remember in the early days, pulling your helmet today because of health and safety regulations,

nobody's going to allow you to. Ricky Ponting won't allow his son to pull without a helmet, man. His wife certainly won't.

But there is Ponting, good enough, young, facing short fast bowling not wanting to get hit on the face. There might have been 10 kids who got hit on the face because of that and are working as bankers somewhere in Australia because they've got hit on the face and the nose and been frightened of the ball.

But one Ponting has emerged from there.

It is also not a surprise that the West Indies, Australia and South Africa keep finding these players. They have pace, their batters have to face it. Some of the best contests are when the two cultures clash.

There is a sickening sound at Centurion Park, it stops everyone in the ground. It sounded like the helmet, and then skull, broke. The batter was Ryan McLaren, a South African all-rounder who was out in the middle facing Mitch Johnson.

But not any version of the Australian left-arm speedster, the southern summer of 2013/14 edition. McLaren was more of a bowler who could bat. In first-class cricket coming in down the order he was good enough to average 33.9. But he was a domestic No. 7, which is not a full-time batting position, and at the higher level he struggled to make an impact. It was almost unfair to bat against Mitch Johnson at that point if you weren't at least a specialist batter.

McLaren survived that huge blow on the head, but later that year faced Johnson again in an ODI and had his arm broken.

In the same game that he was struck on the helmet, three other batters had to face Johnson – Hashim Amla, Graeme Smith and AB de Villiers – three undisputed greats of the game whose careers for South Africa overlapped.

Amla had a very slow start to his career and probably played on a little long. But in the middle, he had a 10-year period of averaging 52. He had nine good years, and four of them were great. He averaged 59 in Asia, 45 in Australia and 60 in England. He should average more away, but has random failures in Bangladesh, New Zealand, Pakistan, West Indies and Zimbabwe. It's almost like the better the bowling attack, the better he went.

In this match, Amla faced only three balls from Johnson. Two he handled fine; the third he ducked into, and Johnson hit him very hard. Amla was a fantastic player of pace and spin, and he was surely great, but this was different gravy in terms of pace. The entire South Africa side was either hit or terrified by Johnson – except one.

De Villiers is a great batter; you can start with his 50 average away from home where he also averaged over 40 in every place he has played more than five innings. He also had to keep wicket for a while and managed to average 57 when doing so. He was really a No. 5, but he had to bat everywhere from opening to No. 8. He averaged 49.4 versus pace and 53.1 against spin. He also played some cricket as the Wobbleball was dropping averages everywhere and managed to score over 600 runs at 53.2 versus quality Australian and Indian attacks. There is a part of his career that feels like he ended earlier than he should have, but he had 11 good years and eight of them were great.

If there was one thing that vaults him up this list, it was his batting against high pace. There was an Indian Premier League (IPL) match where de Villiers was playing against his usual teammate Dale Steyn with his team RCB needed 28 runs in two overs with five wickets down.

The first ball was a straight slower ball on a decent length; de Villiers swept it for six. The next ball, Steyn went for the yorker at 90mph; de Villiers went back and slapped it straight over Steyn's head for another maximum. There were two singles that followed, so when Steyn had de Villiers back on strike, he moved the entire field, including bringing mid-off up into the ring.

The ball was full and straight, and de Villiers was set up to hit it to mid-on, but his hands changed late, like he suddenly remembered where the field was, and the ball flew over mid-off's head.

Steyn changed his field again. Fine leg came up. This time Steyn went full and wide of off stump. De Villiers had already faked like he wanted some room, but as the ball was out there, he went to meet it, and his feet were now on the wide demarcation line. De Villiers was scrambling, maybe even slipped a little. It was looking like he should have stayed at home and hit over cover. But in the middle of him faking to give room, Steyn going full and wide with de Villiers almost losing his balance, he somehow seemed to stop all time, take a break, recompose, and then from two feet inside the line of the ball he swept Dale Steyn into the second tier at the Chinnaswamy Stadium. Steyn's over went for 24 of the 28 required.

CricViz has stats on how players do against bowling of 87mph and quicker. De Villiers averaged 61 against it. Most of the players higher than him on the list faced fewer balls or a lot of theirs in Asia. De Villiers played his on hard South African wickets.

This pitch at Centurion was quick, and probably felt like lightning when Johnson was bowling on it. Smith had lasted two balls against Johnson. Faf du Plessis was not on the level of the other batters mentioned but was clearly an above-average talent, and he was out to the fourth ball against Johnson. So de Villiers entered at 23/3.

The wicket was odd, Australian top order player Shaun Marsh made a hundred, but the wicket was a little inconsistent of pace and bounce. Keeper Brad Haddin would take one ball well above his head and the following one at his feet. De Villiers from the start was so far in behind the ball, his movements are syncopated to some music the rest of us can't hear. His body moves into line as if he and the ball are in it together.

Of course, that ease can be deceiving as the endlessly elegant Mark Waugh knows too well: 'It's just the way you play. It's just the way you move. Yeah, everyone's different. Some people look a bit jittery at the crease and their movements are a bit sharper and a bit more jolted than other players. They move languidly into the ball'.

Waugh continues: 'It's no easier to me to score runs than for Stephen (Waugh) or anyone else. It's just as hard for me. It's just that I look different. Or David Gower looks different. His body movements are a bit of an optical illusion, it's certainly not easier.'

But that leads into time. It was a conversation that every batter mentioned. Why do some players have more time? Previously, I talked about why batters like Don Bradman and Ross Taylor can see things ahead of time, so it appears like they are reading the bowler's mind. Beyond that, there is the athleticism, that ability to match the decisions with the movement.

That is what you see with de Villiers, the two coming together. His history shows that de Villiers could have picked from several sports; he is a great athlete. When speaking to old-timers, they often compared de Villiers to West Indian all-rounder Garfield Sobers, another incredible athlete. They saw the game like the great batters, but they had even more time because when they made a decision, their bodies could execute it more quickly.

So, when de Villiers faces Mitchell Johnson, he makes him a medium pacer. The left-armer thunders down a 90mph delivery, back of a length, on de Villiers' hip. It's not really a place for an attacking shot; it's made to be nudged to fine leg. But de Villiers is inside the line, because as Johnson has come in, he has already moved into position. In the previous over, he faced a bunch of balls back of a length at his hip, and he was trying to whip them across the line but couldn't get the connection he wanted. So, anticipating the same ball, he is now inside the line, and it gives him a free swing at the ball.

The shot he plays is a work of art. It is like a pick-up pull shot, but with a straight blade. It is as if he's playing a back foot lofted straight drive but facing square leg. You can play this shot in tennis ball cricket, against a medium pacer. De Villiers was facing one of the most destructive bowlers ever at his peak, and he treated him like a kid at a barbecue as he hit the ball on to the grass bank. As Ross Taylor says, 'A ball could land in one area and literally he could hit that in three different areas, in all forms of the game.'

De Villiers played this innings after an operation in which they took a plate out of his wrist, and he hadn't really had much preparation.

Later Johnson will bowl a delivery at the top of off stump; de Villiers is waiting for it for such a long time. When this 86mph ball finally arrives, he moves his hands at an incredible speed. Like many in cricket, Nasser Hussain is obsessed with de Villiers' mitts, 'No one's yet explained it to me perfectly, but where do fast hands come from? I asked de Villiers that, you know, he said, "I just trained the brain to do it. I do drills with it."'

This doesn't look like the shot of a well-drilled man. Younger players at RCB would often remark that in the nets, the difference between de Villiers and Virat Kohli was massive. Clearly, the Indian legend worked hard – and smart – but their movements and time were very different. Kohli looked like a top-quality batter who was working so hard to perfect his game; de Villiers looked like batting was invented for him.

In a podcast with Danish Sait on the RCB YouTube channel, Virat Kohli explains the difference: 'It is beyond belief the kind of things he does. I have probably worked five years to get to this level and this guy comes with a six-month layoff of not having played any cricket, and he's batting five levels above you. It's phenomenal. I don't think anyone has had or has the kind of ability AB has.'

Another thunderbolt from Johnson is fired in. The ball is less than a metre from de Villiers and it is honestly hard to tell if he is going to defend or leave. Bob White would often say the same of Sobers: he moved late, but at such a speed that he was still ahead of the ball. He decides to let it pass, and there is a moment where it feels like he could have taken the hand off the bat, grabbed the ball, looked at it and tossed it to the ground.

If that sounds like something from a science-fiction movie, you are not alone. 'Oh, man, it's like watching *The Matrix* movie,' said Dale Steyn on his teammate at a press conference:

There is Neo for you right there. Like he just doesn't understand how good he is.

I think he's actually figured out now that he is like – there is no roof or cap on how good he can possibly be. He's limitless in what he can do. He's one of those players that's proven in this year especially just how good he is. I think he's starting to realise that now.

Players around the world, bowlers are struggling to find a way to get this guy out. The only way to get him out is when he gets himself out.

You watch the ball from Johnson go past de Villiers and, like Neo in *The Matrix*, you think the world works in a different way for him. The way Neo stopped the bullets in mid-air is what de Villiers bats like in peak form.

Johnson drops one a bit short and wide later; de Villiers goes up and over gully for another boundary against another ball at 91mph. What is noticeable is his eyes; most batters do not watch the ball until it hits the bat. It's hard to do from a medium pacer, but at this speed you're seeing his eyes follow the ball on to the middle of the bat. Again, this is not how people play high pace. The science tells me that he was picking up clues earlier, that he knew the rough area the ball would pitch, what kind of delivery and how it would bounce. But the science also tells me that his eyes saccade; that they pick up the first few metres and then find where the ball should be arriving. Yet watching him play this shot, there is no evidence of that.

De Villiers sees the ball from the hand, studies every inch of its journey then watches it fly away to an empty boundary. He's like a hawk; he can see it at all times. De Villiers is somehow seeing into the future and the present at the same time.

Eventually, Johnson would get de Villiers, his sixth wicket, from a slower ball as he slogged with the tail. The second top score in this innings was 25. De Villiers made 91. Johnson took 7/68. De Villiers made 43 of those runs, scoring at a strike rate of 86. South Africa got slaughtered in this match. De Villiers was the best player on show, combining technical brilliance with his own remote control to stop time.

The South African shares a lot with a West Indian legend as well. There is a delivery that the fastest bowler in the world – Australian Jeff Thomson (Thommo) – bowls to Viv Richards that best shows how he goes about it. Thomson was at that stage the fastest bowler in the world – and compared to other bowlers, probably no one has ever been faster than their peers than he was. At this point in the ODI he has conceded 16 runs from 6.1 overs, but with Thommo it was never about numbers. His athleticism is on full show as he comes into the crease and his action is unfurling his human catapult.

This ball is fired into the top of middle and leg. If there is an issue with it, maybe it is too straight; another player would get inside the line and turn it to leg. That is what Viv would normally do, but with the score on 97/4, Richards has had enough. He leans back to the full ball and pulls it violently over deep square for a boundary, like the ball has done something to him personally. Commentator Bill Lawry says, 'Richards has decided to take over.' There is no other way to see this.

The fastest bowler in the world has been treated like an underarm from a toddler. It isn't even a proper shot because you can't pull a ball this full, but it's not a slog. Instead, what Richards has decided to do is hit the ball where and how he wants. He wanted to pull the ball; it wasn't his issue that the delivery was wrong for that, so he executes it perfectly anyway.

In the 1983 World Cup, Thomson bowls the exact same delivery. If anything, it is more down the legside because he delivers it from very wide, probably to get Richards to hit to the longer legside boundary. Richards is not interested in where it has come from, just where he wants to hit. This time he picks cover, he backs away, gives himself room and plays a lofted cover drive for six.

Shortly after this, Clive Lloyd hooks a boundary from Thomson, and while he gets a boundary, the difference is obvious. Lloyd is a fantastic player, but he plays the shot off his face and is rushed all the way through. That is the normal way – even for a great. You are supposed to be rushed, just catch up with the ball and manage a boundary because of the pace. That is not at all what Richards is doing; he has so much time he can decide if he wants to play a cover drive, even if the ball is pitched on his legs while he is still backing away. It's not just these shots that show you what Viv Richards can do, but the one that shows his technical mastery of fast bowling is also against Thomson in that game. The quick delivers a length ball well outside off stump, and Richards meets it on the up. It's again the wrong shot for the ball, but Richards' technical mastery and commitment to attack means he drives it with ease back down the ground for a boundary. Most players – if they dared to attack – would slash this ball to the point or cover region. They wouldn't play a proper drive, and it wouldn't go straight.

Again, Viv has time. He could have used this skill alone, but he matches it with being more aggressive than the fast bowler coming at him. He changes the equation. He is now the killer, and they are the prey. They bowl fast, and he scores faster.

If de Villiers was the person stopping bullets, Richards was the one whacking them back at bowlers.

4

TESTLESS

Some of the best female players have never played Test cricket

'I feel like I'm kind of missing out.' – Suzie Bates

There is a hand in her face, with the idea of somehow stopping her from scoring. The problem is no one has ever stopped her before. She was the leading scorer in 2006, and then again from 2008 to 2011. It is because of her scoring that her team wins a lot. She is a star, and known the world around precisely because she can score.

Diana Taurasi is a guard for the USA basketball team. Her career would end with three Women's National Basketball Association (WNBA) championships, one Most Valuable Player award, six EuroLeague titles and five Olympic gold medals. She has 10,000 points in the WNBA, and second best has not yet reached 8000. When it comes to basketball, no one scores like her.

But the hand in her face is from a great scorer as well. The difference is the sport. Taurasi is playing the sport she is great at: basketball. Her defender is Suzie Bates, a guard for the New Zealand basketball team. In basketball, Bates is undersized; in cricket, she is a giant.

To watch Bates at the crease is like watching someone who can take a step down and meet any ball while also being strong enough to dismiss it. In women's cricket, the keeper often stands up at the stumps, and often, that just makes Bates look even more imposing. Then the ball comes towards her and she takes a step down. She has that kind of physicality that makes it look like she can play any shot she wants from her front foot.

She could not stop Diana Taurasi from scoring, and the rest of cricket knew how she felt.

Suzie Bates is the all-time leading Twenty20 International (T20I) scorer, with over 800 more runs than Australian No. 3 Meg Lanning in second place (1 July, 2024). In ODI cricket, the Australian legend has 15 hundreds, two behind her is Suzie Bates. She was also the third player to score more than 5000 runs in that format. You can look at averages or strike rates in these formats, but she has an incredible run tally, which on its own has to get her into the conversation for the top five greatest women batters ever. In 2016, she won the International Cricket Council's (ICC's) top awards for ODI and T20I.

If you dive deep into her career, England is clearly the team she's struggled with, averaging 25.1 in ODIs. Bates put that down to the opening bowlers. 'I probably wouldn't have admitted this, but now they've retired, I do not miss Katherine Brunt or Anya Shrubsole. So I just felt like as an opening combination, they were so relentless with their lines and lengths.'

The only other blemish on Bates' career was a poor record away from home. However, she averages 39.4 and 44.7 in Australia and India. In the seven years she was ODI captain, she went at 51.8. She's incredible at chases ('I feel like I batted my best innings when I batted first'), at 45.6, but when New Zealand wins, that mark rises to 73.2. In World Cups, she averages more than 50, and just opening, she is at 45.2.

That is ODIs. In T20Is, she has passed 4000 runs, the only woman to do that. She also averages 29 as a very dependable anchor. Her record is almost flawless, but there is one thing missing.

Suzie Bates has no runs in Test cricket.

Not because she isn't talented enough, but New Zealand cricket has never scheduled a match for her to play in. The last time the

Kiwi women played a Test was in Scarborough in 2004. Bates made her debut in 2006 for the ODI team.

How good is Suzie Bates in Tests? We will never know. She muses:

When I watch it, there are those feelings and there's a little bit of envy. There's a little bit of wonder of how I'd go. If I got out first ball, I'd be a nightmare. I just feel there should be sort of equal opportunities. And for whatever reason in New Zealand, we haven't had that. […] I'd like to think, though, that if I'd played a few more games, I would have learned. I love batting so much that the idea of me just going to bat for days and days is incredible.

That is the romantic side of missing Tests, but there are more practical sides as well. When West Indian middle order T20 player Nicholas Pooran decided to make it as a professional player without first-class cricket (due to falling out with the Trinidad and Tobago board over medical treatment), he was left in a weird position. How do you grow your game just playing T20 tournaments?

For Pooran, it was a conversation with West Indian all-rounder and T20 legend Dwayne Bravo. Pooran says, 'Dwayne was telling me, "Pooran, you can still learn from franchise cricket, man. You just have to learn quickly, stop making the same mistakes over and over. And you have to know what you want as a cricketer."'

But Pooran understands how rare this situation is, and how for many players the lack of red ball cricket stops your development. For many women cricketers, this is a normal occurrence, as Bates notes:

You're stopping and starting all the time in limited overs cricket. Whereas if you're playing multiple red ball games, you have a lot more ability to get yourself into that rhythm and feel more comfortable and natural with what you're doing. Patience with the ball. Patience with the bat at times. It's that time in the middle that helps you access that.

Bates, like Pooran, admits that not playing red ball cricket stunts a player's growth:

You have someone like Annabel Sutherland, who sometimes gets limited opportunities in the Australian team, but she's able to bat and score 200 in a Test. Mostly she's batted at No. 5 or No. 6 in franchises. She's got a chance to play in a number of different tournaments, and she might face a handful of balls. But in an international game, she gets to face hundreds and hundreds of balls in one game.

I just think it's the mental toughness and resilience that comes with Test match cricket as well as an advantage, and it's a bit more of a mental challenge.

And so I find it hard when not everyone's playing, like I'm so supportive and I love it, but it's harder when you're in the same competition and you're at the same level, but some people are (playing), it does feel a little bit unfair at times. That's no one's fault, that's just how you feel when you're missing out.

The top five run scorers in Tests for women are Jan Brittin, Charlotte Edwards, Rachael Heyhoe-Flint, Debbie Hockley and Carole Hodges. New Zealand has one player on that list – Hockley – who averaged 52 in Tests. The rest are English. Despite Australia's domination of women's cricket for decades, their highest run-getter is Karen Rolton at No. 10, though Ellyse Perry will probably surpass her.

The real issue here isn't the missing Australians but the lack of runs. Not a single woman in the sport's 90-year history has 2000 runs. Brittin has 1935, and the only current player within touching distance is Perry, who played 13 matches in 16 years. She would need to play for another 16 to get close at that rate.

There are men in this book without many Test runs – W.G. Grace has 1098 – but for them, there is always first-class cricket. Grace made 53,113 runs in that level of cricket. It wasn't until 2018 that the ICC recognised women's domestic red ball cricket as first-class. The decision – made retroactively – was a step to redress the idiotic decisions of previous gatekeepers in cricket. According to the website *Cricket Archive*, Brittin does have 16 first-class matches as well as 27 Tests.

Brittin averaged 39 when not playing for England and 49 in Tests. But this provokes more questions, like what was the quality of domestic pitches made for women? It cannot have been good. Was Brittin great, or just an ordinary player who batted on some nice wickets?

The lack of data also makes it difficult to discuss Australian Betty Wilson, who in 11 Tests made 862 runs at an average of 57.5. She had six scores over 50, including three hundreds. But with no first-class record to troll through, it is hard to know how great she was.

There are 39 batters with more than 500 runs in Tests, and of those, Denise Annetts has the best average – a stunning 81.9 – but it is from only 10 matches for Australia. She also played 43 ODIs, but her average was an excellent – but more normal – 41.7. How good was Annetts? Well, she is barely mentioned at all anymore. That is because when she was dropped from the team, she claimed it was because she wasn't gay.

Her dropping got more headlines in Australia than women's cricket had ever received, yet barely a word was written about her batting.

It is worth looking at the best ODI players as well because that is the format of cricket that women have played the most. While no woman has 2000 runs in Tests as of the end of 2024, 48 (as of 22 April) have that many ODI runs. Mithali Raj has 7805; Bates and Edwards both have more than 5000.

This means the sample size is much bigger, and the players at the top make a lot more sense. Meg Lanning averaged 53.5. Many would consider her the best batter in modern women's cricket, and maybe all time. Lanning seemed to take women's cricket to another level.

'Ricky Ponting was my hero growing up. I love the way he batted and took the game on a lot. I'd mimic him in the backyard,' Meg Lanning told me in 2017. But she didn't need to; you could see Ponting in her eyes when she played.

When Lanning grew up, she did so at a time when women's cricket was hidden, amateur and barely thought of. People turned to the men's game. Her batting – and the team she led winning – was a big part of why the game changed.

Lanning represented her state Victoria at just 16 before making her debut at 18 for the Southern Stars (as the Australian Women's side was known back then). In her second ODI, she made a hundred as Australia chased 215 with nine wickets in hand. It made her the youngest to score a ton for the Aussies. When she retired in 2023, she left the game with 17 centuries across all formats in international cricket. Ten of those were in ODI chases, scoring them at a similar rate to Virat Kohli, who has the greatest number of centuries batting second in ODIs – 27 in 152 innings.

One of Lanning's most iconic knocks also came in the 2017 World Cup against Sri Lanka. The Australians were very heavy favourites, but Sri Lanka made 257/9. No one had ever chased a total like that in a World Cup.

It should have been tough, but Lanning didn't see it that way. Her first boundary is a ball swinging into her stumps on a yorker length, and she still guides it to point for a boundary. Another ball is overpitched, but somehow she still cuts it for another four. The third is full and she drives square to pick up one more. Everyone knew she was going to hit the ball to point, but the boundaries are still inevitable. She would end with 152 from Australia's 262.

It may not have always looked like that, but Lanning was pushed that day, and the person who did that was Chamari Athapaththu. The left-hander played what many at the time called one of the greatest knocks in ODIs, pumping the most highly rated bowling attack in women's cricket at the time to all parts on her way to 178.

It was not even the Sri Lankan's greatest knock – that would be her 195 not out when chasing South Africa's 301 in the 45th over. Both innings were better than a run a ball. Athapaththu's ability also showed how much the women's game was changing. When she was coming through the system, women's cricket was almost entirely dominated by England, New Zealand and Australia. This means that women stars will come from a far wider pool in the future.

Importantly, these innings were televised. The women of before might have been great, but they exist mostly in scorecards.

Women's cricket is changing so fast that Lanning's 8352 runs, 17 hundreds and 38 fifties were all achieved in just 241 games at the age of 31. She was a great by her mid-20s.

But Lanning was not technically correct, while previous generations of women's cricketers had been. Ted Dexter said of England's Molly Hide that she was 'enough of a stylist not to bother with a lust for power.' As the men's game drifted further from *The M.C.C. Cricket Coaching Book*, women's cricket stayed with big forward presses and high front elbows.

Lanning was one of the few to buck that trend early on, as was Claire Taylor. For England, Taylor would average more than 40 in both ODIs and Tests. But she would do so with a grip partly inspired by her time representing her nation in junior hockey. Players like Taylor and Lanning couldn't be kept in place by length balls and straight fields. Their technical twists meant that setting fields to either was a nightmare.

The women's game has less power than the men's, so the ability to manipulate the field through angles is even more important. Taylor did that brilliantly in the T20 World Cup semi-final at the Oval in 2009 to destroy an Australian team who were run ragged in the field trying to stop her twos.

But these new techniques were about scoring runs quicker. It is not the only development because power has come in as well. In the 2009 World Cup, 27 sixes were hit. South Africa's Lizelle Lee hit 118 in her international career.

In the space of a year, I was in the ground when Lizelle Lee hit sixes at the Melbourne Cricket Ground (MCG) and Leicestershire's Grace Road ground – two of the biggest playing areas in the sport. Lee didn't just clear the rope; she cleared the fence on both occasions.

Sixes are quickly becoming a big deal in women's cricket. Alex Blackwell debuted in 2003 and hit eight sixes in 144 ODIs. She smacked three sixes against India in the 2017 World Cup semi-final at the end of her career. Blackwell's hits bouncing off the Derby press box was the sound of women's cricket changing.

After seeing the hit of Lizelle Lee at the MCG, I spoke to her Melbourne Stars coach David Hemp (a former Glamorgan and Bermuda player):

> They are now backing themselves to have a go at it. They are practising it more; in the past that hasn't necessarily been done. Lots of people now practise range hitting, so they see how far they can clear. At the international level it happens all the time, and now it's filtering down the domestic game. Before they were doing a gym session a week, and now it's two or three. And they are getting better bats.

The bigger bangs weren't just from one big bang. Women's cricket has changed massively in the last two decades, more than the men's game ever has in a similar timespan. In 2012, any woman playing domestic cricket was completely amateur. She would study or go to school, then hit the nets for practice. At the end of that, there was almost no chance of them also putting in a gym session or extra range hitting. As many countries are moving towards professional women cricketers, and the best players hop between franchises, so many more are becoming great athletes.

When Lanning beat Sri Lanka and Athapaththu with that 152 not out, her final shot was a big straight six. This new outlook has changed what is possible for women's cricket.

But it doesn't tell us who the greatest batters in the women's game are. For instance, as good as Lanning has been, she averages 31.4 in Tests.

Tests were the most important format for a long time, but ODIs took over. The simple solution is to look at combined averages, but that brings up many other issues. In ODIs, strike rate matters a lot and it is not always easy to get for earlier women's matches. Even if we had access to it, factoring that in would be tricky. Also the 50 over game brings up unique differences. Like sometimes, you throw your wicket away to chase runs at the end. Women are far more likely than men to run on the final ball of the first innings in white-ball cricket until they are dismissed, sacrificing their averages for one extra run.

The other issue is that the women's game has developed so quickly that a quarter of the data is from an amateur era, when there were only two or three good teams. Of course, the men have this too, but it is stretched over 130 years. However, it is all in one format, so combining both makes the women's game even trickier to work out.

Then there is the Michael Bevan dilemma. The Australian lower-middle order batter is one of five players who have averaged over 50 in men's ODIs after scoring at least 5000 runs alongside Virat Kohli, Babar Azam, MS Dhoni and AB de Villiers. Each of them is a modern batter who has benefited from the run inflation of the modern era, and that limited overs batting is just better than ever before, except Bevan.

Indian wicketkeeper MS Dhoni debuted in 2004, and Bevan is the only player here to start before the year 2000 (1994). In the golden era of ODIs, Bevan was like nothing we had ever seen before, a middle-order player who could not be dismissed. More than that, Bevan changed the way limited overs batting was thought about. He combined the Australian running between the wickets and fitness with Javed Miandad's angles and found a way to handle yorkers others hadn't.

Bevan's main skill was really his brain. He saw limited overs cricket in a different way than others. For him, it was like a formula he could calculate. In the first innings, he would study the conditions, look for a par score, and then keep his wicket in hand for a late blast over with a great bowling line-up backing him up.

In the second innings he was even better, averaging 57 compared to 52 in the first. It is because of this he became known as the first finisher.

That all started on New Year's Day in Sydney, 1996. It was Bevan's 19th match. In his first 16 innings, he was not out in half of them. However, he was also dropped from the team, in part because there was a feeling the short ball could work him over.

The Australian team was not yet fully formed, especially the ODI version. So, chasing 173 against the West Indies, they fall to 38/6.

Bevan had played three matches in the series already, all of them not outs, scoring small totals at better than a run a ball.

This is a different kind of innings because Bevan enters a collapse, and it keeps happening. So he digs in and rebuilds the chase on his own, at first partnering with Australian wicketkeeper Ian Healy and later their seamer Paul Reiffel. But they are batting; Bevan is doing something else, calculating, working like an algorithm. Each two or four is part of his plan to chase this.

With 16 needed from 11 balls, he loses Reiffel. Soon, it is 13 off 8. None of these numbers are huge by today's standards, but once the chase became more than a run a ball in this era the bowling team were usually on top.

These days the same chase would be two boundaries and done. But as Andrew Miller wrote for *The Cricket Monthly*, 'Bevan's options were framed by the zeitgeist.' He was brilliant at running so fast that he put pressure on the fielders, so he brought the equation to 11 from 7 with a stolen second to long-on. Finishing the over with a boundary off Phil Simmons, an opening bat who bowled medium pace. The reason was the West Indies have used their frontliners trying to finish the game earlier. Teams from this day forward would learn not to do that with Bevan at the crease.

The last over, Shane Warne was on strike, there was a dot ball, a wide, and then the leg-spinner ran himself out to get Bevan back on strike meaning Glenn McGrath was in. The score needed was now six from four when Bevan took a single – something that wouldn't happen now. But luckily the gangly No. 11 got an inside edge, and Bevan was back on strike with four needed from two.

Roger Harper was the bowler, a defensive off-spinner who played as much for his fielding as his bowling. So when Bevan backed away to give himself some room and struck the ball back straight, Harper was there to stop it. Bevan looked at the pitch but really was giving himself a moment to find the boundary pockets.

The difference between him and other limited overs players of this time was that he wouldn't just go for his best power shots. He had such a rounded game and great wrists to find openings that he would milk the field with five men out. Harper went for a full quicker ball, and Bevan went straight again, but this time over the bowler's head with an extra bottom hand to the part of the ground that rarely blocks the straight hit.

Bevan became the finisher that day, and players like Meg Lanning still follow his formula.

But Bevan was dropped the summer before, not because of ODI cricket, but Tests. In 18 matches he never made a hundred, and outside of a great series touring Pakistan, he never looked like he could make runs, despite averaging a staggering 57 in first-class cricket.

Many blamed the bouncers. When Jimmy Adams was asked about this, he responded:

> Michael Bevan batted well enough against short pitch bowling. The easiest thing to say is, "Oh, he couldn't play the short ball." I disagree with that. I have done a lot of research on YouTube. There's evidence there against his attacks in Sheffield Shield, where they think the same thing, and they had more. And he was churning runs, like proper churning runs playing the short ball well for New South Wales. Look at his record in Perth.

Australian wicketkeeper Brad Haddin said on the *Willow Talk* podcast, 'I've seen him do things on the cricket field that others can't do. I remember everything was about the stigma about the way he played fast bowling. I've never seen anyone take on fast bowling as good as Michael Bevan in state cricket.'

Adams and Haddin are right; Bevan only has 1000 first-class runs at three venues. Two are the Sydney Cricket Ground (SCG) and Bellerive Oval, his home pitches. The third is the WACA; the fastest and bounciest wicket in the world during Bevan's career. Shield matches were played like Tests, and visiting players to Western Australia would often get peppered by abnormally tall local bowlers looking to get the attention of the national selectors.

On that pitch, against those bowlers, Bevan averaged 47.

Adams has another theory:

Let me call some names, right? Bevan is one. English guy from Zimbabwe, Graeme Hick, is another. Mark Ramprakash is another. No technical reason why they couldn't or shouldn't have performed better at the international level. There's nothing in the technique.

If Michael Bevan had issues with the short ball, then I can recall Mohammad Azharuddin and Sourav Ganguly were worse against it. But those guys at the highest level had a different mentality. They had an "I am going to find a way" mentality. And nothing is going to cause me to freeze mentally. For Hick, Bevan and Ramprakash, something happened to these lads when they took that step up. I think Steve Waugh played the short ball worse than Michael Bevan.

But Waugh never suffered from freezing when he got to the international level. In fact, he expanded himself because his mission in life was to dominate.

I take a very simplistic view to say that something in Bevan's mental or emotional wiring just didn't click when he stepped out with that baggy green.

Looking at that list of players with more than a 50 average in men's ODIs, and you also have MS Dhoni. The Indian keeper was an above-average keeper batter, but he was one of the greatest ODI bats ever. West Indian Shai Hope also had an average above 50 for a long time in ODIs, but he had a shockingly low one of 25 from his first 38 Tests.

So, is Meg Lanning another ODI superstar who couldn't translate or just someone who played six matches and never got a big score? The latter seems more likely, but with someone like Suzie Bates, we can only assume she would have played great Test innings.

In making a list of the greatest women batters, we must leave out some brilliant players.

Players unlucky to miss out include Australian opener Lindsay Reeler, who has a great record but not many runs. Around a quarter of them are from five ODIs against Ireland and the Netherlands as well. Karen Rolton – Australia's No. 3 – has a similar record to Bates, but her average is a little lower. England's all-rounders Nat Sciver-Brunt and Jan Brittin are both right up there, but don't quite have the number of runs or average to displace anyone. If I was factoring in strike rate, Sciver-Brunt might move into the top 10 as she finishes her career.

She also deserves special mention for being one of three players to play the draw shot, or as we now call it, the Natmeg.

Because Sciver-Brunt is a power hitter, she often sets her base wide and she's stuck with one option to hit down the ground. That is fine if she can get under the ball, but otherwise she's probably getting a single. So Sciver-Brunt started hitting through her legs, just helping the ball on its way. With short fine leg up in the circle throughout much of the women's innings, all that was needed was a fine tap and it was a four.

The actual shot is not new, even if the moniker has been updated. Rev. James Pycroft wrote about it in his 1862 book, *The Cricket Tutor*: 'No man can play underhand bowling well who cannot draw. And with round-arm bowling, for a left-handed player – I speak feelingly – the draw is quite indispensable, because so many balls, for which he must prepare as if straight, work away to the leg.'

There is no great description of the draw, but it feels like it was a back foot shot that was played when batters were cramped trying to score to the off side. That is certainly how it looks when illustrated for Nicholas Felix's book, *Felix on the Bat* – a back foot defensive shot with the face set up for the leg glance. In Ranji's *The Jubilee Book of Cricket* there is a photo of a shot called 'W.L Murdoch's under-leg stroke'. Ranji has his leg cocked like a dog near a tree and is trying to guide the ball to fine leg through the gap. It was a silly idea, and you can see why it faded away when players stood inside the line, put their pads in front of the stumps and turned to leg.

Once round-arm and under-arm bowling faded out, the draw did as well. But Sciver-Brunt and Steve Smith have brought this back. What is interesting about that is the fact they are vastly different players. Sciver-Brunt is a power hitter, and Smith is a master manipulator. But Smith has never found a ball he doesn't want to drag to behind square leg and it suits Sciver-Brunt as an escape shot.

Cricket's recent history with the yorker is fascinating. During the Joel Garner era, the West Indian giant fast bowler made it feel like the yorker was seen as the greatest delivery in limited overs. Batters evolved, though, at first through Bevan slicing it away through backward point then through South African Lance Klusener's big bat and raw power, the many Marillier scoops and ramps, MS Dhoni's helicopter shot and lower middle on his bat, and modern players moving around in their crease each ball.

The Natmeg is yet to catch on, but if pulled off it could be another arrow in the war on the yorker.

The other player unlucky to miss out is Enid Bakewell. Her average of 59 in Tests looks great, but she only went at 35 in ODIs. And she averaged the same against Australia in Tests; her runs are all against New Zealand and the West Indies.

It is also hard to compare eras. In men's cricket, there has been a gradual evolution of the game, but they all at least played Test cricket. The standard of the finals at the Women's T20 World Cup of 2009 was way lower than the franchise leagues of the early 2020s. The bowling talent had been supersized.

Suzie Bates lived through both eras:

Every pace bowler is a lot quicker. It's interesting though, because I still think back to Cathryn Fitzpatrick, who I played against once, and she was as quick as anyone that I've faced.

But she was out on a limb, and then everyone else was 10-15k slower, whereas you play in the WBBL [Women's Big Bash League], and any opening fast bowler is above 115. Before that you had dibbly dobbly medium pace bowling at 100k. There was a lot of less than 100k, a lot of them.

The athleticism of all the domestic players, especially in Australia and England, has improved. So whenever you now play in The Hundred or WBBL, every fast bowler gets the ball through. There's none of that wicket-to-wicket bowling that we perhaps had occasionally before. I feel like there's going to be a couple of young players that really max out their potential because they're going to have been in a fast-bowling system since the age of 15.

The systems haven't been in place quite long enough, but you'll have females hit that 130 mark because they've actually trained to be that type of player.

For a long time you could be a bit of a front foot bully. Your technique has to change a little bit because you can't pop on the front foot to some of the quicks around the world.

Many of the great early batters never had to face bouncers at all. The women's game has had a development boom that men's cricket has never witnessed. National players from the early 2000s often remark how they wouldn't even get into domestic teams today.

When looking at the quality of the batting, we are looking at how you do in your era. There would be no Nat Sciver-Brunt if Betty Snowball and Myrtle Maclagan hadn't paved the way.

The challenges in coming up with a list of the best batters in the women's game is endless. The old players have almost no footage to go back through. We can't see their domestic records. And they didn't play enough cricket. To come up with my list I consulted John Leather, the legendary women's cricket statistician, as well as the great cricket writing team of Raf Nicholson and Syd Egan from the *CRICKETher* website.

The top 10 I have settled on is: Mithali Raj, Charlotte Edwards, Meg Lanning, Rachael Heyhoe-Flint, Belinda Clark, Stafanie Taylor, Ellyse Perry, Suzie Bates, Denise Annetts and Debbie Hockley. Laura Wolvaardt looks destined to join that group, but you could make the same argument for Marnus Labuschagne early in his career, and that has slowed down.

Heyhoe-Flint is now more known for her pioneering ways, like how she started Cricket World Cups. But as a batter, she was a legend. She hit the first six in a Test (and ODIs), batted for 521 minutes in making 179 against Australia at the Oval to force a draw (a world record at the time), and averaged 45 in Tests. She made three hundreds. When she retired, she'd made 33% more runs than any other woman in Tests. Yet in ODIs she went beyond that, averaging 58. Her place is secure.

Belinda Clark was the first person of any gender to make a double hundred in a 50-over match. But if you stop there, you don't understand how incredible this was. She ran 141 of those runs, because she had no sixes and 22 fours. So she legged the first-ever ODI double hundred in 65 singles, 32 twos and four threes. Her professionalism when the game was amateur was beyond belief.

She averaged over 45 in both formats but did struggle in England, averaging only 28 in her four Tests – even in ODIs she was not great. However, she is one of the few women to play enough games to go into that detail, and there is no doubting her overall quality. She went on to work in player development for men and women in Australia.

Stafanie Taylor was one of three West Indian women to change cricket there. But she was the best at consistently making runs. Again, not one was in Tests, but averaging 43 while scoring 5000 ODI runs, and still retiring early to make money on the freelance scene (before making a comeback for T20Is). Her biggest issue would have been how much she struggled away compared to home; 49.4 compared to 35.3, but in neutral games it was 48.5. However, she didn't make huge runs in Australia (24.5) and England (19).

Debbie Hockley has a great record, that looks better the more you delve. From her ODIs in Australia, England and India, she averaged over 50. But at home, only 32. So her combined average of 44 is earned on the road. In Tests she made runs at home, but in England she averaged more than 70. Her combination of runs, average and record on the road makes her case very good, despite her not being as well known as others. Oh, and she played in the 1970s and the 2000s.

Then there is Mithali Raj, a batter of such timing and calm that during the 2017 World Cup she was reading a book when she was next in. You watch her bat and you think she almost has enough time to finish the paragraph before playing another grammatically correct cover drive. At the end of her career she was seen as too slow for T20, a relic of another generation.

She played across four decades – a 23-year career. Kids were complaining about her strike rate, unaware that before they were born she made a Test double century against England when no one else passed 62 for India.

Statistician John Leather said of her:

> It always impressed me that 'form' didn't exist for Mithali. Her career was famously long, but also contained huge periods of inactivity (she went 300+ days without playing an ODI on eight occasions in her career), but she always returned from them as if she'd never left. If you asked Mithali in 10 years' time, she'd probably still be able to reel off a 75-ball 50.

A couple of decades later, when she retired, she had doubled the number of runs scored by any other Indian woman – making 17% of India's runs in ODIs in total.

Raj was the face of Indian women's cricket. Even those who didn't watch it knew who she was. Australia's version of that was Ellyse Perry.

On average alone, Perry has a great record. But she is a not out legend. In Tests, she has been not out in seven of her 22 innings. Her average of 61 from 13 matches is incredible, but that is helped by a small sample size.

In ODIs that ratio goes up even higher; 42 not outs from 120 innings. That is barely believable. In T20Is she has 37 more not outs from 97 innings. If you want to dismiss Perry, bring an army. There are higher quality batters than Perry, there is no one better at not being dismissed.

She's also massively consistent. In ODIs, of the places she's batted more than three times, she averages 39 and above in each country. But it gets freakier. She averages 50.6 at home, 50.8 away and 50.9 at neutral venues. You can set your clock by her batting.

She is like a very high-performing version of Imran Khan's batting. Both got into their teams as bowlers, but over time worked out a method to stay in. Perry's batting is well beyond Imran's, but he averaged over 50 for the last decade of his career by being a master of the not outs. Perry has batted every spot except opening and No. 10. But she is at her best at No. 4, playing very long – and slow – anchor innings. In that spot she has 19 not outs from 52 innings, but only one hundred and a strike rate of 74.

On raw averages and overall runs, she could claim the title of best batter. The issue with that is that she was batting beside Lanning, who was just better. Even Australian wicketkeeper Beth Mooney might be more talented – although with far fewer runs.

Raj and Lanning are probably the two greatest batters of modern cricket, and perhaps all time. But I would like to mention one more of the top 10.

England opener Charlotte Edwards has the lowest average of those I have picked, coming in at just under 40 across formats. But she has the second most runs. Her career was epically long, just like Raj. Making her debut at 16, but not as a future prospect, before turning 18 she had the ODI world record score of 173 not out against Ireland. This followed another hundred against South Africa. Before turning 20 she added a Test hundred against India. She would average 53 in World Cups and win one as a captain.

In ODIs she would average only 32 at home but 40 away, and because of her incredible World Cup record, 46 in neutral matches.

Her home record keeps her from achieving incredible numbers, but only Mithali Raj is close on total Test and ODI runs. In Tests, she averaged 44 and scored four hundreds in her 23 matches.

When women's cricket was still struggling for any notoriety, Edwards' name was known by cricket fans.

There will be a time when others outscore Edwards and her legacy fades. Her average won't look as good, and much of her best batting was before cameras covered her games.

But there is one thing that shows just how good Charlotte Edwards was. When she started representing England, the players had to pay for their blazers, and they lost money representing their side. Because of Edwards and many of the great batters, the men in charge could no longer ignore the talent. So, in the last years of her career, Charlotte Edwards was in the first group of professional women to represent their team. She stayed at the crease making so many runs, the game changed because of it.

She even changed her opposition. Suzie Bates almost quit in her prime:

I honestly thought at the 2017 World Cup that I was going to have to give it away because it almost wasn't sustainable in terms of what we were earning.

After each four-year cycle, it was like you reassessed. I was captain at the time, and that came with other pressures and stresses.

I wasn't always enjoying all the off-ground stuff that came with that, so my enjoyment level wasn't as high as I felt it should be.

The captains I played under finished at 27, 28, because they had to either think about their career, think about a family and all those sorts of things, which cricket didn't really support. At the time I was going to have to maybe step away and do something else just in terms of financially supporting myself.

Then a franchise came up and I was like, "Oh yeah, I want to be a part of that." And then another World Cup and then another franchise tournament came up. And opportunities kept coming that I wanted to be a part of, and that's probably why I'm still here.

Even someone like Suzie Bates, who never played a Test, gets to be a professional cricketer now. But to get to her level, she behaved like a professional – thanks to her time in basketball – for a long time on her own. It was that mindset of 'I always felt like I trained like a full-time athlete' that built her into this player.

But with everything she has achieved, she still missed out:

I love watching cricket. And when you watch the fifth day of a Test match and they've toiled away, and there's been ups and downs and ebbs and flows. And that team moment when the team wins the fifth day, knowing kind of what they've been through together. I'm really envious of that feeling and to have played for so long and not been able to experience that with my teammates or as an individual or batting a whole day and you just being mentally exhausted. I feel like I'm kind of missing out.

In 2024 the New Zealand women lost 10 games on the trot coming into the T20 World Cup. During the tournament they played decent, if uninspiring, cricket. Their bowling was incredible, but their batting was dour. Never ideal in T20. But their bowlers forced them into the final when the three favourites (Australia, England and India) all bombed out. Against South Africa in the final, they decided to attack. The player who did that was their opener, Bates. She'd had a horrible tournament, the runs hadn't come, and it had been slow.

The World Cup final is an occasion, people can be nervous, especially with a young New Zealand team who did not expect to be there. It was Bates swinging away that really showed this was a team trying to win, not hoping they didn't lose. In the end, Bates didn't score fast, she got stuck. But made her highest score of the tournament. All the young players around her swung as well, and they made 158. Their bowlers defended it easily. Meaning that Bates has more World Cup trophies than she does Test runs.

In 2008, Suzie Bates was a young woman hanging out with LeBron James, Dwyane Wade and Kobe Bryant when not battling Lisa Leslie and Sue Bird, not to mention her nemesis, Diana Taurasi. But to women's cricket, Bates is that level of giant.

But like too many greats of the women's game, she did it without playing Tests.

5

HIGH FRONT ELBOW

Exploring the many different techniques for making runs

*'I'm not really going to fight fire with fire. I'm
going to find my own way.'* – Chris Rogers

Art. Simple as that.

You do not need to understand the symbolism or meaning of the work. It is simply a thing of beauty. Straight lines, balance, poetic movement and flourish. It's a cricket shot, but coming to life as if from a painting.

The elbow is pointing directly at the bowler and in front of the body, waiting to unfurl a bat that is held next to the right shoulder like a clock about to strike 11. The head is peeking over the elbow, allowing the eyes to peer into the soul of the bat. The balance shifts like a bowl of jelly in the back of a minivan, until the foot is landing under the head and elbow like they're all magnetised. The feet and ball land on the ground simultaneously, like two ballroom dancers who have been working together since childhood.

Then the bat comes down – straight, pure and righteous. Nothing barbaric or grammatically incorrect. It was made to come down on this path and meet with this ball. That was its destiny, and it was as beautiful as anyone could imagine.

Someone has painted a cover drive, or maybe that famed manual *The M.C.C. Cricket Coaching Book* has come to life.

The final touch to make it look like another era is the fact that the batter has a wide-brimmed hat and not a helmet.

This is the Indian Mithali Raj playing just one of her thousands of perfect and textbook cover drives.

She stood out so much in modern cricket because by the time she started her career, most techniques had changed completely. In fact, *The M.C.C. Cricket Coaching Book* was stopped in 1994, after Harry Altham first had it published in 1952.

The question about that date must be that Don Bradman already existed by then and if he wasn't a perfect batting machine, it is hard to see what was. He didn't bat like the manual at all. If you were judging like people do with diving, then Mithali would regularly get perfect tens while Bradman would get some sevens.

In an interaction with the ICC YouTube channel in 2018, India's Smriti Mandhana called her 'the most technical batter', and said she was 'really strong mentally'. She also thought Mithali had 'the best cover drives in the world'.

Bradman's hook shot could be a little like someone swatting flies, while his pull shot would often end up with him off balance. His drives were incredibly well-balanced, but he didn't get a long way forward. He would sweep squatting rather than getting down low. After using his feet to loft spinners, he'd sometimes topple back a step. He would defend off the back foot with his bat a long way in front of his body, often a shot he would also play off fuller balls. He would occasionally get himself inside the line of a ball to help it on the way, or even just flick it to the legside, no matter where it was pitched. There was a gap between his bat and pad at certain times.

In the old *That's Cricket: Don Bradman* film, Bradman explains the correct technique. In his forward defence, his bat is nowhere near the pads (he does mention this), his back foot is outside leg stump, and his hands go through the ball instead of dead batting it. There is no coaching manual that has all these things in it.

His back foot defence has his head right behind the ball and the blade is straight, but his elbow is not in line. His first straight drive shows that instead of pointing his toes at the ball, his feet often point towards square of the wicket. He plays a front foot square cut, but the bat blade is on an angle.

The best bit of his clips is that he plays a back foot leg glance (clip off the thigh pad) to a ball from the stumps, and then explains that this is a risky shot in a game. But footage of him shows the many times he would drag the ball across from off stump to leg stump with this shot for easy singles.

If this all paints a picture of something less elegant, exact and correct than Mithali Raj, that is the truth. But while Mithali might be one of the greatest to ever bat in the women's game, she was nowhere near Bradman's level. To him, *The M.C.C. Cricket Coaching Book* was little more than a 'based on a true story' message at the start of a film. He learned cricket his own way. The pulls were often messy because he would play that shot to very full deliveries. His bat was away from his pad because he didn't need the pad as a second line of defence as much. He kept his elbow to the left of his body for back foot defensive shots so he could turn his wrists on the ball for easy singles.

Don Bradman is not a textbook coming to life. He was a mess of contradictions and variations that made him the incredible batter he was.

In cricket, the three most incredible techniques by players have been: Jeff Thomson's fast bowling, Murali's inverted off-spin and Bradman's batting. It is weird that none of them have been copied. No one ever mastered the action of Thomson, or at least matched it with that level of athleticism, bowlers who came after Murali with his action were discouraged or shadow-banned from cricket, and Bradman's technique has never been copied.

The M.C.C. Cricket Coaching Book is, at best, incomplete. But the game has also changed.

In modern cricket, the forward defence is barely used in Tests. Trying to get as far down to the ball against a six-foot-eleven left-arm pace bowler like Pakistan's Mohammad Irfan is impossible.

England middle order player Kevin Pietersen gave a batting masterclass to Sky Sports, where he openly says he doesn't care about the front foot getting to the ball. He uses South African stylist and No. 3 Hashim Amla as an example – a player who took small steps, kept his balance and head over the ball, but never overcommitted. Mark Waugh, Damien Martyn, David Gower and VVS Laxman are some of the most beautiful batters of the last 50 years, and none of them have big front steps. Legendary Pakistan No. 4 Inzamam-ul-Haq was a player who was shuffling, not batting, but with an incredible stillness came batting poetry.

'It's very subjective what technical excellence looks like to different people, right?' says former West Indies quick Ian Bishop:

> I have a particular fetish for straight lines, batters who've got that pendulum bat swing that is up and down the line. And that's why Sachin Tendulkar for me was one of the excellent ones. It's why I love watching someone like Virat Kohli bat or the late Martin Crowe playing in straight lines, that sort of thing.

Many former players share Bishop's love of someone who plays in a straight aesthetic way, rather than across the line. Playing straight is a more textbook method.

What about the less pretty styles? Ijaz Ahmed held the bat like an axe murderer and strangled his way to almost 10,000 international runs for Pakistan in the '80s and '90s. England's defensive opener Alastair Cook defended with an angled blade outside off stump as if he was daring the ball to be edged. MS Dhoni would often shuffle across his stumps and force his bottom hand at the ball. Virender Sehwag played shots as if his feet were set in concrete.

In modern cricket as bowlers (spin and pace) get faster, it seems that techniques are minimising even more. Mithali Raj's technique worked in women's cricket because of the drop in pace.

Perhaps cricket's last pure technique in a great was Sri Lanka's No. 4 Mahela Jayawardene. But as his brother from another mother, fellow Sri Lankan legend Kumar Sangakkara points out, it was not a great way of playing extreme pace:

> Technically extremely correct. Even with his backlift, you'll see that it's not an open backlift. It's a very closed backlift. And going back straight, and if you watch him and how his front shoulder and head works all the time, you always see that if you have that back so straight, it's really difficult to be good on the short ball or good on the legs. But because of that easy

movement of that front shoulder, how early he saw the ball, his complete game was incredible.

Jayawardene overcame his technical flaws through genius. And his technical flaw was looking like a coaching manual.

Many of the game's greatest batters blatantly hit across the line. Bradman did it, but the true kings of this are Viv Richards, Kevin Pietersen, Victor Trumper and Steve Smith. No coaching manual would be bold enough to even suggest this.

Neither would they have suggested that Australian batter Simon Katich should scuttle across his stumps like an elderly man trying to hide his wallet from an intruder.

What about Shivnarine Chanderpaul? The Guyana legend started as what cricketers would call a two-eyed batter; someone who is chest on to the bowler. India's Mohinder Amarnath used this after struggling with short balls. English batter Peter Willey had a similar style. Discussions about this technique have existed since the method itself.

The Queensland cricketer Dr Robert MacDonald was a defensive player and dentist who made 2069 runs at 31.8 in first-class cricket. When playing for Leicestershire against Sussex in 1902, his innings of 33 was 225 minutes long. He wrote in the *Daily Mail* in 1924 about eyesight and the two-eyed stance because it was starting to take over English cricket. 'Is it judicious in cricket to face the bowler full with two eyes?' he asked. While he writes about batting, it really is more about eyesight.

> The eyes, while giving expression to stereoscopic vision, are also range-finders. Stereoscopic vision is concerned with three dimensions, range-finding with two dimensions, and the well-known mathematical principle of triangulations being applied when two eyes are used.

This is not a man who has come to this theory that looking with two eyes is better than the standard one-eye technique of side-on batting. What he is saying is that you want a combination of two eyes and feet in the side-on position, and he talks about great players like Jack Hobbs, Victor Trumper and Ranjitsinhji and how the baseline of their eyes is at right-angles to their line of sight:

But note also that they all incline the face of the bat towards their legs; this is due to that slight twist of the body, chiefly at the hips, which enables them to keep the feet and legs in a correct position.

What exactly the good dentist would have made of Chanderpaul's technique, we will never know.

The left foot is in front of middle stump, but instead of the toes aiming at point, they are aiming at extra cover. It would be the thing to notice for most batters, but it is Chanderpaul's front foot, the right, that is bizarre. As a young boy, his father prepared him for fast bowling by pinging balls quicker than he could handle. It meant that Chanderpaul had to develop a method for rapid bowling. 'I just had to be a little open and get the bat up in front of my face every minute. It was just to protect myself,' is how Chanderpaul explained it.

It wasn't the only odd thing about his method. Despite his body being so open, he felt like he was facing a bowler from midwicket. When the bowler got to him, his feet were often in a normal place, but from there he would move into a side-on position as the ball was being delivered, going from two eyes to a better feet position to play the ball. Then he would play with perhaps the softest hands in the game. There were times when it felt like his bat was made of whispers, so soft was each touch. Even a normal edge would die on the way to the keeper.

On top of all that, he was the opposite of straight lines. When he did hit down the ground, it was begrudging. He wanted to play square, late and soft. He did it with a two-eyed crab-like technique. And he scored 11,867 Test runs at 51.4.

Yet, there will still be cricketers somewhere saying, 'Imagine what he could have done if he batted properly.'

There was one legendary batter who told a group of cricketers about his conversations with Sachin Tendulkar. The great Indian batter would get ready in his stance by holding his bat up, whereas many players around the world keep their bat on the ground until the ball was being delivered. This former player told Tendulkar that he should keep his bat down. The Indian player decided to keep his own way. And the legend said, okay, but if you listen to me, you'll be even better.

The truth is there's no perfect technique. No answer to the question. There are only runs.

'Sometimes people talk about my backlift. I found more problems with moving across my stumps too much,' says the West Indian left-hander Brian Lara.

His backlift was extreme; there was no way you couldn't see it. When the bowler was coming in, his bat would be down. As they hit delivery, he would have it above his head. If a small kid comes through with that technique normally, they would be stopped. He explains:

As a young man through school age group cricket, I felt that everybody was just more in awe and happy that I was playing the way that I was playing. I think the West Indies have a certain flair about it. I was lucky that way. You see now the present-day golfer [...] they'd win a major or two, and then they'd change a swing by the end of the year.

With players like Brian Lara or Steve Smith, they can have all the flaws they want because they make a lot of runs from an early age. The stories of Smith being a leg-spinner first are not true. He was picked for Australia as a leg-spinner because they had no other options. Australia also chose Marcus North and Cameron White as Test spinners, but no one thought they were bowlers. They just had some – not much – spin talent as well.

But Smith's leg spin was helpful, because it meant there was less pressure on his batting. If Lara had some quirks to his game that runs overcame, Smith's technique was so bizarre that the ability to take a seven-wicket haul one time in first-class cricket actually helped him.

Even when you look at Smith taking guard, there is something off. His bat face is really closed, facing into his pad. The reason for this is Smith holds the bat in what is called the semi-western grip from tennis. This was set up for topspin, so it's not an ideal way of holding a cricket bat. What it allowed him to do was to turn every ball to the legside.

On top of that, Smith played from a different spot on the pitch. His childhood coach, Trent Woodhill, told him that the off stump for him was actually leg stump. This meant that he would move right across the wicket, standing in front of the stumps, even exposing leg stump at times.

Then there is his backlift, which is not the right way to put it – Smith has a sidelift. As the bowler hits the crease, his bat is aiming at point. When the bowler comes in, he lifts it up and turns it back so that the face of the blade is facing one metre behind the stumps while aiming at gully. It does not look like he's about to face a ball at 90mph.

But when the ball is delivered, Smith's backlift is normal. His hands are near his body; his head is still. Yes, his bat face will aim towards square leg, and he's standing in a position that would make anyone else an lbw candidate.

So incredible were his numbers that hundreds of pro batters across the world started taking guard on off stump like Smith around 2018. Virtually, none of them make it work.

His technique made Australia's opener Chris Rogers doubt his entire outlook:

> He almost played just off the back foot; he would just stand on his right foot. He'd never fall over. He wouldn't get hit in the pads because his head wasn't tipping over as he was only standing on one foot. If you only stay on one foot, you have to be completely vertical. I even think to myself, all the times I fell over as a leftie and got hit in the pads, why didn't I just stand on my back foot and play like that at times?

In 2013, when Smith was picked to tour England, I compared his chances of success to that of a dead donkey. His technical style of moving across the line, his hands and bat whirling, turning and pushing, should not have worked with everything we know about batting. It felt like there were purely too many moving parts for the lateral moving ball. As of the end of 2023, Smith averaged 55 in England.

Most judges thought Smith's style couldn't work consistently. Chris Rogers says, 'There'd be a lot of us who'd probably put their hands up and say, "look, we didn't think that it would have longevity, and it did."'

His hundred at Edgbaston in 2019 was perhaps his greatest innings – and that could be either of them, as he made two in that Test.

Australia fell to 122/8 under grey skies, Smith was on 43 at that time. Straight after this to combat the movement, Smith faced Ben Stokes and moved so far across his stumps that you could see the middle stump as he glanced the ball a foot from the keeper's gloves. Stokes went short to him, but outside off, and he played a cross-court tennis forehand past mid-on. When he faces a back of a length ball, he stands inside and swats over his left shoulder. After a couple of bad balls from the spinner Moeen Ali, he scores his hundred from a conventional cover drive.

Yes, he's a bit further across his stumps, but that means he is closer to the tempting ball allowing his hands to be more in line with the ball. His foot is out towards the pitch and his bat comes through straight.

He finishes the innings by clearing his front leg and swinging the ball away to the legside like a golfer. Finally, he misses one. Australia are out for 284, so they added 162 runs after the fall of the eighth wicket and Smith made more than a hundred of them.

In the second knock, Australia started with a 90-run deficit. Smith came in at 27/1, yet Australia ended up scoring almost 500 and had a 398-run lead. Smith made 142 and carried the top order.

That Test was his comeback after Cricket Australia suspended him for a year for his role in the ball tampering scandal known as 'Sandpapergate'. Those two hundreds were also Smith's second and third straight on English wickets.

Smith's version of batting was not made to be aesthetically pleasing or easily copied by other players. It was simply for him to make runs and take on the most delivered ball in Tests.

'That's pretty much the art of batting, isn't it?' says Chris Rogers:

> The higher up you go, the more predictable it gets in some respects. Because you know exactly that the bowler is going to hit the top of the off stump five, almost six times out of six. Steve Smith worked that out early and decided I'm not really going to fight fire with fire. I'm going to find my own way.

Even though there is a lot of spin bowled in Tests, each kind of spinner has a different angle and method. But seamers are pretty standard, right or left arm, over or around the wicket. They are mostly trying to attack you at or around off stump.

If Smith and the batters who played across the line took the biggest risk, how did the other players take on what England opener Geoffrey Boycott called the corridor of uncertainty?

The Yorkshire batter himself defended with a straight bat. But Rahul Dravid and New Zealand No. 3 Kane Williamson did so with a slightly open blade, knowing that they could use soft hands, play the ball right under their eyes and find runs to backward point.

Graeme Smith had a closed bat face, allowing him to drag balls towards square leg even when defending, again to find gaps. Virat Kohli takes a big stride out and drives on the up, or even pushes through the ball, which means he always has a chance of scoring. Javed Miandad would rob the bowler of his length, allowing him to drive or force from the back foot. Alastair Cook would leave the ball all day.

These players would often do this, even though each seam bowling type produces a unique challenge. Taller bowlers always have the opportunity of hitting a slightly angled blade and ending up with a catch behind. Shorter bowlers keep lbw and bowled in play by skidding the ball through. Outswing bowlers can drag you into shots that are away from your body. Inswing makes you play more balls than you'd like. Fast bowlers can rush through before your foot or head is set. Seam bowlers can keep bowled, lbw and caught behind all in play on the same delivery. Left-arm bowlers usually swing the ball one way, but they bowl 20% of seam balls in Tests, and you never play that much of them on the way up. Right-arm bowlers often use the crease better and have more skills.

This doesn't even allow for the fact that bowlers have different natural lengths, from 5 to 9 metres. They come from different angles and have varying release points. Yet one way or another, the ball is still going to be at or just outside off stump – on a length or just slightly back of.

How you handled this zone outside off stump was the difference between you being a good player, who might have time, a good eye and straight lines in your bat swing with the most magical feet against spin, and a great player who could just handle a bowler digging a trench on a line and length outside the off stump. Each ball in a position it was hard to go forward or back to, angled in, but just missing the off stump, slightly outside the natural eyeline of a player who has to defend their stumps first. How you play that delivery, and the thousands of them you will receive at Test level, is more important than any high elbow or gap between bat and pad.

That delivery is the ball that needs to be conquered. Everything else is a distraction.

6

RAG

Fast bowling scares, spin embarrasses

'Mentally, you are keeping ready for the flighted delivery.' — Sunil Gavaskar

There is a predator out in the middle. Most people's eyes would be drawn to the bleach-blond Australian leg-spinner who turns the ball so much you hear it coming like a ticking bomb in a bad action movie. He's athletically strong, has incredible stage presence and the world watches his every moment.

But right now, he is not the predator. It is a far less strapping figure, a hunched-over Indian man who appears to be using a thigh pad he borrowed from an older brother and an arm guard — even though he's on a spinning wicket. The chin strap of his helmet dangles down as he's attached it incorrectly. Indian opener Navjot Singh Sidhu was not someone who screamed predator, but that all depended on what you bowled.

Sidhu against spin seemed to inhabit two states: complete stillness or a mad dash down the wicket. This occasion, he is on the move with a purpose. It doesn't matter to him that Shane Warne is bowling around the wicket. Sidhu is just getting down to the pitch of the ball. Then he punches the ball through the line in the air to the long-off rope.

It's a standard lofted off drive to a spinner, except that Warne has dropped the ball into the footmarks and it's pitched around a metre outside leg stump. In his haste, Sidhu has overrun the ball and almost yorks himself. He is also standing 1.5 metres outside leg stump when he plays his off drive. It looks like someone has moved the stumps behind him using Photoshop.

Warne and Sidhu exchange words. This is not the first time the Indian batter has treated the Australian leg-spinner like he's a net bowler. There are so many occasions of Sidhu running at Warne, just to unleash a huge shot against him. Usually, they end up in the stands. Warne was a brilliant bowler but too slow for the Indian wickets and feet.

But it wasn't just the pace and precision of Sidhu's footwork. He would wait and watch forever. Like an ambush predator, letting the spinner get more comfortable, almost forgetting he was there. Prod, push and leave them, until that ball went up out of their hand just a little too much, he would attack them and someone from the crowd had to retrieve the ball.

Navjot Sidhu played 136 ODIs, and he managed 44 sixes. In 51 Tests he cleared the rope 38 times. The difference was in the extra time. That is what he wanted. It is hard to bowl to someone who can wait all day for the smallest error, and then destroy you for it. He was called a 'Strokeless Wonder' early in his career, and it was perhaps all part of an epic ruse to set up spinners he hadn't even played yet.

Sidhu was a fantastic player. He made a double hundred in the West Indies against their pace legends Curtly Ambrose and Courtney Walsh. But he averaged 26.6 outside Asia, even with that score. He was almost a single-use player. When the ball was turning, he was as good as anyone in the world. He made seven centuries in Asia while averaging 52.8, and a great deal of those 38 Test sixes were against Murali and Warne.

No one who saw Sidhu playing thought he wasn't a great player of spin. But clearly, fast bowling wasn't his thing.

Years ago I was the Scotland analyst, and we were talking about taking twos in a team meeting and how we'd been struggling to find them from the seamers. Scotland's No. 3 Calum MacLeod said, 'That is because it's easier to hit twos from spinners.' Until that moment, I had never even thought about such a thing. So I looked it up later and found that the rate of twos from spin and seam was the same. The reason MacLeod thought this is because he found spin easier to face. It hadn't occurred to him that others couldn't do that easily.

When MacLeod made his famous 140 not out from 94 balls to defeat England at the Grange in Edinburgh, he really went after their spinners Moeen Ali and Adil Rashid, who not long after would be part of England's World Cup winning squad in 2019.

Brad Haddin told a story on the *Willow Talk* podcast about playing with Mark Waugh in a game for New South Wales where they discussed playing spin. Haddin was getting bogged down by a left-arm orthodox bowler, so Waugh told him to simply come down the wicket and loft him over cover. Haddin tried to tell him that wasn't even an option for him.

Kane Williamson averages almost 50 in Asia, and almost 50 against the turning ball on those tracks. He has Test hundreds in Sri Lanka, India, the UAE, Pakistan and Bangladesh. He's not made runs consistently in all parts of Asia, struggling to make any kind of consistent runs in Sri Lanka and India. But to think a player from New Zealand would have hundreds in five different Asian nations is almost unthinkable. The land of the long white cloud is where spin goes to die.

We see facing fast bowling as this thing you can either do or not based on eyesight, courage and reflexes. But it is easy to forget playing spin comes to people just as naturally. MacLeod, Waugh, Williamson and Sidhu probably have similarities in terms of wrist play and footwork. But Glasgow, Sydney, Tauranga and Punjab are four very different places in which to grow up. It's interesting when you look at the nature versus nurture debate. Clearly the best players of spin come from Asia, but it doesn't preclude players from outside.

Yet we'd be lying if we said that conditions played no part. Sri Lanka had Mahela Jayawardene, the middle order batter

Thilan Samaraweera and Kumar Sangakkara at the same time, the generation before had Aravinda de Silva. Looking at Hawkeye data, the ball spins more in Sri Lanka than anywhere else. Not to mention that the percentage of spin bowled there is huge. The ball used to spin more in other countries. Before covered wickets became the norm, Australia was well known for its use of spinners and how they played it.

There are a lot of things to notice about Australian left-hander Neil Harvey straight away. His sleeves are folded immaculately, his shirt is unbuttoned to give you a lovely view of his chest and his hair is Brylcreemed back to show it in its wavy, perfect glory. But the most extraordinary thing about Harvey were the things no one focuses on, his feet.

Neil Harvey had fast feet. It wasn't just that he could get down to the ball to spin, it was as if at times he was so far down the pitch it was cheating. But he was just as quick moving back. He would take a step forward in defence then change to moving his feet down the wicket again. He could also sweep, often playing it standing up.

Harvey was a fascinating player who averaged 86 over his first three years, which would be incredible if he started his career at 28 – instead he was only 19. After that, he never played at that level again. After turning 32 he played on for four more years without ever making runs consistently again. He also struggled playing on English wickets, but on Indian decks he played eight Tests for three hundreds while averaging 55. He also made runs in Pakistan, but that was on matting wickets.

The majority of the runs were against South Africa, and even then, he had to conquer spin as he faced Hugh Tayfield in 14 Tests. Yet the great off-spinner only picked off the southpaw Harvey four times.

Harvey was a natural right-hander, who, as a kid, picked the bat up as a leftie and stayed that way. Many batting experts debate if what we call right-handed for cricket batting is correct, as the dominant hand when batting on the standard side of the stumps is the left, not the right. Harvey, like a lot of Australian southpaws, actually might be on the correct side of the bat, even if that is the left.

The left-handed thing does matter a lot for spin, especially in Tests, because in five days (or some matches that went even longer), the footmarks of Test bowlers get very dusty. And with most seamers being right-armed, it is the left-handed batters who must deal with footmarks.

Harvey once wrote in his book, *My World of Cricket*, of an exchange between him and Len Hutton (the legend played spin from the crease and is often credited for the fact that England players used their feet less), where the England opener had complained to the umpires about the footmarks from Australia's left-arm swing bowler Alan Davidson. 'You ought to turn around and bat left-handed and see how tough it is then.'

But it's England No. 3 Ted Dexter's book, *From Bradman to Boycott*, that wonders if Harvey's fast feet against the spinning ball were from the footmarks and his need to get down to the ball to ensure the bowler couldn't spin one back through him.

Again, perhaps conditions play a part.

We also know what happens when something changes. From the early 2000s, something changed dramatically in playing spin bowling in Tests: umpires started giving lbws. Before, a large forward step and putting your bat roughly near your pad was enough to stop that as a possibility. What it really allowed for was finger spinners who turned the ball away from batters to have the options of lbw, bowled and caught behind all from the same delivery. This was all because of the invention of Hawkeye, which showed umpires how often the ball was likely to be hitting the stumps. Because of that, how you played the ball spinning away became way harder. Modern spinners, when bowling to someone turn the ball away from the bat, land it on the stumps, and then the batters have to work it out.

It meant that batters worked out how to walk across their stumps a little more against bowlers spinning it back in. South Africa had so many batters like Jacques Kallis (a very underrated player of spin) and Hashim Amla who would walk across their stumps in this period as off-break bowlers would have to pitch outside the line. So, it wasn't as if it was all bad for batters.

There were two kinds of batters who struggled with this change a lot: left-handers who now had all off-spinners coming around the wicket to target them, and right-handers who liked to hit the ball to the legside.

Chief among them was Kevin Pietersen, who became a victim in the great pie-chucking wars when he lost the ability to face any left-arm spinners. Yuvraj Singh was a batter by trade who by the end of his career was more than handy with the ball (despite Pietersen referring to him as a pie chucker). Over 402 matches he took 148 wickets, and five of them were Kevin Pietersen.

It became such an issue that teams would pick random left-arm orthodox bowlers when playing Pietersen. Australia took it a step too far in 2010/11 trying two different bowlers just to get into Pietersen's mind.

Looking at his record over those few years shows the issue with left-arm finger spin wasn't new to him. Across all international cricket in 2005 and 2006, he averaged 26.2. In 2007 he scored 153 runs for only three dismissals. Then 2008 came around and he was dismissed 11 times and averaged 26.1. As he was fed more of it, he worked out a small game plan for it. But he never conquered it.

So he called the big guns in to help him, emailing his former RCB teammate Rahul Dravid. Years later, Pietersen would reproduce this letter from Dravid in *KP: The Autobiography*:

Against guys who bowled a bit quicker (and I grew up playing Anil [Kumble]) I would look to go forward without committing or planting the front foot. What can happen is we look to go forward which is correct but because we are so keen to get forward and not get trapped on the back foot sometimes you can plant that front foot too early. It sends the timing all wrong and forces your bat to come down too quickly (because once your foot is planted it is a signal for your brain to deliver the bat) resulting in you pushing at it rather than letting it come to you. Also then if it turns you are more liable to follow the ball rather than holding your line and letting it spin past. (Nobody counts how often you get beaten.) Also that results in what we call 'hard hands', which is nothing but pushing out. If your transfer of weight brings your bat down, then that's perfect because it always puts the bat in the right place. I have in fact struggled a bit with that in Aus as my timing has been a bit off and has led to me pushing out at ball and created a gap between bat and pad. That's the bummer with timing – it's impossible to teach or train.

Anyway, all this stuff is happening in the subconscious and you can't think about it.

You can practise a few things though – in the nets try and pick up length from the bowler's hand, that will force you to watch it closely. Look to go forward but recognise that a lot of the scoring opportunities are off the back foot, so while you're looking to go forward you are not committing, the key word is looking, you are ready to rock back and pick up some runs if you can.

One good practice is to bat against Swann and Monty without pads or with just knee pads (maybe not a day before a game!). When you have no pads it will force you, sometimes painfully, to get the bat forward of the pads and will force you to watch the ball. Also the leg will be less keen to push out without any protection. My coach would tell me you should never need pads to play spin!!

KP, you are a really good player; you need to watch the ball and trust yourself. You'll be able to pick up length and line and spin a lot better if you're calm and trusting at the crease. Under stress we miss vital clues especially early on. If you get beaten and it spins past you so what... you're still in, and realise that you'll pick up the next ball better if you can forget the earlier one. Don't let anyone tell you that you can't play spin, I have seen you and you can!

Anyway, I probably rambled on too much ... all the best, go well!

Rahul

There are a lot of things to love about this letter. It shows you how batters talk to each other. This is so technically heavy, there is of course a little bit of psychological stuff in there too. But it is about the hovering front foot method, playing inside the line and hard hands. It shows the science of the method from one of the best to play spin.

And he was. *CricViz* has the records of all players against spin from their database. Rahul Dravid throughout his entire career had an average of 68.4, but those numbers can be slightly misleading at times. In the records of people playing 90mph and quicker, they had Tamim Iqbal as the highest average, with 369. But many of those deliveries will be in Asia, where it is naturally easier to face. So, with their list of the greatest players of spin, there is Australian No. 4 Greg Chappell averaging 81.8. There is no doubt he was a fine player of the turning ball, but he only had four Tests in Asia, one in Sri Lanka and three in Pakistan. He may have been a great player of spin elsewhere, but Asia is a whole different challenge.

In the database I checked, Rahul Dravid has played 5304 balls of spin on Asian pitches. He averages 75.9 against spin, the third-best in modern times.

Dravid learned a lot from a coach at under-19 level called Hanumant Singh. A prince who made a hundred versus England but who never fulfilled his incredible talent. His theory, now called the hovering front foot, was 'be in readiness to move, but move as late as you can'. This method makes it look like a batter is coming forward, when they are delaying the action based on where the ball is going.

According to Dravid, 'You don't want to commit. Once you've planted that foot, then it becomes very difficult to make an adjustment. Even though spin is so slow, like people say it's easier to make the adjustment. But when you're playing spin on turning tracks not committing too early is really important.'

The issue here is about how you learn this. Did Dravid pick this up from his coach, was it inherited knowledge from Indian cricket, or was it something that came naturally because he played on these wickets? Dravid elaborates:

If I was trying to teach, I don't know if I'm gonna teach some young kid: don't commit too early. I can't tell him, okay, now move at this particular point of time, move just when the ball is at this point in the air. If I start going into that, then that's something he has to learn. You have to learn it yourself.

There is another thing that comes up with Dravid and spin: his interception points. It is a new phrase in batting, but something players have discussed in one way or another for generations. Where does the player hit the ball, in Dravid's case against spin? It was either very far forward or right back on the stumps.

But Dravid never realised this himself:

I read this book, *Hitting Against the Spin*, where they write about my contact points against spin. In the sense that I got fully forward and I got fully back.

Now I never ever thought about actually, oh, now I should go fully forward, and I should go fully back. I think just playing in India, I learned that if I didn't get fully forward when I played forward against spin I allowed the ball to spin a lot. And then when I wanted to go back, if I didn't get fully back and it kept low, it would hit my pad.

Maybe I just naturally learned that, and I never, honestly, until I read that book, I never even knew I did any of that. But I do remember what some bowlers told me. Like playing against Anil Kumble or playing against international bowlers, you do pick up the length, and balls that other guys are not cutting, you are cutting. It's nice to know about this thing, I don't think I actually consciously thought about it.

Dravid's method was partly passed on to Joe Root. The English player is an unusual batter because he is a great player of spin, even in Asia. He averages 48.9.

Root is one of the best players of spin from outside Asia, and he is certainly right at the top for English players. He may not be at the Zimbabwean wicketkeeper Andy Flower, Brian Lara and Neil Harvey level, but he is close to that.

Root has had an interesting career. He has kept his average hovering around 50 despite how poorly England have batted ahead of him, even during the Wobbleball era that eroded many great batting averages. He is a great player of seam bowling as well. His biggest issue for parts of his career was a failure to convert. And his career average is probably lower because of the number of times England have needed him to bat No. 3, when he is a four.

Part of the reason he is so good at four is how he plays spin.

Like Dravid, Root is a player who either plays spin a long way from the stumps, or way back. It's not just his use of feet; like many English players, he loves the sweep.

The Bazball England side swept twice as much as other teams in the first two years. Shots have only been tracked in recent times, but when you look at old cricket footage, the shot was never more prevalent than today. As covered wickets come in, players outside of Asia lost many skills to play spin, and the shot takes off. Limited overs make it even more critical; you need to be able to hit boundaries everywhere off good balls.

Rahul Dravid didn't sweep. But he was India's coach during a recent series against England. And even he was so obsessed with England's usage that he wanted modern Indian batters to round their games out further.

The sweep is a disrupter shot, which makes it perfect for the Bazball England side. But it was an English shot beforehand. Pakistan is another country that plays it, whereas countries such as India and Australia never tried it as much.

If you look at old clips of English batters, their players used their feet a lot more traditionally, even if they still swept. But English players do play spin in their own way. Footage of England middle order player Ken Barrington shows him incredibly crease bound versus slow bowling, and *CricViz* have him down as averaging 76.1 against spin. Many of his shots are cuts and turning the ball to leg. But his main shot is standing in the crease and swinging hard through the line to crash the ball over mid-on. It would look like a tail-ender swinging if it wasn't done so neatly and on demand.

England's cricket changed because the wickets did. As covered pitches came in, there was less help for the spinners and England weren't developing their batting in the same way.

It wasn't just them; Australia also lost a lot of spin bowlers when the pitches got covered. But Australian players kept using their feet, and England went to the sweep. The difference is probably in the bounce. Playing the sweep on Australian wickets, you are in constant danger of getting a top edge; that isn't the same in England.

That may be a perceived threat because looking at data from 2014 to 2024 the sweep shot had a healthy average in Australia, but in England it was even better. This might explain why English players use it so much, just because of how much it works at home. It might also explain why England batters struggle when touring Asia at times. The sweep is not as effective as using your feet there.

Virat Kohli takes the knee for no spinner, sweeping 1.7% of the time in Tests from 2019 to 2024. Almost all of those are slog sweeps, from the traditional, lap and reverse he has a combined two runs. He and England are playing two different sports.

This is exemplified by Joe Root, who has scored 10.4% of his career Test runs playing the shot, including his runs against seamers. He had nearly double the amount of runs of the next most common sweeper in my database, fast-scoring Sri Lankan keeper Niroshan Dickwella. From 2019 to 2024 he scored 37.3% runs from spin playing sweeps against spin.

Part of the reason Root plays this shot so much is that when he was young he was also small, meaning he couldn't hit the ball off the square. The sweep really helps smaller players when they are young.

On top of that, despite coming from Yorkshire, he also grew up playing for Sheffield Collegiate, a club where the ball spun a lot. Root had access to Nadeem Khan there, the brother of Pakistan keeper Moin Khan, who also played two Tests. So, Root was a sweeper with a world-class coach and a wicket that spun. He was trained to be this good against spin; it's not an accident. So, when he made three consecutive scores in Tests over 180 (Kumar Sangakkara is the only other player to do that), they were all in Sri Lanka and India.

When a non-Asian player gets good against spin, there is often a background like Root's. South African Heinrich Klaasen had a late-career surge where he became one of the best T20 batters in the world. A lot of this had to do with his play of spin. C. S. Chiwanza has written about why in his recent article 'Heinrich Klaasen's World' for Cricket8. 'Klaasen learned to play spin in the bush,' he states.

In 2001 Etienne Birkenstock turned his piece of land close to the Roodeplaat Dam (north of Pretoria in South Africa) into a cricketing nursery. Soon after, he was visited by Klaasen's mother:

> She wanted to know if Birkenstock could take on her son as one of his students. At the time, Willowick Academy had more grass growing than it did future stars.

Willowick was a dust bowl. There was barely any grass on the field or any of the pitches. Birkenstock was bootstrapping with limited resources. It was less of a spiffy-and-prestigious centre, but more of a rough-and-ready academy. There were no structures or support staff.

So, to help, Birkenstock asked his few students to learn how to prepare pitches. It wasn't just cost-cutting:

He felt that understanding the nature of batting surfaces would help his students as they developed their game. Klaasen was one of the few who embraced the opportunity. The youngster spent every Wednesday afternoon attending to that task, and other days of the week helping out with other chores when he was not training. Willowick Academy was his home away from home.

Heinrich soaked up everything I told him like a sponge. He often came to help with the rolling of the eight pitches at Willowick and never shied away from hard work on and off the field.

Like any youngster, Klaasen loved batting and would have preferred to roll out batting surfaces, but two of his best friends were tweakers and prevailed on him to curate turning wickets. As a result, Klaasen spent a significant portion of his formative years learning how to navigate spinners.

At the start of 2024, Klaasen had scored more than 1000 runs from spinners in T20. He averaged 48.7 at a strike rate of 180.

Of course, there are many players outside Asia who were incredible against spin who also grew up on turning tracks.

Brian Lara is from Trinidad, and the wickets turn there. He explains:

If you go back into time, to Guyana and Trinidad, which was where a lot of the indentured labourers from India came from. Guyana and Trinidad again, the soil content is not the coral or the bauxite that you have in Jamaica, the coral in Barbados.

It's more marshland where the pitches were not as solid. It didn't have that firmness, that concrete feel that you see in Jamaica and other places. We created a lot more spinners in Guyana and Trinidad compared to the other islands. From street cricket to playing on a dust ball in the Savannah, in my village I learned to play spin much quicker than fast bowling.

There can be little doubt that he is one of the greatest players of the turning ball ever. According to *CricViz*, he averages 77 against Warne and 124 versus Murali (this dataset is not complete, but does have the vast majority of their matches up). Kumar Sangakkara says:

I watched him score 680 runs in three Tests against us in Sri Lanka with Murali, Chaminda Vaas, all of them in top form and a series where he scored 680 runs by himself. The West Indies lost 3–0.

And he did all of that on less than, I think, three or four hours of sleep a night. It's hard to describe his level of genius.

Brian Lara is a cricketer that you feel grateful to have watched score runs against you.

I challenge you to find anyone who has watched Brian scoring runs and walked away without being completely overwhelmed by how brilliant that man was.

His mastery of spin was so much that it cost South Africa a chance at winning a World Cup in 1996. Matched against the West Indies in the quarter-finals on a wicket due to spin in Karachi, they dropped their best bowler Allan Donald to fit in the left-arm wrist spinner Paul Adams.

At this point Adams was known for the frog-in-a-blender action that made him hard to play. That was pretty much all anyone knew, as he'd only played six international matches. He'd taken eight wickets in his first two Tests, but five in four ODIs, while going at 3.6 runs an over. He was a mystery bowler that no one had worked out yet. And so, on a spinning wicket, he should have been trouble.

Instead, Lara dissected this unknown frog species limb by limb. There is a ball at one point that is almost a half-volley outside off, it is spinning back in sharply, yet even from a full length and the quick turn, he is cutting it fine for a boundary. Later he'll get another wrong 'un spinning back on to middle stump and he'll cut that through the gap he had opened with the previous shot. The ball never bounced above three-quarter height on the stumps.

Just as Adams should have been troubling the West Indies, South Africa had to yank him from the attack.

That left the canny off-spinner Pat Symcox to deal with Lara, who at one stage saw him as so little of a threat that he backed away to square leg and drove him over point for a boundary. That was with Symcox bowling over the wicket and pitching it more than a metre outside leg.

Lara would end with 111 from 94 balls. His average against spin in Tests according to *CricViz* was 82.5.

If that number seems high, what about the Zimbabwean keeper Andy Flower? His number was 97.5.

If you are thinking that he struggled to play the best teams in his career, that is true. He barely played against Australia, South Africa and England. But he did play against Pakistan, Sri Lanka and India a great deal. In fact, he played on Asian pitches in 21 Tests, scoring 1614 of his 4794 runs.

He struggled on Sri Lankan wickets (23.4) and was fine but not spectacular on Pakistan pitches (38.7), but he made 820 of the Asian runs on Indian tracks. This wasn't one big series; he went to India three times but played only five Tests. His first match was in 1993, then two more Tests in 2000 and 2002. So it's spread out enough, but it is only five matches.

Yet, against Murali in Sri Lanka he was out five times in seven Tests. Murali took Lara three times in four Tests on his own pitches, but the West Indian batter averaged 100.8 in them.

Not that this means he wasn't a great player of spin, but a lot of Andy Flower's reputation is built at home (Zimbabwe wickets do turn) and India. While that makes it harder to work out how great Flower was against the turning ball, we know that he could play it, and that coming from Zimbabwean wickets that turn certainly helped build him.

If that helps the odd batter from outside Asia, imagine what it does to those from there. Sri Lanka is a place where the ball doesn't just turn; it rags.

That breeds incredible players, but even then, having Kumar Sangakkara, Mahela Jayawardene and Thilan Samaraweera from one small island at the same time is insane.

Of those three, two are accepted greats. The other is much more complicated. Samaraweera is often forgotten just because he was the third-best player of that era. 'He was always the kind of player easiest to drop in terms of a batting line-up, and he knew that,' says Sangakkara. 'That made him a lot more determined.'

Samaraweera was first in the side to bowl off-spin at No. 7 before his batting took over.

His career is interesting; he played in a great era for batting. The average of the other top six batters in the games he played was 40.5. He also only averaged 17 in Australia and 27 in England. Outside of that, he was strong across New Zealand, South Africa and West Indies. As a great spin player, he averaged over 50 on Asian wickets, but only 24 in India.

He scored only 5462 runs over a 12-year career. Part of that was batting down the order; he usually batted at five or even six. Another was that Sri Lanka didn't play many Tests. Samaraweera appeared in 81 Tests, and while he missed some during his career, Sri Lanka only played 26 more.

Cricketers are affected by many kinds of injuries but Samaraweera experienced something different: he was shot.

Many cricket teams have set seats on the team bus, and Sri Lanka was one of those. On 3 March, 2009, the team was travelling to Gaddafi Stadium in Lahore for the third morning of their Test against Pakistan. Sri Lanka were well on top in the game, having scored 606 in the first innings. Sangakkara and Tillakaratne Dilshan had made hundreds. But next to Sangakkara on the bus that morning – in his usual place – was Samaraweera. He had just made 214, his second double century against Pakistan on that tour.

Samaraweera was relaxing after two hard days of making runs, wondering if his bowlers could take any wickets, when the bus was jolted and then stopped. A car had cut off the bus, but the real danger was the gunmen firing at them. Soon it was a grenade as well. There was blood on the floor of the bus. Shrapnel was everywhere.

Ajantha Mendis and Tharanga Paranavitana were both bleeding badly. The latter passed out. Just behind them were Sangakkara and Samaraweera. The blast sent Sangakkara to the floor, and Samaraweera fell on top of him. Because of this he wasn't low enough, and so the bullet came through and struck him on the top of his thigh.

He wasn't out long. By July he was back playing, against Pakistan, in Galle this time. He only made a couple of 30s, but it was still an incredible return so soon after a major injury – physically and emotionally. A few Tests later, he made a big hundred against New Zealand at Galle.

Quite obviously, this is not a usual injury. But to a player like Samaraweera, who uses his feet, any leg injury could have slowed him down and changed his trajectory. It didn't. Some of that is because even if it slowed him down – and there isn't evidence of that – his hands were incredible. He was a master manipulator of quality spin. Watching him at times you think he could have batted with a stump and still found the gap. Sangakkara reflects:

I remember his debut; he scored against India on a turning pitch at the SSC. He worked hard, brilliant against spin. He was really great with his wrists, great driving down the ground, hitting against the spin, which I always think is a hallmark of a great player.

And Samaraweera was just that. He started as an off-spinner and developed into one of the best Test players that we ever had. For him it was about determination, really buckling down and being able to absorb pressure. He was very different to Mahela or Aravinda, but as effective.

Samaraweera was more than a player who tried very hard against spin. *CricViz* have him averaging 72.7 against the spinning ball and 79.8 on Asian pitches against spin, which is the second best recorded in modern cricket. Those are incredible numbers, higher than either of his legendary teammates.

Mahela Jayawardene was also an incredible player of the spinning ball. While others might have been more effective, it was Jayawardene who appeared as if he was playing it in a dream, like he could read everything that came from the hand and was already floating on a cloud to get there.

In his career, Jayawardene scored 9399 runs in Asia – only Sachin Tendulkar has more. He averaged under 40 in Australia and England and under 30 in New Zealand and South Africa, but went at 56 in Asia. That was 66.5 in the ball-by-ball recorded era against spin, but 42 in the Americas is the next best average. At home, his mark was 60; away, it was 40.

For all that, his teammate and friend Sangakkara says, 'I wouldn't consider myself a special talent. I think I'll reserve that for the likes of Jayawardene. Players like him, they have that genius in them.'

In 2012 at Galle, England were touring and Sri Lanka batted first. England's great seam combination Stuart Broad and Jimmy Anderson took three early wickets – including Sangakkara for a golden duck – with only 15 runs on the board.

After handling the new ball threat, Jayawardene went after Graeme Swann and Monty Panesar. That is the way he plays; there was always a little more risk in his batting than other great players of spin. He wasn't working out a great method, he was ensuring that they were never quite settled against him. It wasn't like Sehwag, who against the turning ball in Asia averaged 72.1 while striking at 91. Jayawardene was scoring at a fairly normal rate of 53. But within that was the fact that if he wanted to, he could play any ball inside out through the covers, even if he struck it from his pads, or he could just take an easy step down the wicket and dump the ball over the long-on fence. In fact, he could just come down and slog it with the turn.

The thing about him is that it never looked like he was attacking or hitting the ball so hard. It was as if his bat was made of rubber. It would make a different kind of noise, like he was helping the ball away, placing it on its rightful journey.

Off the back foot, he could cut almost any ball at will, fine or well in front of point. Setting the field was almost impossible. He could drive from point through to midwicket and he could also sweep, conventionally, and the lap. It meant he could score from slip all the way around to leg slip as he had so many boundary options.

In this match at Galle, England kept putting people on the boundary, and Mahela kept hitting it 30 metres away from them like he was tormenting a kitten with a toy. England felt like they had everything they needed: their greatest pace pairing and one of their best spin duos. They were the No. 1 team in the world. At the other end, no one could make runs. Dinesh Chandimal's 27 was their second top score.

Sri Lanka made 318, Jayawardene made 180. In response, England scored 193.

Yet that was a first innings. One thing that showed his absolute class was how well he played spin in the fourth innings in Asia, where he averaged 69.3. That is where the real technicians stand up, when there is dust, footmarks, uneven bounce and everything else.

Only one player with 350 runs in the fourth innings of Asian Tests has a higher average: Pakistan's Younis Khan with 73.8. AB de Villiers told me he learned a lot about playing spin just by watching him.

There are people in the game who believe Younis is the greatest fourth-innings player ever. He made 1465 runs in the last innings of Tests and has the record for the most hundreds: five. His average is also 50.5 in that innings.

That is not the highest – that belongs to South African Bruce Mitchell. A player barely talked about now, but on paper he has a similar record to Graeme Smith. He averaged 48.4 at home, 32.2 in Australia but 55.6 in England. Sadly there are two what-ifs about his career.

The first is the Second World War. He played 42 Tests: 32 before the war and 10 after. In those last matches, all against England over two series, he made 1072 runs at 59.5. He was 40 when he retired, so this is a player who missed his prime. It is extraordinary that a player of his talent would have a 20-year Test career and only end up with 42 matches.

The second issue with his career is that South Africa didn't play non-white teams. We only have his record against England (great) and Australia (terrible) and a few matches against New Zealand. The West Indies of that era were a dominant fast-bowling team. But India would have been a different kind of challenge – spin.

According to *CricViz*, Mitchell averaged 78.5 against the spinning ball. The one team that did cause him problems was Australia. He faced the great leg-spinner Clarrie Grimmett in 10 Tests and was dismissed five times. England's leg-spinner Doug Wright also took him on five occasions. And England's No. 4 Denis Compton used his left-arm wrist spin for another three. Yet Hedley Verity and Bert Ironmonger, the world's two best finger spinners, and Tich Freeman, who took 3776 first-class wickets with his leggies at 18.4, caused very few issues.

The best tweaker – and bowler – in the world then was Bill O'Reilly, and he dismissed Mitchell only once from seven Tests.

Where Mitchell ends up against spin is fascinating because India would have given us another clue. But one other thing in his favour is how good he was in the fourth innings. In 12 innings, he scored 629 runs with five not outs. Even if he was dismissed every time, he would still have averaged over 50. It's a small sample size, but you run into that a lot in the fourth innings. Mitchell was a warrior in what was an ordinary South African team, batting all the positions.

Mitchell's numbers more than hold up against spin, but despite his average he is not the greatest player in the fourth innings, at least in part because he wasn't tested.

There are few players in history who batted more in the fourth innings, often on low turning wickets, than Younis Khan.

At 13/2 he was in against Sri Lanka (in July 2015) on a Pallekele wicket in Kandy that helps seam. So much so that both teams went in with one fewer spinner than normal. On the final day, it was turning. Off-spinner Tharindu Kaushal never made it as a Test bowler for Sri Lanka, but domestically he took more than 300 wickets at under 26. He was a fine bowler, on a wicket helping him, with Pakistan in trouble. The Sri Lankans had one more thing in their favour; they were defending 377.

After seeing off the quicks' opening spells, Younis moved on to the young offie. He moved inside the line to find gaps on the legside that weren't there. When the ball ragged, he used the spin to find the rope on the legside some more. After the 27th over, with figures of seven overs for 43, Kaushal was taken off. The prodigious spin didn't seem to bother Younis, or his batting partner Shan Masood, at all.

Sri Lanka kept Kaushal out for a while, but when he came back on, Younis stopped looking for boundaries, and started milking him. It was the final day of a Test in Sri Lanka, the ball was really spinning and Younis was batting like it was the 23rd over of a flat pitch in an ODI. Every now and then there would be a big shot.

When Younis plays a big shot to a spinner, it is often like a club cricketer against a long hop, full throated. When Kaushal overpitches to him, he swings incredibly hard through the ball for a sweep to bring up his hundred. Later he will bring the sweep back, but this time it is after he walks outside the line of off stump and plays it. The ball's position to great players of spin doesn't matter; they have already decided what their plan is against it.

If Younis Khan had one elite skill against spin it was his ability to play all the shots. He could sweep and reverse, cut and pull and use his feet. While at times he almost looked ungainly, it was because he saw an error and would throw himself into that boundary.

'So with spin, we knew he would sweep and sweep, and it got difficult,' remembers Kumar Sangakkara. 'Brilliant to watch and just scored a lot of runs. Perhaps slightly different to Mohammad Yousuf. Younis was very easy on the eye, standing up tall […] He scored a 300 against us in Karachi. He went on to just absolutely flay us.'

There are parts to Younis' career that make him unlike anyone else. The Pakistan Cricket Board banned him from cricket for his role in locker-room infighting – quite a claim from a board known for its own never-ending issues. In the Test when Samaraweera was shot, Younis was due to bat very soon and instead he would never face another ball in a Test match at home. His last innings was the 313 that Sangakkara mentioned.

Looking at his record, he averaged 58 at home but 49 away and 55 in the UAE, playing for empty stands so television audiences could watch him back in Pakistan. No cricketer has ever had a career like that, never making more than 2500 runs in one place, despite passing 10,000 runs.

He was not a one-dimensional player and he did brilliantly against pace. He averaged more than 50 in Australia and England. It was only 32 in South Africa and weirdly – despite how bad they were during his career – the West Indies. But he made hundreds in all 11 countries where he played Test cricket. Yes, he averaged 76 on Indian wickets but he was still at 43 in New Zealand. He was a master of spin, but like his play of the ball in Pallekele he was completely rounded.

In that match, Pakistan chased 377 runs, losing only three wickets from 103.1 overs. Younis Khan was 171 not out.

Younis is just one of the many players from Pakistan who play spin incredibly well. Mohammad Yousuf is another. However, most of his runs versus spin came at home, and when the ball turned a lot more for Indian and Sri Lankan wickets, he averaged a combined 33. He still has the most runs ever in a Test year, but he made the most of his reputation playing on very flat Pakistan wickets, especially in draws, where he averaged 83 at home.

Yousuf and another Pakistan legend, Inzamam-ul-Haq, struggled in South Africa and Australia. That has been a common problem for Pakistani batters, no matter their talent. Inzamam averaged 31 in these countries, but his record against spin is far stronger outside of home, averaging 54.9 on Indian wickets and 58.7 in Sri Lanka.

That means Inzamam conquered them all across the three main spinning venues of his day. Unlike Yousuf, when he made runs at home they were not in draws (39.8) but wins, where he averaged 94.4 when Pakistan won 20 matches at home.

The main difference between the pair is the impact they had. Yousuf had 'genius' according to Kumar Sangakkara, but Inzi had presence. Not only was he a big guy, but when he arrived at the crease things seemed to change.

A man of his enormous size could be incredibly nimble and get himself into the exact position he wanted – all the while with his head completely still. He often changed his mind after using his feet and still played the perfect shot. He could hit the ball incredibly hard without losing any shape or trying to slog.

'He averages basically 50. How many Test matches he played?' asks Jimmy Adams.

The answer is 120. Anybody who can average that much, for that long, wow. Wide range of shots, equally adept against pace and spin. Nothing flash, but just very effective. He had a really rock-solid defence against pace and spin, he scored runs against all the attacks home and away for decades. Inzi was the epitome of solidity.

My experience with Inzamam is that he can take the game away from you in a session. That is all he needs.

You can see all of this in his incredible knock in the 1992 World Cup semi-final against New Zealand. The Kiwis, in scoring 262, thought they had enough runs that they could rest their captain Martin Crowe in the field. At 140/4 after 34.1 overs, Pakistan needed 123 runs, at more than eight an over. This was a period where if you required more than a run a ball it was seen as a death sentence.

One big issue for New Zealand was the tournament where they pioneered opening with a spinner, Dipak Patel. Usually they would bowl him out early. The previous match – against Pakistan as well – he bowled his 10 overs for 25 runs. They didn't this time, he still had overs left late and so they had to bowl him again before the death, which usually would have been a sedate time. Inzi tore him apart. Patel's figures were 1/50 in a tournament where the games prior he'd never gone for more than 36 runs in a spell.

When Inzi was run out, he had cut the rate down to almost a run a ball again and in that partnership of 87, he added 60 runs from just 37 balls.

But Pakistan's best spin player is the one who ran him out in the innings: Javed Miandad.

It is impossible to express in words what a genius Miandad was. His impact on batting was as great as anyone's after the First World War.

Just purely as a player of spin, he is incredible. At Old Trafford in 1992, he went up against England leg-spinner Ian Salisbury. This was a huge mismatch based on talent, but Salisbury had taken Miandad in the previous game.

This time the leggie offers up a ball just outside off stump, and Miandad strokes it through the covers. Salisbury lands the next one on off stump and is whacked over mid-on. The next ball arrives around middle and is worked through midwicket. Back to off stump and hit past mid-off. Finally, Salisbury gives up on the stumps and goes wide; this one is square-driven. Five fours in the over, with barely a risk taken. Simply, Miandad was bored; it was time for the spinner to go. The delivery was not important, it was more about which boundary could be found next, like he was a raptor in *Jurassic Park* systemically checking its cage for weaknesses.

This was not Miandad at his best. At his absolute best over his first 101 Tests, Miandad would average 57. He played on for another 23 matches and struggled so much, his final number was 52.6. A look at his record in the first 101 games shows he was around par in England and Australia, averaging either side of 40. In his four Tests against the peak West Indies on their wickets he averaged roughly the same. The bulk of his touring runs came when he went to New Zealand, who he loved destroying (that World Cup semi-final he was the second-highest run-scorer) and India, where he played 13 Tests averaging 49.9. That shows what a great player of spin he is. If you add that to his average of 71.2 in Pakistan for that period, you have a player who was just untouchable at home.

Bowling to him was a nightmare as a spinner, like when he was facing Indian left-arm finger spinner Maninder Singh in 1983 at Hyderabad. You can see him jab-stepping towards the bowler quite violently, and because he was so quick and seldom missed a drive, you had to accommodate that. No spinner – and few quicks – ever felt comfortable bowling to him.

At the Oval in 1987 he was facing off-spinner John Emburey. He had already scored his first hundred against England earlier in the innings. The offie had just been brought back into the attack; it was a relaxing first ball of his spell, outside off stump on a decent length. Miandad saw it early and skipped at it almost quicker than the camera could pick up. It could have been a simple drive, but Miandad was making a statement using his feet like this and launched into a running slog at the ball that went back into the members. It was his only six in that knock of 260.

His 154 in his first Test against India in 1978 at Faisalabad has him looking completely wild. Hatless with this shaggy bonce of hair, shirt unbuttoned, and his movements so quick and dynamic it looks like the footage has been sped up. You see him come down the wicket to India's off-spinner Erapalli Prasanna, and it is perfect technically until he just decides to hump the ball away over wide long-on.

While Miandad could be elegant and precise, sometimes he just enjoyed being loud and dirty. He averaged 81.4 against spin.

That use of footwork is no longer as in vogue. When you look at the data of the players who use their feet to spinners the most since 2005, the list really has two standout players: Cheteshwar Pujara and Michael Clarke. India's Pujara was a fantastic player of the spinning ball, averaging 55 in Asia. He struggled more against pace, but his stoic defensive knocks helped India tire out Australian quicks for victories down under.

Clarke was another player from the Sydney wickets who learned to play spin incredibly well due to the mentorship of Neil D'Costa. Clarke's play of spin on his maiden tour to India in 2004 is still talked about. As a young batter, he danced down the wicket to Indian spinners Harbhajan Singh and Anil Kumble in Bengaluru for 151 runs in his first Test. He would average 54.3 against spin in his career. Clarke's incredibly nimble footwork was sadly slowed down towards the end of his career by back injuries. This hurt because it took him a long time to mature into the player he was born to be, and once he got there his body let him down.

While he still has a very good overall average of 49.1, he did it in matches with a bucketload of runs in an era during which everyone was scoring a lot. He averaged 62 at home, but never more than 43 anywhere else, other than New Zealand. He went at 39.5 away and in his era other Australian top-six batters went at 39.1, meaning he was a great in Australia but a par player on the road.

Despite great footwork to spin, he would end up with a disappointing average of 37 in Asia.

Pujara is another who looked destined for greatness but never got there. Against the turning ball he went at 64.4 in his career. However, from the start of 2016 until the end of 2019, he made 1732 Test runs against spin, averaging 96.2. Pujara made 202 against Australia at Ranchi, where he spent more time down the middle of the wicket facing spin than he did at either end. He was a fantastic player.

The physical courage you need to face a 90mph ball is talked about, but what about the mental fortitude you need to run down the wicket knowing that if you miss, everyone will laugh or be angry at you. To do it all the time, without fear or doubting yourself, it is quite something

It is cricket's boldest move, changing the length of the wicket, running at the bowler and then trying to whack them out of the ground. These are two aspects of a dying art. Slow bowling is no longer that slow. Spinners are getting quicker every year, and moving down the wicket to them is almost impossible now.

Rahul Dravid noticed this when trying to coach the Indian players:

How do we get our guys to play spin better?
And they're saying, oh, we need to get them to use their feet more. […]
The trajectory of spinners has changed. That whole thing of going above the eyeline, the old spinners would talk about, throw it above his eyeline, make him look up. I don't think people look to throw it too much above the eyeline.
They're looking to spin it hard. And they're looking to bowl it a lot flatter. So maybe they're becoming stronger as well. So allowing them to spin it, and fitness, and all of these things mean that they're able to impart a lot of sidespin. A lot more sidespin than maybe overspin.
I think telling people to just step out is not giving them enough options. You need to have other shots now to be able to play spin well.

There are incredible highlights of old spinners online but the one that illustrates this the most is Bishan Bedi. He is unquestionably a great bowler, as his bowling average of 14.5 in the fourth innings confirms, but when looking at Bedi through modern eyes you cannot help but notice the slowness of his bowling. While this is more obvious for quicks, there is little doubt that before DRS and lbw took over for spinners, it was a different game entirely.

There have always been some faster and slower spinners. The best players of spin need to be able to handle all kinds. Sunil Gavaskar grew up in an era – much like Viv Richards and fast bowling – where he had to go up against India's quartet. Erapalli Prasanna and Srinivas Venkataraghavan were both off-spinners, Bhagwat Chandrasekhar was a fast leg-spinner and Bishan Singh Bedi a sweet lullaby left-arm spinner. Combined, they played 231 Test matches with 853 wickets.

Gavaskar told *The Indian Express*: 'I always looked at the release of the ball. See the air that is being given, mentally you tell yourself that if there is some air in the ball I will go down the pitch. Mentally, you are keeping ready for the flighted delivery. And be ready to go back too.'

Gavaskar puts his great play against spin down, at least in part, to going up against so many great Indian spinners domestically. India had four legends, but also a host of high-quality options on often turning wickets meaning that to survive you had to play spin incredibly well.

Within that is what we know of Viv Richards facing fast bowlers, or W.G. Grace going up against over-, round- and under-arm bowling. A genius who has to overcome something extreme will be built differently.

This was showcased when Gavaskar batted for 320 minutes in the fourth innings of a Test at Bengaluru's M. Chinnaswamy Stadium in 1987. It was a ragging pitch, Pakistan did not make it to tea on day one, as they were rolled for 116, Maninder Singh taking 7–27 with his left-arm orthodox.

India lasted slightly longer in their innings, where Pakistan used pacemen Imran Khan and Wasim Akram for seven overs combined before letting their spinners Iqbal Qasim (left-arm orthodox) and Tauseef Ahmed (off breaks) take all 10 wickets. India managed 145 in reply. Mohammad Azharuddin – who averaged 67.1 v spin – made six from 30 as India lost six for 19. Pakistan managed to make 249 in the third innings, despite the fact no one made a 50. India required 221 to win.

The problem was that the wicket kept getting worse. The ball was turning square, which is hard enough, but the wicket had tremendous bounce as well. When you hear that, it doesn't mean much if you're facing spin, but at one point Gavaskar has to duck a ball from Tauseef like it was a regular bouncer.

There is a stat that gives you a good idea of how bad this wicket was: there were 22 byes. Saleem Yousuf was like a toddler trying to hold a bursting dam behind the stumps.

It was nothing like a normal wicket. Gavaskar looked like he was playing Bodyline as the ball kept spinning and lifting up at him. He tried to get his hands out of the way as the ball would hit his thigh pad or chest on the way through to a legside catcher. He spent much of his time with his arms above his head like he was afraid a couple of kids were going to steal his wedding rings. The entire thing was made to look more dramatic as Gavaskar had on a wide-brim floppy hat with padding inside instead of a helmet. With an early form of arm guard, wrist band on the other side and something tucked into his trousers that looked like a bandage from a First World War bunker, he looked like a character in a John Carpenter film.

At the other end, people came and went after each unplayable delivery. Again, Azharuddin struggled, making 26 in 81 minutes before he was caught and bowled by a diving Qasim. This meant that India were five down, with 98 required.

Gavaskar didn't have his own way either. He pushed the ball through waiting slips, poked the ball past short leg, had heaps of inside edges and almost spooned the ball back to the bowler. Even when he played what looked like an attempt at a leg glance, the ball struck his pad and the umpire called it a dead ball because he was so far from the actual delivery. Pakistan put a fielder at third because so many edges went past the keeper and slips.

At a certain point, Gavaskar makes the most subtle change in his technique. As the bowler is about to deliver, he just squats down a little, like a wicketkeeper. His thoughts were that he needed to be closer to the ball, and that being lower like a keeper would allow him to rise with the ball. He never got too low; but this wicket needed an extreme method to counter it.

He also changed his grip on the bat, holding it higher so that when he drove the ball, it would always go down. When defending, he would slip his hand back down the grip. The idea is that the bottom hand decides the power of the shot, and he was choking his defensive shots with soft hands so that the many catchers couldn't get under the drop of the ball.

India – Gavaskar mostly on his own – edged towards the total. It wasn't just a close Test, but this was the last match of the series, and the score was 0–0. This was the deciding moment of the series.

There are no extravagant shots. Many of his runs are simply turned to the legside. On rare occasions, the spinners make a mistake, lose their length and there is a cut or drive. The tweakers are bowling quickly. They know they don't have to worry much about spin, as the pitch will do that for them. Most deliveries are simply too good, on the right spot. Gavaskar leaves and defends while looking on occasion to steal a run to the left hand of a ring fielder, or just beyond a close catcher.

There are many people who regard this as Gavaskar's greatest innings. The pressure of playing Pakistan on this wicket, to win the match and the series with no support from his fellow batters. It does make this one of the toughest situations he'd ever batted in, and that is amazing because this was his last innings in Test cricket. The first man to make 10,000 runs, the little master, was at the very end of his innings. He might not have been as sharp or fast as when he was young – Wasim Akram once talked about how Gavaskar had so much time when he played the ball – but surely this was his innings with the least of that. Yet there he was, finding a way when no one else could.

Gavaskar is nearing his milestone. The Indian crowd cheer each forward defence, which is quite the effort in a Gavaskar knock that has now reached its sixth hour. Pakistan have appealed around 50 times, and they have raised their hands in disappointment more than a hundred. Normally in an innings of this length, a player of his talent would have spread the field. There is no real need for Pakistan, though, as even when Gavaskar pierces the field, he must be so careful that the ball barely goes 40 metres. He has managed only eight fours in his mammoth stay.

With 41 runs to get and three wickets left, he faces Iqbal Qasim. The Pakistani left-arm spinner starts his run up from over the wicket and gently strolls around between the stumps and the umpire. He lands the ball around off stump and, like he has more than 100 times in this innings, Gavaskar comes forward to smother it, but the pitch has its final say. The ball spins and bounces (both verbs undersell it). It darts sideways viciously and lands on a trampoline. It may have taken bat shoulder or glove, and then appears to hit the keeper Yousuf in the shoulder before ending up at slip. The umpire gives it out.

Later, Gavaskar said the ball hit his wrist. But maybe the umpire just thought he hit it, because in 264 balls and 320 minutes on one of the toughest wickets ever, he really didn't miss many. Pakistan won by 16 runs. Gavaskar never batted again.

In his career, Sunil Gavaskar averaged 101.3 against spin. A Bradman-like number, which is apt, because he is the only other man to average more than 100 against the turning ball.

7

RUN

How players use running as a weapon

'Good running can change the whole atmosphere of a game.' – Dean Jones

Joe Root is standing at the non-striker's end. He looks relaxed, his bat is leaning on his thigh pad and at the other end his partner is dealing with the bowling. The juxtaposition of the two players couldn't be greater. Root is standing at a bus stop on a Sunday afternoon listening to a podcast. The striker is trying to handle a bowler who is a little too quick and skilful for him.

This isn't one match; it is most of England's.

If you asked me how it happens, I couldn't tell you. He usually has 20 runs, and I couldn't tell you how or why. But if Root has a truly elite skill in batting, it is simply his ability to get to the other end.

There are better players of pace and spin; others can handle the short ball better and dominate more when in the middle, but Root is the hardest batter to bowl at, simply because he doesn't allow you to bowl to him for a long time. He scores 27% more singles than other No. 4s. He faces 5.2 balls per single. Keeping him on strike is like trying to capture a butterfly on a windy day.

Test batting can be so hard because if you face a bowler for long enough, they will get you out. Even the best players will struggle if a bowler can group deliveries together, build up the pressure and set the batter up. Joe Root overcomes all of this by simply getting to the other end.

Chris Rogers uses Root in his coaching:

> He has the ability to get to 20 without you noticing. He has that skill to deflect, pushing the gaps, get down the other end, and then put the odd bad ball away. He can score off good balls. And I think that's what he likes to do – getting down the other end, taking the pressure off himself, but keeping the scoreboard just ticking over without having to play a risky shot.

Those skills are not as flashy as Virat Kohli's cover drive or Neil Harvey running down to a spinner, but Root's ability to get off strike is as important. He also combines three important parts of running: the ability to find gaps, make and react to the right calls, and he's quick.

English running between wickets has not always been this way. Root's method has always been more in the Australian style of running between wickets. The Australian method has always been for batters to look for a boundary first, then a three, two and one, before settling on a dot ball. Great batters from other nations have been good at finding gaps and even running between the wickets at times, but so many Australian players have been that way.

Perhaps the best illustration of that is the Australian opening partnership of Bill Lawry and Bob Simpson.

Lawry was a tall, elegant left-hander who liked to take his time. He was christened 'the corpse with pads on' because of his defensive tendencies – which were overblown by his friend and fellow commentator Tony Greig as part of their schtick on air.

'There's a lot of bullshit spoken, and particularly by Tony Greig, who really didn't see much of Bill Lawry play,' says Australian No. 3 Ian Chappell:

I would never call Bill Lawry a defensive player. He wasn't a slow scorer. I batted with him a lot. I had a lot of big partnerships with Bill and there was never any problem getting the strike. The only time I would say that Bill got a bit negative in his thinking was in India and obviously, South Africa, we all struggled there, and then against England in 1970/71.

And I think that came about because we were struggling as a team, and I had the feeling that Bill thought, if I don't stay in, there could be a collapse. So I thought then that he probably played more defensively, but I never thought of him as a defensive batsman. Bill was a very good player with a ton of courage and he really had all the shots.

But Bill was the sort of guy who could cut a shot out for an hour, or a day, or even a Test match because he felt that it might be dangerous.

Lawry also had an exceptionally straight blade. Ted Dexter talked about how even with wide half volleys he would hit the ball back down the ground. One mark for (or against) him is a particular record:

I remember Greigy going on about how Bill was never given out lbw in a Test in Australia. And I remember saying to Greigy, not on air, off air, "Mate, there's one requirement with lbw. The ball's gotta hit your pad without hitting your bat. And very few bowlers could get the ball past Bill's bat."

Lawry was out lbw seven times in away matches; albeit three of them on disastrous tours of South Africa when he was struggling with form (he averaged 27 in two tours there). Also, Lawry was a tall left-hander, so you do assume that he would have fewer lbws than other batters. He was lbw 11% of the time away from home; most players fall to leg before at 14%. In his era, there were local umpires, so this does suggest that Lawry was harder to dismiss lbw, even if the home record is a bit extreme.

But that isn't the fascinating thing about his batting, it was his running. Ian Chappell says:

He was very good at getting singles and I always got a lot of strike when I was batting with Bill. If you looked at his career, he probably scored a hell of a lot of singles. But you would never have a prolonged period bowling at Bill because of that ability to get the singles.

In 1964 at Old Trafford, Simpson and Lawry opened together. Simpson made his first hundred, and the two batters put on 201 for the first wicket.

Here is a part of the transcript from the *British Movietone* recap of the day's play:

'Simpson put the board up to 181, so they'd beaten the record for an Australian opening partnership against England. When Lawry was so unfortunately run out for 106, the score was 201, a new record opening stand.'

We know Lawry was run out. But when you watch the footage, you really understand just how often they were running, and crucially, how hard they were going. Their first scoring shot is a stolen single, the second ball shown is a hard-run two, the third is another single, and the fourth as well. Even when they show a dot ball, they both look for the single as Lawry drops the ball at his feet. Later, there is a hard-run three as well.

The reason for this being in the highlights is that movie cameras did not film all day, so they can only show you what they happened to record. But also, this was the partnership. In total, both players made 417 runs in that Test – Lawry's 106 and Simpson's 311. They did an awful lot of running, as only 136 of those were from boundaries.

The two batters played 129 Tests between them. Simpson was run out five times in those matches and Lawry six. Eleven is a lot, especially for opening batters who are less known for their running as they face the new ball and take their risks that way. Openers in the 1950s and '60s were usually run out 3.5% of the time, including Simpson and Lawry, who were run out 8.5% of the time.

West Indies opener Chris Gayle (aka the Universe Boss) had a single run out in 103 matches, Geoffrey Boycott had seven in 108, Sunil Gavaskar had five in 125, Alastair Cook had one in 161, England's opener Herbert Sutcliffe had one in 54 and his partner Jack Hobbs had two in 61. West Indian Gordon Greenidge was never run out in 108 matches; his partner Desmond Haynes six times in 116 matches. This is an eclectic list of some of the best non-Australian openers ever – old and new, two partnerships, and a bunch of others known for their work alone.

That is 23 run outs in 836 matches combined. One run out every 36 matches. Simpson and Lawry were dismissed that way every 11 games. They were playing a different sport to other great openers.

While Lawry and Simpson are known for running well between the wickets, especially as a pair, Australian cricket was also known for this. Simpson pushed this even further in ODI cricket in the 1980s and '90s, when he was Australia's coach.

Running between the wickets became a way the Australian team believed they could score more runs in the 50-over format.

Australian batter Dean Jones was a huge catalyst for this. He was a natural athlete and very aggressive. But more importantly, he loved running between the wickets in a way few players before him had. In the book, *One Day Magic*, he explains how it can change a game by putting pressure on the fielders and bowlers:

> You can actually see and hear your opponents getting frustrated. At first the bowler will stand there, hands on hips, staring at the guilty fielder; later he'll shout a curse; the captain will stare coldly at the offender.

Jones would also talk about how he'd get more fun out of stolen singles or unlikely twos than hitting sixes. The idea that stealing a one is as important or exhilarating as hitting a six just didn't exist before players like Jones. He didn't come to this naturally; he would work in the nets over something he called 'phantom running'. He also practised hitting the ball softly, dropping it at his feet: 'If you think about it, the fielders from cover or square positions have to travel at least 15 metres to get to the ball, ample time for the batters to get home.'

Before going out to bat, Jones would also look at fielders to work out who had the better or worse arms. Which players could he target because they were slow to react? There was a science behind what he did.

Jones did not have the same impact on Test cricket as he did on ODIs. But from 52 matches, he averaged 46.5. In a weaker playing era – the Australian team was stacked – he would have had a full career. Twice, he scored double centuries: once against a very strong West Indies attack and another in the second tied Test in Chennai, where he made 210 and got so sick that he ended up in hospital on a saline drip.

But whether subconsciously or not, the style of running that Jones and the Australians had used did come more into Tests as well.

Steve Waugh was not an attacking player in the five-day format after his disastrous start, but he was between the wickets. His ability to drop the ball on the legside against the short ball and find a gap and take off was incredible. Somehow, he was only ever run out four times in Tests, but when he retired, he held the record for the most at the other end; a staggering 23 partners he sent off early.

Two more Australian captains have incredible records of run outs, Ricky Ponting holds the all-time record with 15 times dismissed, and for a long time Allan Border (another disciple of Bob Simpson) was two clear of his nearest rival. Dean Jones referred to Border as someone who got himself in trouble because, instead of running in and out of the crease, he would travel in a circular motion.

Matthew Hayden is also in the top four of all time, meaning that of the batters who have been run out the most, three of the top four are Australian.

Even Australian players like David Warner and Hayden, who were known for their power and aggression, loved to steal runs. When Warner's shoulder gave way and he lost some of his hitting ability, he became one of the world's best runners between the wickets. He told me once that he loved to get into his innings through stealing ones and twos early on. Warner scores 32% more singles than expected for a batter with a similar over distribution as him.

By the 1990s, Australia was being matched by South Africa. They were less aggressive in their running, but with athletes like Jonty Rhodes coming through, they were looking for singles a lot more. Limited overs – with an assist from Australia – really changed how players ran in Tests.

Limited overs batting has often been criticised for a decline in Test batting. During the 1990s, former players often said it was ruining techniques. Weirdly, they said little when cricket arguably had its best batting period ever from 2000 to 2015. Now T20 cricket is getting much of the same blame. There are technical changes, though people seem to ignore the fact that players find it much easier to score now. Even if they might also get dismissed quicker, the number of runs does seem to stay the same.

But limited overs cricket did improve running between the wickets in Tests by a huge amount.

By the 2010s, while Australia still had some great runners, England had Joe Root and their occasional wicketkeeper Jonny Bairstow. Martin Guptill from New Zealand was probably one of the best, which is unfortunate as he's remembered for the run he didn't make in the Super Over of the 2019 World Cup final.

There was a rebellion against running in T20s, notably led by Chris Gayle. This was probably in part due to his hamstrings making quick singles tough, as well as his view on the game. For Gayle, if he was going to take a risk, shouldn't it be on a six and not one extra run? That style really took over for the West Indies.

But AB de Villiers, England's keeper Jos Buttler and Australian batting performance artist Glenn Maxwell combined the hustling running with the big-shot making to create their own hybrid. The future of T20 batting will probably be stand-and-deliver players, batters who can find constant pockets to steal two runs and hybrids of both.

The requirement to get off strike never goes away; even in T20, many a canny batter has looked for a quick single when Jasprit Bumrah or Lasith Malinga were on one.

In Tests it's a necessity. Virat Kohli is an incredible runner. As of 18 August, 2023, he had run more than 500 kilometres between the wickets from his own and his partners' runs according to Sampath Bandarupalli from *ESPNcricinfo*. He was always a good judge and keen, but he matched that with supreme fitness after his first few years in the game.

Ian Bishop was on commentary when Kohli was playing his 500th international match. After the former Indian skipper put in a dive to complete a double during his innings, Bishop said:

Absolutely superb. That's the sort of desperation you love to see incorporated in your batting and batsmanship. This is a Test match. You sometimes see guys doing this in desperation in a one-day or white-ball scenario, but here is a guy who has been around for 500 international games and in a Test match, knows the value of every run. Putting his body on the line and diving to make sure he's in. That tells you how badly he wants whatever he gets out of this innings.

Kohli would go on to score his 29th Test hundred in that match. But there was one time he could not get off the strike.

Vernon Philander is bowling to him at Cape Town in 2018. That is already bad as this is the South African's home pitch, where he averaged 18.3 over 11 matches. He is also bowing in the fourth innings, where he averages 18.4. Philander is so tough in the final innings because of his accuracy. He can hit a length that trims the bails seemingly at will, and so he keeps the stumps in play almost every ball. His Hawkeye numbers suggest no one is better at hitting the stumps than him.

That is not what he is trying to do to Kohli; he is bowling outside off stump and moving the ball further. He knows that Kohli wants to get some bat on them. So, he keeps each ball between 6 and 8 metres, outside off stump and curving away. Kohli doesn't have length to drive, width to slash, and the movement of the ball doesn't allow a punch on the up. He is stuck because he is looking for a single but is unable to find anything.

Kohli faces three balls in a row in the 18th over from Philander: the first is pushed to a fielder, the second left and the third he drives at a ball that is not there, taking an edge on his pads.

The start of the 20th over, Kohli is now desperate to get off strike. He pokes one towards point and takes off but ends up having to dive back into his crease. The next one Kohli leaves alone as it goes through. He does the same with the following two balls. It feels like Philander is dragging him ever so slightly to the off side. The fifth ball of the over, Kohli goes out to meet the wider delivery and scampers through for a run from a push between cover and point.

The following over, he is back on strike again. Again, Kohli tries to meet the ball moving away outside off stump and pushes it to cover for no run. Next ball is just that little bit wide, he reaches for it and can only push it to cover again. The third of the over is even wider, and Kohli moves across but then leaves it. Philander has now kept Kohli on strike to him for 11 out of a possible 12 balls. His plan is clear – he tried a similar tactic on an Indian tour in 2015 – wide, wide, wide, drag him across, and hit the top of leg stump once he's in the wrong position. This is exactly what he does for the 12th ball of this spell, and Virat Kohli is out.

There are days when one magical ball is enough for a player of Kohli's ability, but most times it would take a brilliantly executed plan. Kohli averaged 44 for his first 41 Tests as he got in the swing of things, then as he hit his prime years from 2016 to 2019 he played 43 more and went at 66.8. Philander was bowling to this version of Kohli. An ultra-competitive and driven individual who spends every spare second in his life trying to better himself. When you bowl to Kohli, you're not just going up against a batter but an entire belief system.

This is a person whose father had passed away during a Ranji Trophy game, yet he'd kept playing.

Unlike many of his fellow great Asian batters, the faster the ball comes, the more he likes it. He averaged over 50 in South Africa and Australia combined. His twin hundreds in Adelaide in 2014 to almost steal a Test from Australia is some of the best batting this century. He does struggle with the laterally moving ball in places like England and New Zealand. His average dropped off when the Wobbleball took over. It also dropped because the wickets at home were set up for their spinners.

Even then, this man is a force. However, no matter how great you are, if you are stuck on strike against Philander on a fourth-innings pitch at Newlands, you either get off strike or are stuck in a trance.

Kohli has spoken a lot about running between the wickets as an important aspect of his game. He obviously played with MS Dhoni, a master runner, even if – like Root – the keeper didn't appear at first glance to be that type of athlete. His sprinting for doubles against Australia in a must-win T20 world cup game in Mohali was breathtaking. But Kohli chose AB de Villiers as the best runner between the wickets he batted with.

He also chose Indian No. 3 Cheteshwar Pujara as the worst runner when talking to de Villiers on his podcast, including a story about how he was run out twice in the same match:

> I was like, 'You were run out in the first innings. How can you be so brave to take on the quickest man on the field and then not be seen on the screen while being run out. That's the worst call I have seen in my life.'

Pujara was run out nine times in 176 Test innings. While cricket has many great runners, there are also batters like Inzamam-ul-Haq and Virender Sehwag who created issues by not really enjoying or being awake during runs. Geoffrey Boycott was involved in 20 run outs in his career (his partner was the victim 13 times). The Indian legend Nawab of Pataudi was never ran out, but there are a lot of reports of him being very keen for runs.

Looking at the number of run outs doesn't always tell the full story. Some players are dozy and bad communicators; others always push for extra runs.

What about the combination of both? For that, we need to get to someone who certainly ran between the wickets well but was sometimes dozy, by his own admission.

Bill Brown was a high-quality batter. Not that he had a huge ego – he said that making it to lunch was a success. He should have been far more famous because he had a 14-year career, but sadly it was either side of the Second World War. Instead of becoming one of the greatest Australian players, he has only 1500 runs. He averaged 46.8 over 22 matches and more than 50 in first-class cricket. His record was more impressive because he played only five Tests at home, and in them he averaged 31.8. In away Tests he averaged more than 50 from 17 matches. He was clearly an elite opener; he just didn't get a chance to make many runs.

And runs, in his case, is the right way of thinking about it. Of all the things Brown was known for, one of them was running between the wickets. He often referred to his batting as tip and run. He stood out, even in the Australian culture; he was a fantastic athlete and lightning between the wickets.

There was another reason he was better at doing this than others; it was because he'd back up a long way at the non-striker's end.

This was an issue when he played against the Indian left-arm finger-spinning all-rounder Vinoo Mankad, who saw Brown do this in a tour match and ran him out. He had given him a warning, but Brown left the crease early at the non-striker's end and Mankad ran him out.

Then the Tests began. Australia smashed India in the first match in Sydney, which passed without any issue. The next Test was in Brisbane, Brown's home ground.

The first day was almost a complete washout. The second, India had to bat on a wet wicket, and luckily it had dried enough for them to make it to 188. This meant that Australia had to survive to the close.

The openers put on 25 runs when Mankad was bowling to Arthur Morris, with Brown at the non-striker's end. Brown backed up too far again; this time, Mankad didn't even warn him. Brown was run out. He flung his bat on to the ground and left the field. Stumps were called soon after.

Usually, when something like that happens, cricket continues the next day, and so the controversial issue is one of the talking points, but eventually, cricket dilutes it.

What followed was actually a rest day, which allowed for more talk about the run out. Then it continued as days three and four were also washed out. Day five was the only one with cricket, and Australia collapsed on another wet wicket. Then day six was washed out. So, after Brown's run out, there were four days of no cricket.

It wasn't really the press who led the attack on Mankad; it was more the letters to the editors. The newspapers were flooded with angry fans voicing their disgust. Most of the pieces seemed to suggest Brown was in the wrong.

An Adelaide newspaper talked about how a similar thing happened in grade cricket there; the bowler on that occasion was Martin Chappell, father of Ian, Trevor and Greg.

The former Australian leggie Arthur Mailey wrote about the first run out in the tour game and actually called Mankad overly generous for warning Brown before dismissing him.

A couple of decades later, when Charlie Griffith – the West Indian quick who loved a run out at the non-striker's end – did it, the Australian press was yet again on his side.

Even articles from Brown's local paper did not blame Mankad for his actions. They interviewed him about the event and let him explain why he'd done it. Essentially, Mankad said that Brown leaving the crease early was getting in his eyeline and causing him a distraction.

Not every former player agreed; Jack Fingleton and KS Duleepsinhji weren't happy. But there were plenty of people on Mankad's side, including Bill O'Reilly, who had no problem with a bowler stopping what he called stolen singles. Years later, Don Bradman also came out on Mankad's side.

We now use the term 'Mankad' in cricket for this run out. It is a contentious term, with some in his family asking for cricketers to stop and others wanting his name to be used. All these years later, it is still a controversial way to dismiss a batter.

Modern cricket sees more of these dismissals, especially in white-ball formats. The reason is simple: batters are looking to get down the other end as quickly as possible now, and bowlers are sick of batters getting an advantage. To modern-day bowlers, why should they be leaking runs because a batter leaves the crease early – either by accident or on purpose? They are reducing the distance they need to run.

That is what Bill Brown was doing. Running between the wickets was one of his superpowers, and he was determined to steal as many runs from India as possible. All Vinoo Mankad did was penalise him for his repeated transgressions.

When Brown threw his bat on the field, it wasn't because he was upset at some mythical spirit of cricket. Brown was fuming that he'd got himself run out by being a bit dozy.

Joe Root got himself to the non-striker's end so he wouldn't be dismissed. Bill Brown found a way to get himself out, even when at the other end.

8

ATTACK

How aggressive batting can change games

'He went round the clock as it were and I stood there thinking, "he's taking the mickey here."' – Bob White

The Fremantle Doctor is a sea breeze that blows in during the afternoon in Perth's summer months. The idea is that there is a temperature difference between the land and sea, and the cooler air will come in and change the temperature on land. On this day at the WACA, there is a breeze, but it is not The Doctor. It is 37°C, but it feels far hotter. On the hottest days in Perth, it feels like the sun sits lower in the sky there, right on top of your head, penetrating your brain.

In December 2013, when covering a Test at the WACA, journalists started putting their laptops in the fridge as they overheated. It was hot every day of this Test, with 37°C the maximum temperature. The sort of heat that melts your soul after a day or two.

Some batters say that it gets harder to think in hot conditions. They resort to trying to get as many runs as they can before fatigue gets them out. This was one of those days as England were well behind in the Test, needing to score 504 to win. At the crease was Kevin Pietersen.

The chances of winning were low, as the heat had split the WACA pitch like a fault line with cracks everywhere. Australia had Mitchell Johnson in peak form, and burly chested fast bowler Ryan Harris almost as good. They were both too fast, too much. With a big total to chase, the wicket and the heat, nothing was on England's side.

But they did still have Pietersen, the player who changed things with his stroke play. His strike rate was 61, which was nowhere near some of the quickest players. But when he went hard, it was violent.

'Kevin Pietersen, he's the best player I've ever seen play for England,' says David 'Bumble' Lloyd:

Sensed the moment, right, my turn now. At the Oval in 2005 that'll stay with me. He just kept whacking Shane Warne. And, you know Warnie, said, "well, he's bound to hit one up in the air." He didn't, got 158. The great players can win a game on their own.

They have no fear, no fear about getting out because they just know I'm better than him. He's got the ball, but I'm better than him 'cause I've got a bat. Whereas the rest of us think, oh Christ, not him.

At the Oval in 2005, Pietersen was yet to make a Test hundred. He was facing Brett Lee and Shaun Tait – two of the fastest bowlers, then and now. As well as Glenn McGrath and Shane Warne – two of the best bowlers, then and now.

Pietersen slog-swept Warne like he was a part-timer in a village team. The champion leg-spinner took 40 wickets in that series. Pietersen brought his hundred up from 124 balls, even though for a period Warne bowled defensively around the wicket into the footmarks, just to slow him down.

But it was the attack on Brett Lee that was the most exhilarating. After 60 balls, Pietersen was on 35, and most of those were boundaries from attacking Warne. The Australian quick decided to bounce Pietersen.

It started with a bruise, clocked at 93.7mph. All Pietersen could do was glove it and almost fall over into his stumps. Straight after that, the Australians smelled blood and Lee went all in on the short ball. Pietersen went on the hook.

The second ball of this plan was hooked for six. Lee's speed was 91mph. It cleared fine leg by some distance. Pietersen was not a great hooker; like many other tall batters, he didn't face as many short balls growing up. He often made the decision late, and it was more of a panicked swipe. He also often tried to play it off the front foot, which he was even worse at. In all, he averaged 32 playing the pull and hook. The top six batters of his era averaged 44 using those shots.

Pietersen used this shot differently compared to other players. He was daring quicks to keep bowling it to him. Lee did. Looking back, it felt like this contest went on forever. Lee kept getting faster and shorter, and Pietersen swung more and more frantically. But in two overs, the Australians bowled only seven short balls. From those, Pietersen hit 21 runs. Lee was forced to give up the plan.

No one who saw that innings live has ever forgotten it.

Pietersen was no one's idea of a perfect batter. His technique involved hitting balls on the up, dragging deliveries from outside off to leg, and hitting the ball in the air. Playing across the line might have been why he struggled in the second innings of matches, averaging only 38 as the ball kept lower. Overall, the risks he took stopped him from averaging 50 in what was a great era to bat. His average was 42 on the road, but he was above 50 at home, which in England is a triumph. However, he was not from England, being raised in South Africa. So it's still very much a great achievement. Looking at his record, he stood up for the big series – averaging 46 in Australia and 44 in India. Weirdly enough, he struggled back home in South Africa, but from only four Tests. He was a fantastic player with an average of more than 40 in Asia, which was made worse by his struggles in the UAE.

He is not an automatic player for the top 50 Test batters of all time, but his ability to turn a match in an innings was like few others in history. It means his average of 47 is more significant than others.

A generation after 2005, Pietersen is facing fast bowling from Australians again – this time on a faster wicket at the WACA. But he is also going up against a new Australian spinner, Nathan Lyon – on his way to 500 Test wickets – bowling with the breeze.

Australia have attacking fielders and boundary riders, an in/out field. Many batters would simply rotate the strike, punish any bad deliveries and keep their wicket intact. Lyon was the bowler to milk, to stay in against, and save your real energy for Mitchell Johnson's thunderbolts or Ryan Harris' Mack Truck-like force. However, it is hot, and the pitch is playable. The Australian quicks are all rotating through their second spells, and to give them more time to rest, Lyon's off-spin is floating on the breeze.

Pietersen starts to attack him immediately, smashing one back to the bowler, which is stopped. Next, he comes down the wicket and drop-kicks a shot over mid-on. He gets three. Australia drop the mid-on back. The next over, there are two more boundaries: one from a fine sweep and another from a cover drive against the spin.

Lyon stays on, and Pietersen wants to emphasise that he should not. So he runs down and smashes the ball over the long-on fielder into the crowd. It is audacious, wild and exactly how Pietersen thinks. One more hit, and Lyon will have to be taken from the attack. Australia will have no choice. Pietersen has scored 21 from 14 balls.

This was also not the first time he'd gone after the Australian spinner. In total, he had struck at a rate of 71 against Lyon in his career, quicker than against most bowlers. And being that the offie was frugal, that was a big jump up. He was also averaging more than 50 against Lyon. He has the matchup, has put him in the crowd and scores off him with ease. One more blow would change Australia's rest strategy.

So, Pietersen runs down the wicket at Lyon one more time and goes for glory. But something doesn't work; his head isn't perfect, the ball doesn't come from the middle, it hangs in the famous Fremantle Doctor and the catch is taken by Harris, one of the quick bowlers he is trying to tire, at long-on.

Even though we were almost a decade into Pietersen's career at this point, and he'd taken that sort of risk so many times, he was still taken to task for it.

People saw it as arrogance, a lack of patience or just plain stupidity. But there was solid thinking to how Pietersen played. If he did knock Lyon out of the attack, Mitchell Johnson would probably have to come back into the attack too early. Getting him tired was the key to making runs against Australia if you'd managed to survive Ryan Harris and the new ball. The third seamer, Peter Siddle, was more of a holding bowler, and Lyon was not a major threat on the seam-friendly wicket. Johnson with the old ball, and Harris with his accurate pace were the threats. Both men could be slowed down in this heat. You could try handling them for hours and do that over time, or you could speed up the process by making the player who rests them unbowlable.

Pietersen often chose the faster, more dramatic option. And when it worked, England won the 2005 Ashes due to his 158 at the Oval. When it didn't, Australia won the 2013/14 Ashes at the WACA. In terms of game theory, Pietersen was risk and reward. He was hailed as a hero when it worked and abused as a pariah when it didn't.

Batters like Pietersen, Garfield Sobers and Brian Lara were not always batting at a high speed. But when they thought it would make a difference, they would hunt a bowler or an entire attack.

Brian Lara commentated for Triple M in Australia a few years ago when he was questioned about a Test he played in Antigua. 'MacGill and Warne played in the previous Test,' says Lara, of the famous Test where Warne was dropped because he hadn't recovered from his shoulder injury. 'But then you got someone called Adam Dale.'

When Mark Waugh asks Lara if he gave Dale some tap, the West Indian replies, 'You were there.' A few moments later, the scorer comes in and says, 'Brian Lara's career strike rate vs Adam Dale was 146.'

Now it was only one Test they played against each other. Looking at the scorecard, Lara clearly realised that the best thing to do against an attack of leg-spinner Stuart MacGill, hybrid bowler Colin Miller and tall seam legend Glenn McGrath was to take down Dale, Australia's medium-fast swing bowler playing in his second and final Test.

In 1966, Sobers played for the West Indies against Nottinghamshire. Playing for the county was a Jamaican bowling all-rounder called Carlton Forbes, who was roughly the same age as Sobers. Forbes took 707 first-class wickets at 25.4; he could play.

'He hit Forbes in six different directions, all six balls,' says Notts all-rounder Bob White:

> He went round the clock as it were and I stood there thinking, he's taking the mickey here. He hit the first one over or past mid-off, the next one past cover, the next one he hit square on

the off side for four, the next one he flicked over square leg. The next one over midwicket and the last one he hit over mid-on and I thought this is a genius. He did it just to take the mickey out of poor Carlton.

The following year, Sobers was signed as Nottinghamshire's overseas player.

Those kinds of players use attack when they need it. It isn't about all-out attack, just when the mood or moment calls for it.

Compare that to the most attacking specialist batter in Test cricket in terms of strike rate, Virender Sehwag. When he was sitting in the changing rooms having been dismissed, he would be watching greats like Sachin Tendulkar and Rahul Dravid and saying to himself, 'four, four, six' as the two legends blocked out balls he would have attacked.

Sehwag has a few flaws in his career. Lateral movement was a big problem for him. The bowlers who dismissed him the easiest were almost all outswing bowlers like Matthew Hoggard, Ben Hilfenhaus, Dale Steyn and Jimmy Anderson. In Tests, when his team lost the toss and was sent in, he averaged 26. It means he was a fantastic opener in Asia, but very ordinary in South Africa, England and New Zealand. But when the sideways movement went away, like in Australia and the West Indies, he was a star again. His career wasn't hugely long, and he was often overshadowed by the legends around him. But when he decided a bowler had to go, they might as well be fed through a trash compactor. There are Test venues around the world with little chunks of bowlers still in the soil.

His strike rate was so much higher than everyone else's that it overcomes his many shortfalls.

Sehwag was pure attack. And his impact on other teams was incredible. Kyle Mills was well known among the New Zealand bowlers for his ability to hit his thigh pad to get him off strike. That was considered a win. Sehwag still scored at a strike rate of 93 against him in ODIs and made 18 runs from the 11 balls he bowled to him in Tests.

In the ball-by-ball database I had access to, Sehwag faced 32 bowlers for more than 100 balls. Not a single one ever kept him to a strike rate under 50. Jimmy Anderson and Chaminda Vaas – two brilliantly accurate seamers – both went at more than a run a ball against him. Muttiah Muralitharan and Rangana Herath were great spinners, who both went for more than five runs an over. Shoaib Akhtar and Dale Steyn went at strike rates of 83 and 81 respectively.

Accuracy, skill, pace – it didn't matter. But Sehwag's impact, at its most, was felt against the new ball.

Teams don't have a lot of plans in Tests with the new ball. Generally, the idea is to bowl whatever length the seamer usually tries, or something slightly different on some pitches. The line will be either at the stumps for lbw candidates, or just outside for most bowlers. If you bowled outside off stump to Sehwag, on practically any length, he would slaughter it through the off side. So, three standard Test balls could cost you 8–12 runs.

As a bowling team, you have a real issue. What do you do now? It is too early to bowl short to him, as it will damage the ball. You cannot bring spin on, as he likes that even more. If your seamers went straight at him, he was just as good at flicking the ball away. If the bowlers decided to go into the pitch, he would slash over the off side and would again turn the ball away to leg fairly easily.

What Sehwag did was take Test bowling away completely. Rahul Dravid explains:

> You can see the pressure that it puts on bowlers and captains. Suddenly, you start seeing fields becoming very defensive. They're not necessarily looking to get the guy out; they're looking to contain runs. Suddenly, it's a shift in mindset. Where there was a third slip, that's deep point now. They're sometimes willing to give away easy singles. What Sehwag can do when he is playing well is shift the mindset. If Test cricket's all about taking wickets – which it should be – suddenly it becomes, oh, it's just about saving runs.

Sehwag inverts the roles of batters and bowlers in a few balls. The opening batter as victim does not apply to him, as he's the killer out there. It's not about whether the bowlers can dismiss him, it's whether they can survive.

The former general manager of the Jamaica Tallawahs is a man named Mohammad Khan, an American who comes from a financial background. One thing he looks for when constructing teams in Test cricket is an attacking opener. His reasoning is quite simple; many of the best cricket teams of all time have had someone who goes in first and bashes the ball.

Ian Chappell and Bumble Lloyd are old–school cricketers from a different universe, but they also have the same theories. If you were to make a list of the best cricket sides ever: Australia in the 1990/2000s, West Indies in the 1970s and '80s, and (while they didn't play as much) South Africa of the late 1960s. All these sides had an opener who could take the game away from the opposition and would create havoc for plans. Sri Lanka is another team that often has attacking openers.

Getting a great, or even two, standard or defensive openers, is fantastic. But one player who can mess with team plans, bowling rotations and change the match in an hour is priceless.

Ian Chappell says:

I was fortunate that I played for South Australia with Les Favell and Barry Richards and then for Australia with Keith Stackpole. Very aggressive openers. Obviously, they score quickly, which is very good for your team. The fact that he's scoring quickly makes things easier for the batsman he's in with, and the following batsmen. And importantly he plays a great role in getting a decent score as quickly as possible, so that the bowlers have got time to get the 20 wickets.

And then there's another thing that a quick scoring opener does. He can deflate the opposition. Let's take David Warner as an example. If you go out there and you know that if Warner has a good two hours, he could almost take the game away from you.

In the first session of a Test match, if he plays really well, he could be well on the way to doing that. The fellows who worry you most as a captain are the fellows that get decent scores, but they get them quickly. There are certain blokes who can keep you awake at night.

Warner is such an interesting batter because he has a terrible away record for a player of his quality. He was fantastic in South Africa and Australia, and awful everywhere else he played a lot in. By the end of his career, his form really fell off completely when right-arm seam bowlers started bowling around the wicket with the Wobbleball. His poor record against Stuart Broad became one huge reason to dismiss his greatness. Yet during his career, his wicket was huge for the opposition. Because they knew on the day he made runs, they came with such force and speed that he could wipe a team out.

Technically, Warner was such a weird player. He was a small, powerful man who played the game so differently to others and was one of the few white-ball specialists to make a successful transformation to Tests.

Chris Rogers, Warner's former Australian opening partner, speaks about him:

> I think a lot of opening batters are top-hand dominant, look to play straight. Whereas he was a bottom-hand dominant player. I felt at times, it's almost like he was playing a bit of tennis.
>
> He could get on top of the bounce and hit the ball in front of point, where most openers would be cutting that behind. He had such strength to go with incredible skill and timing that he hit the ball into different areas as an opener.

At the WACA in 2012, India batted first and were rolled cheaply for 161. Australia went in to bat, and Warner, in his fifth Test match, was ticking. A young Indian seamer on debut called Vinay Kumar came on to bowl. Warner went down to chat to his then opening partner Ed Cowan about how they would take their time with him. Warner smashed his second ball from Kumar into the crowd over long-on. Cowan asked what happened, Warner replied, 'It was in my wheelhouse.'

At the close of play, Warner had 104 and Cowan 40. Australia were 149/0 from 23 overs. In far less than a session, India's entire score had almost been wiped off.

Chris Rogers was a fantastic late-blooming player himself, averaging 42 in his mid-30s as a traditional opener.

> There was one game where he was on 40 and I was on two and the crowd were going berserk and you're almost standing there thinking, uh, no one's paying to come watch me bat while this bloke's down the other end. I have to get off the strike or I

have to match it. I thought I was a pretty good player and to be overshadowed like that was a little bit challenging.

He just put so much pressure on the bowling team. Both from a cricketing aspect, but from personality as well. So batting down the other end took a little while to get used to because it was almost like you got the feeling of being a little bit second rate. But eventually you realise that you could use him to take all the pressure off yourself.

Then it was fantastic because the opposition players almost forgot about you. I'd imagine in the team meeting they just spent 20 minutes preparing about Warner and one minute preparing about me.

What Rogers is describing is what Chappell talked about before; attacking players take up more air. Their ability to shift a game quickly means that they force you to prepare anxiously for them, and once they start to go, the panic follows, as Rogers recalls:

The best I ever saw him bat was against South Africa in 2014. He had a great tour. We were facing Morné Morkel in the first Test, he hit me in the shoulder first ball. Then I tried to ride the second ball, and I got caught at short leg. Then we went to Port Elizabeth, I was probably under pressure for my spot and he was bowling beautifully, and it was just so difficult to face.

And I remember Davey hit him for four fours in four balls. I think it was like two of those kind of punching half cuts in front of point, and two of those half pulls, in front of square on the legside. And Morné got taken off the next over. And I just remember thinking that's just some of the most incredible batting I've ever seen. When he was on, there weren't many bowlers who could bowl to him.

That was Warner's greatest away tour, but he couldn't replicate his batting outside Australia all that much.

Rogers, now Victoria's head coach, says:

He could play those kind of half cross-bat shots better than everybody else. And so when the ball bounced, he could score boundaries from balls at the top of the stumps. Most batters are trying to defend them but he's punching them in front of square for four.

Maybe it just came down to the fact that when there was bounce, he stood out.

Matthew Hayden and Virender Sehwag also struggled when the ball was moving to have the same impact as they did on the wickets without lateral movement. South Africa, New Zealand and England have always struggled to produce this type of player. While Australia has had a lot, India have Sehwag and now Rohit Sharma, and the West Indies have Gordon Greenidge and Chris Gayle.

Gayle has two Test triple hundreds and was a brilliant opener, even though few think of him as a top Test player. Gayle made a bunch of runs in Australia, New Zealand and South Africa. He didn't always attack, though his strike rate of 60 was very high, but he could be an extraordinary dead batter when he wanted. He was the first person ever to hit a six off the first ball of the match when he launched off-spinner Sohag Gazi in his maiden Test over long-on at Dhaka.

The search for a player who could scare you like this means teams try attacking openers, often from white-ball cricket.

England once tried their T20 hitter Alex Hales to open with Alastair Cook. In 11 Tests, Hales had a strike rate of 43.8, which was slower than Cook's by quite a bit. New Zealand used Brendon McCullum as an opener, but he was slower there than other positions. South Africa's most aggressive option was probably Herschelle Gibbs, a very underrated batter at the top of the order who averaged 47.2 in the 68 Tests he batted first. Sadly, the rest of his career he struggled in most other spots he was also forced to play. But despite striking the ball so effortlessly, his strike rate at the top was 52. So, we know that conditions do play a part.

Warner finished his career averaging 26 and 13 in England and New Zealand. When Australia lost the toss and were sent in, he averaged 29. Like Sehwag and Hayden, Warner could attack but he needed the conditions to be in his favour to last long enough to make it count.

On top of the tactical side, attacking openers help with the most important thing in batting, the ability to age and soften the ball. While a defensive opener may, to quote the tragically taken too young Phil Hughes, 'Dig in and get to tea', an attacking opener can pave the way for everyone else by simply stopping the ball swinging by crashing into fences, or softening the ball so much that any lateral movement is slow.

But the reason we see so many attacking openers is simply because it is the time when the ball is at its hardest, meaning it races off the bat, and the field is at its most attacking. If you have the skills to score quick, this is the time to do it.

Looking at *CricViz*'s historical strike rate database of top-seven batters with 2000 runs, nine of the fastest 20 are openers. Sehwag and Warner are at the top. But on that list are also two more from India; the 1980s dasher, Kris Srikkanth, and recent slasher, Shikhar Dhawan. McCullum and his English protégé Zak Crawley are also on the list, along with Sri Lankans Tillakaratne Dilshan and Sanath Jayasuriya.

Obviously, this list leans towards modern times, but it does show how likely someone with a high strike rate is going to open, which does go against how we usually see that position.

Roy Fredericks was a West Indies opener from the 1970s who liked to attack. 'I like to get good little 40s,' he told Ian Chappell. Chappell says:

He was a better player than that. When it came to square driving, he was a bloody nightmare. Particularly at his home ground [...] if he hit it well, you couldn't stop it. But I think because his mentality was, "I like to get good little 40s", you always had a chance of getting him out before he got away.

Fredericks did average 42 in Tests as an opener; his strike rate is listed as 48 in some places, but that is not complete. Because of one game, that seems unbelievably low.

His attacking shots were ebullient, not least because Fredericks had the most fascinating footwork. It was as if he never left his original place in the crease. His feet standing slightly less than shoulder width apart would stay there even as he played a back foot drive, hook shot, straight hit or flick off his pads. All the action was in his backlift and fast hands. Even when coming down the wicket, his feet would somehow get back into that position. All this was made more obvious by his small stature and the fact his pads always looked a size too big.

It was the pull and hook that the five-foot-six player was best at. As fast bowling took over, it was a perfect time for Fredericks to shine with his ability to read the length quickly and get into positions to smash the short balls away. He was the first batter ever dismissed in a men's World Cup final – a bouncer that he hit for six but swung so hard he trod on his stumps.

Fredericks at the WACA was a symbiotic relationship. In 1975, the man who liked to play the pull shot and make 40 went large against the fastest opening bowling combination ever in Dennis Lillee and Jeff Thomson. Viv Richards talks about Thomson as someone who would 'spread the eagle and fly'.

The only thing that flew when Thommo bowled to Fredericks was the little man's bat. When he was out, the West Indies had 258, of which Fredericks had 169 with 27 fours and a six. He faced only 145 balls. In the innings, Thomson went at 5.6 runs per over, Lillee 4.6.

Australia had scored 329 in the first innings, and Fredericks simply erased it. That is what attacking openers do.

His batting partner for many of those years was Gordon Greenidge. Despite Desmond Haynes and Greenidge being the famous coupling in cricket, when Gordon batted with Roy, they averaged 54.9 – good enough for tenth highest of all pairings with 1500 Test runs.

'Gordon on the square cut, even if you were third man and you were square and you had to run five yards, he was so powerful, it would only be three yards wide of you and still four,' remembers his old Hampshire batting partner, former South African great, Barry Richards.

Of the attacking openers, Greenidge stands out as someone who could play everywhere. He was a great player of lateral movement, averaging 56 in England and New Zealand combined. He also made runs on Indian wickets (though not Pakistan). He did struggle a little in Australia, averaging only 30, and his overall mark dropped a lot because he played on well past his peak, managing a mark of 36.5 in his last 28 Tests, until then he was at 48.

His record is full of wonderful work, like averaging 10 more in wins than draws, showing the impact he had. He averaged 48 in the

West Indies and 42 on the road. But he wasn't really a West Indian batter, at least his teenage years and professional development were not there, so this was some record. He was perhaps one of the first truly international players; raised in Barbados until 14, he would eventually move to Reading, England, and develop further there.

Barry Richards says:

I think he was a West Indian that had an English technique. He learned to play on wickets which weren't quite as trustworthy as they were in the Caribbean. And even though he had the English technique, he still attacked in a more of a West Indian style. He became better when he played for the West Indies. Once he threw his hat in with them, the style of play was very much part and parcel of the way he wanted to play. He could have gone the stodgy route if he wanted to, because he had the technique to grind it out like a Geoff Boycott, but he didn't, he chose not to do that.

It did mean, that unlike Warner, Matthew Hayden, Fredericks and Sehwag, he could play the moving ball more and would often defend for long periods and then attack.

But Greenidge is best known for one innings at Lord's in 1984.

It was a low-scoring match – neither England nor the West Indies went past 300 – and at the halfway mark, the West Indies were 41 runs behind. They started well with the ball, but England's middle order batter Allan Lamb scored a century which, coupled with an 81 from their all-round legend Ian Botham, meant England were the first side in the match to make it to 300. This meant the West Indies needed 342 from only 78 overs on the last day. A run a minute, on what was a good pitch that hadn't fallen apart.

Botham had taken eight wickets in the first innings, while he and Bob Willis bowled 47 of England's 66 overs. The home side had lost faith in their bowler Neil Foster, and Derek Pringle had been injured.

Because Willis had bowled a lot in the first innings, a beautiful pattern became visible on the grass at Lord's. This was his run-up arc. Starting behind the umpire then arcing out towards mid-off before coming back in straight – it was almost parabolic in its perfection.

When he strays too close to the pads of Greenidge and is powerfully flicked for the first boundary of the innings, Willis already looks tired though barely into his spell.

If Willis was tired, Greenidge was limping and looked sore. Throughout his career he struggled with a back complaint (this happens to many batters who make a lot of runs – bending over the blade is not good for you). Often when he was stiff, he attacked more. As Greenidge told Subash Jayaraman on *The Cricket Couch* podcast:

> I like to feel that I am going to take the fight to the bowlers [...]
> I believe personally that when I take the fight to you, I make you change your game plan [...] It didn't always work, of course, but I thought this was the best game plan for me.

It also helped (as it did for Warner, Sehwag and Hayden) that the batting behind him was incredible. So, he went for England. At one stage he hit a cut so hard that all Richie Benaud said on commentary was, 'That is hitting the fence now.' There was no time for a description; it was happening too fast.

When England went wide, he punished them with his drives and cuts. He would stand very legside of the ball, hoping for some width. The ball was swinging too. Foster delivers a decent outswinger and Greenridge seems to wait for it to move exactly into his arc and then slams it through the cover gap.

But he was also so quick in his first step, so if you got it too straight, he would move into position and flick away violently. He did this against Botham and lofted it. He brought up his hundred from 135 balls. West Indies were 160 when he raised his bat.

Once he was on top, and the fact England had taken one wicket (the run out of Desmond Haynes), he really went for them. England resorted to slowing down their over rate, but after tea, Greenidge and his partner Larry Gomes took 29 runs from Botham's first three overs. One straight drive from Botham almost destroyed the bowler and umpire in one go. By the end of the day, Botham was broken. He had made 81 and took an eight-fer, but he finished the game bowling off-spin as the West Indies won with 11.5 overs to spare.

Their total was 344/1; Greenidge made 214 from 242 balls. He scored 66% of the runs the West Indians did from the bat.

This innings also helped give Greenidge his highest average in the fourth innings. However, there are 12 not outs there. He once had four in a row, and in total eight out of ten, but they included 79 not out, 120 not out, 214 not out and a 49. While he got a boost from not outs, it was clear that he had a technique that could handle the wickets at the end of a game and the power to destroy when he felt the need.

West Indies have produced many attacking openers, all the way through to Chris Gayle, but the history of attacking openers goes way back.

When making a list of the greatest batters of all time, Victor Trumper is one of the most curious cases. Because, for all the exaltation of the man, he averaged 39. But before we pull out Neville Cardus quotes that speak about Trumper like he invented foreplay, we can do something similar with numbers.

In Tests Trumper played in, the match average was 32 by other top six players. So he was 21% better than those he was playing with and against. If you look at him by era, he was 30% better than other top six players. Both numbers have him firmly in the frame for greatness. Purely as an opener he struck at a strike rate of 77 from the 37 innings we have data for, and as a non-opener, his strike rate was of 63.1 in 27 innings. He was the original big bang.

There are players of his era with a better record: Jack Hobbs, who is one of the greatest batters ever, and Aubrey Faulkner, who played on matting wickets. But there are two stories of Faulkner and Trumper that show the difference in class. The South African scored his team's first-ever double hundred at Melbourne in 1911, which gave South Africa a first innings lead of 212. This was supposed to be South Africa's first away victory, then Trumper came out. He scored better than a run a ball to make 159. The next highest score was 48. Faulkner's innings had been brilliant, methodical and stoic; Trumper blew it away like it didn't even happen. South Africa collapsed to lose the game.

On the same tour, Ian Peebles writes of a time that Faulkner was given a bat from Trumper's sport store. Faulkner was overwhelmed

THE ART OF BATTING

at the generosity and couldn't wait to try it out, but when he did, it was a dud. The bat just didn't have any kind of middle at all. When Trumper asked Faulkner about it, he sheepishly admitted that it wasn't any good. Trumper took it back and apologised, then he used it in a tour match and smashed the ball everywhere with it. He told Faulkner that he had now knocked it in. But when the South African used it, it was terrible again. Faulkner may have averaged more than Trumper, but even he didn't think he was better.

One other player needs to be mentioned here: Clem Hill. In the same era, and often on the same wickets, he averaged an almost identical mark to Trumper. They both preferred playing at home and facing the weaker South African attack. Hill might have had a better career had he not been out so often in the nineties (96, 99, 98 and 97).

Most importantly, they were both attacking players. Hill is the 19th quickest scorer in Test history, yet there is no mention of scoring speed in his obituary. There is a chance that the strike rate *CricViz* have for him (63) is inaccurate, or his left-handed nature of scoring on the legside was not attractive enough for comment.

We know that Hill could go, he was the fourth man to hit a hundred runs in a session, a massive 116, against South Africa at the Old Wanderers ground. Hill is one of two players on the 20 fastest scorers list that didn't play a Test after 1980 (the other is Trumper).

Victor also liked to make a hundred in a session. He did that three times, including the first occasion of scoring a hundred before lunch on day one of a Test at Old Trafford in 1902. Even if Hill's strike rate of 63 is accurate, Trumper's is 69.

During his career, the bowling economy was 2.8, meaning that players scored at a strike rate of 46.3, including bowling extras like wides. This meant that during his career, Trumper scored at 50% quicker than cricket. He was a lot better than the batters of his era, on the same wickets, and did that at the fastest rate of any top-order batter, until Viv Richards arrived.

C. B. Fry said, 'He is a poet of cricket; he has a poet's extra sense, touch and feeling. Trumper can play, with his bat, a cricket ball as Paganini played his violin.' But let's not mistake this – Trumper was a thumper.

Jack Hobbs once said, 'He is the most perfect batsman in his scoring methods I have ever seen. He makes every orthodox stroke quite after the best models, and in addition he has several strokes of his own, which is quite hopeless for other batsmen to attempt.'

Trumper essentially unlocked the legside by hitting from the off side, which meant that in a world of Test and first-class players with only a few shots, he had them all. There was no way to stop him in the pre-bouncer era. You just had to hope he touched the sun by trying to score too fast.

We know through an interview conducted by cricket historian David Frith with Wilfred Rhodes that Trumper didn't like the ball spinning away as much. Rhodes once famously said, 'I wanted to get at Trumper.' That was probably in part because his ability to hit across the line meant his bat swing came across his body.

Rhodes did dismiss him nine times in Tests, though they played each other in 31 matches and Trumper's median scores in those dismissals was 59.7, suggesting he had already tormented the quicks by then.

Syd Barnes had Trumper 13 times in 17 matches, but he was also the best bowler in the world at that time. Clearly you needed to be a legend yourself to keep him down.

Trumper was a player who loved the front foot, was not afraid of lofting the ball, had a huge back swing, played across the line and scored very fast. There were players who did some of these things. Trumper did them all.

He also did them first. Openers of his era were just coming out of their bowlers' dominating defecated pitch era. The idea was to survive, and Trumper did far more than that. He made batting fun in a way that not even Hill, Faulkner or Hobbs could do. His batting was joyful. So much so that 35 years after his death there were still old heads saying he was a better player than Bradman.

Only in cricket could 39 beat 99.94 But Bradman was a calculator, and Trumper was all the colours of the rainbow. It is unfair to compare the two.

The most interesting fact about Trumper is that although he was known as an opener, he batted down the order quite a lot, making nearly as many runs from batting positions 3–7 as he did up top. Some of this would have been through injuries and wet wickets, also batting orders were not so dogmatic before the Second World War. But the interesting thing is that as an opener he averaged 33, but batting 3–7 it was 49.9. And that is from 1496 runs – a decent sample.

Would Trumper have sung his songs even louder from down the order? Was he a misdiagnosed opener?

The rest of the fastest scorers ever does have a different pattern. Most of the non-openers are players with a second skill: Kapil Dev, Sarfaraz Ahmed, Rishabh Pant, Quinton de Kock, Niroshan Dickwella, Matt Prior and Freddie Flintoff.

While this is still impressive, there is a freedom with knowing you have another skill to be in the side with. It means you can play the attacking way, and even if you fail a little more, you can make up for it with your second job. As talented as all those players were, they are not all all-time great batters. In fact, most of them are No. 7s, which again is a lower pressure batting position that lets you swing a little wilder.

When coming up with a long list of nominees for greatest batters ever, I only looked at players in the top six. The reason is that players further down the order – no matter how useful they can be – are not on the level of true batting greatness.

There is one exception – the only man to make more than 2000 runs averaging over 45 at seven or lower is Australian wicketkeeper Adam Gilchrist. Seven is an easier job than anyone else on this list had, but Gilchrist had an incredible average with the fastest strike rate of anyone in Tests.

England's Darren Gough explains the conundrum of Gilchrist by saying he was the toughest to bowl to in his career. Not just due to his immense talent but because of when you bowled to him. By the time you got Australia five wickets down, the bowlers were tired, and there was often well more than 200 on the board. So, adding the most destructive hitter in Tests to that was terrible for bowlers.

In Gilchrist's first Test he came in at 345/5. He was not an unknown by this point; he'd forced himself into the side with runs (even being booed in his first Test by the Queensland crowd who were upset their man Ian Healy had lost his spot), including an explosive start to his ODI career.

When he arrived in the middle of the Gabba, he was well known by Pakistan, and he attacked straight away. He was a different kind of attacking player than many of the openers or attacking players further down the order. The top-order players relied on a string of boundary fours. The guys further down looked to hit over the top. Gilchrist did both of those things and looked for quick singles. He was a triple threat. He also was someone who could hit pace or spin, played back and front foot, and like the best aggressive batters, a play and miss never seemed to affect him.

His mantra was 'just hit the ball' and that is what he did that day at the Gabba, attacking the leg-spinner Mushtaq Ahmed. Pulling and cutting every time the quicks Wasim Akram and Shoaib Akhtar dropped short at him. It was an incredible start, and when Shoaib Akhtar finally dismissed him with a yorker from hell, Gilchrist had made 81 from 88. Australia made 575 and won by 10 wickets.

The next Test, Pakistan were on top after 50s from Saeed Anwar and Ijaz Ahmed to support Inzamam-ul-Haq's hundred. This meant in the fourth innings, Australia had to chase 369. At 126/5, Ricky Ponting was out and Justin Langer was joined by Gilchrist. Pakistan was well on top, Gilchrist was playing his fourth Test innings, and the Pakistan bowling attack was Wasim Akram, Saqlain Mushtaq, Waqar Younis and Shoaib Akhtar. Between them they cover swing, reverse swing, off-spin, doosra, leg-spin, wrong 'uns and express pace.

Yet, it was Pakistan who defended. They saw Gilchrist come out and they moved fielders back to cut off his boundary options almost immediately. That soon into his career, he was already psyching out the opposition just on the thought of him.

Saqlain had two players out on the sweep; the quicks had two players for the pull and a guy for the cut. It didn't matter because Gilchrist didn't see boundary riders as obstacles to runs. He saw the ball, and he wanted to hit it hard.

After one over of a powerful cut and pull combination, Wasim Akram is walking down the wicket talking to himself and shrugging. Australia still need way more than 100 runs, but he looks out of ideas.

Waqar Younis bowls to Gilchrist from around the wicket. It's a length ball well outside off stump and Gilchrist pulls it to the boundary like it's a normal thing to do. Not long after, Younis overpitches and is slammed back down the ground, Gilchrist has his hundred from 110 balls. Now one of the best strike bowlers in history is bowling with four men on the boundary.

Eventually Pakistan brought the fielders back in, but it didn't matter. Gilchrist played the same way, he just had to run less. Australia won, losing one more wicket. Gilchrist hit the winning runs, finishing with 149 from 163 balls.

From his debut in that Gabba Test in 1999 until the end of 2003, Gilchrist averaged 57.4 in Tests. He made his debut just before reaching peak years, and so most of his Tests were in that peak period. From the start of 2004 until his retirement, that dropped to 38.8. He also averaged 27 on Indian pitches, yet from only seven Tests he scored two hundreds.

There were other things that are certainly in favour of him being a top 50 batter of all time. One is the fact he was also a keeper, and because of that he averaged 15.5 runs more in the first innings than the second. The other was his record on the road; Asia was the only continent in which he didn't average 40, but even that was only 37. Everywhere else he was above 50, outside of two poor Tests in the UAE.

There was also the fact that while he was a No. 7, he was clearly the greatest one by a wide margin. He averaged 46.4 batting there; in his era he made 12% of all runs scored at No. 7 in Tests. But he also averaged 67% more than a normal No. 7 who only managed 27.7. In games he played, that mark dropped to 25, meaning he was 85% better than the No. 7 on the opposition.

One of the big myths of his career is that he inspired teams to pick keepers who could bat over pure glovemen. Keepers' averages had been rising steadily for years, but he certainly made teams look for faster scoring options.

So many keepers are on the list of great strike rates: Quinton de Kock, Sarfaraz Ahmed and Niroshan Dickwella fit the bill. Rishabh Pant and Matt Prior also have outstanding averages. But perhaps the player most like Gilchrist was not a clone but someone who came out of that same era: Brendon McCullum.

It might surprise people how low his strike rate of 65 actually is, because when he went, it was carnage.

The ball is full and McCullum swings through the line. On one shot, England have gone from in front to behind. The score was 68/3, with England swinging the ball everywhere at Leeds in 2015, but that one hit shook the home team.

Alastair Cook instantly starts to defend, despite the fact he won the last Test, and is in front on the scoreboard; the captain is defending the boundary after McCullum clears the cover rope first ball.

This innings only lasted 28 balls and he made 41 runs. But when he is out, the ball has stopped swinging, New Zealand are 123/4 and now it's about getting out players with a ball not being all that helpful.

Something even more incredible happens next. McCullum is replaced at the crease by Luke Ronchi, a man who somehow ended up as a backup keeper in Western Australia for Gilchrist and then in New Zealand for McCullum. He keeps attacking like he's inhaled the spirit of his captain. He will make 80 from 70 balls and New Zealand end up winning that match by 199 runs.

McCullum's actual career is a mess. He started as keeper, averaging 34.2, then as a specialist batter that mark moved to 43. But that wasn't straightforward either, because he opened, batted three, five and six, having started as a No. 7 when keeping. His position in the order was as random as his shot selection. No. 5 was probably his spot, there in 28 matches he averaged 43.9 (49 as a specialist batter).

He was also terrible away from home, averaging a surprisingly low 29. He only made runs on Indian and UAE wickets, which for a Kiwi is a strange place to be at your best. At home he averaged nearly 50; on the road he was like a handy keeper bat. He also did a fun thing of getting faster as his career progressed. Perhaps inspired by his own white-ball success, or more likely as he realised his normal technique was fading, he decided to play out his twilight years by destroying bowlers. There is no debate that he should be anywhere near the list of best batters of all time, but influence is another thing.

No one really copied Gilchrist; he was a one of one, part woodchopper, part accountant late to the office. No one could copy McCullum; he was a sawn-off shotgun firing lollipops to sugar-obsessed kids. A whirling dervish of screams and ejaculate. The single most entertaining batter of modern cricket.

There were times when it was like McCullum was running down the wicket to chest the ball away, like he had forgotten his bat and was hoping that just by charging at the bowler they would wilt and give him runs. His method was to take away the bowler's line, length and slip cordon. It was kamikaze batting that somehow refused to die.

He was the most must-see batter of all time. Because he was glorious in hitting boundaries, playing and missing, his cricket possibilities were endless. He could save the world, chop his own head off or clear a stand at cover. It is all possible, it is all probable, in that final moment. The 400th millisecond between delivery and McCullum was as thrilling as any batter before or since.

When you see a player who hurls himself down at a ball, runs legside of it, gets a short fast one at his left shoulder and still slashes over backward point for six, you are changed.

When McCullum had finished changing his own country, he decided to take the head coach job of England's Test team in 2022, and here he handed out cigars and champagne while telling the team to whack the ball. They called it Bazball. The phrase was coined by Andrew Miller at *ESPNcricinfo* to easily explain Brendon McCullum's philosophy using his nickname.

Bazball is now in the *Collins Dictionary*: 'Noun – a style of Test cricket in which the batting side attempts to gain the initiative by playing in a highly aggressive manner.' It is a little more than that, and we felt its impact first when Jonny Bairstow went wild at Trent Bridge in 2022.

New Zealand's stand-in captain Tom Latham made a mistake not putting nine men on the rope – and if that sounds like a ridiculous statement, you didn't see Bairstow in that fourth innings.

England were chasing 299 in 68 overs. We knew they would go hard, because they promised it just as aggressively. It was weird how much England told New Zealand they'd chase anything, regardless of the equation, because that gave a big tactical advantage to the Kiwis.

But England delivered on their promise. The first over has three fours. New Zealand fought back, and they took three wickets, including Joe Root, the most important. They fell to 56/3 when Bairstow came in.

The innings progressed further for England and then Alex Lees was out, meaning they were now 93/4.

With the accurate New Zealand seamer Tim Southee on, Bairstow does something that Test batters in the fourth innings don't usually do. He runs down the wicket and drives hard for a boundary.

At this stage it had no name, but later we would call this 'the Bazball shuffle'. It might seem like needlessly aggressive behaviour, but McCullum had worked something out in his playing career. If you allow Test bowlers to hit their length, they will eventually get you out.

That Wobbleball was matched with another change in the game: seam bowlers were bowling fuller and straighter because of DRS so increasing the number of lbws they could get. So, quicks were now bowling around the six-metre length (a whole metre fuller than before) and aiming at off stump, not the channel outside.

The Bazball shuffle is one way of counteracting that, because you know roughly where they are going to pitch, and if you move quick enough, you ruin their ability to bowl fuller. This wasn't the only method used to counter it; Pakistan and New Zealand players batted further out of their crease as well. You also don't need to do it every ball. Once or twice every two overs is enough to keep a bowler guessing.

That was the first part of Bazball, but there were others.

England took to reverse sweeping spinners a lot. In with Bairstow was his captain, Ben Stokes. Not a great player of the ball spinning away because his bat flow comes across the ball from outside off stump.

Stokes goes with two reverse sweeps. A shot invented to manipulate the field. This was another big part of England's aggression, just moving away catching fielders. To go back to Kevin Pietersen, you take a risk to get a reward.

The reverse sweeps had more than one impact, as it was also against New Zealand's part-time spinner, Michael Bracewell. Since the 1970s, teams have targeted the fifth bowlers in ODI cricket. From 2015, England turned it into an art form for the 50-over game. They even expanded to specialist bowlers who they saw as weak. Traditional batting may have a player looking to just milk a couple of safe runs an over off the worse bowlers. But in modern white-ball cricket, the idea is to smash them out of the attack so the team must change their plans. For New Zealand it meant overbowling their main guys as their giant seamer Kyle Jamieson was injured.

England landed these blows before tea, and that meant after the break they needed 160 in 38 overs with six wickets in hand. It was winnable, just. Drawable, certainly. And losable, possibly.

For the Bazballers, there was only one choice: winning. New Zealand tried the short ball, but without the bowlers to back it up, and Bairstow pulls two of them to the rope, then New Zealand Wobblebowler Matt Henry goes too wide and Stokes plays one fine of deep point for another.

Bairstow then uses another tactic; he just smashes the ball straight down the ground over left-arm legend Trent Boult's head for a six. Before the ball has landed, Boult is changing the field. This kind of batting is what McCullum wanted, but it was also what England did best. They had become a horrible Test batting side. In 2021, their fourth leading scorer was extras. But they were the new kings of white-ball cricket; in 2022, they became the first team to hold 50- and 20-over World Cup titles at the same time.

McCullum wasn't rebuilding their Test batting; he was borrowing from their white-ball side.

So, why didn't New Zealand simply bowl like it was an ODI? They had made the 2019 World Cup largely on the back of their seam bowling. The genius of England switching the codes on them was that New Zealand (also Pakistan, South Africa and India in later matches) were not ready for this. They kept thinking that if they did the right things, England would eventually punch themselves out.

The English had discovered a method of white-ball batting that upped their averages and strike rates simultaneously. They did this by hunting match-ups that favoured them, taking down the weaker bowlers, looking for short boundaries and being able to clear boundaries when things were in their favour.

New Zealand were trying Test tactics against an ODI team with a ball that was soft and one bowler short. They looked like this was their first-ever cricket match. This game exploded in front of them. There was no time. New Zealand were playing a Test, then suddenly they were trying to put the Hindenburg back together with things they found around the house.

The only thing that slows England down is Stokes injuring his knee, and Bairstow looks for a safe option to make his hundred. But he can't stop middling the ball; it's like a mania. He finds a gap on the off side and brings up his hundred.

Unshackled from the burden of self-gratification, Bairstow decides to end Bracewell. Sweep, six. Sweep, six. Sweep, four. Luckily, they didn't ask him to try to bounce Bairstow.

This is the bit where Latham made an error not putting every fielder on the rope to allow Stokes to come back on strike. Or at least, made it 30% harder for Bairstow to hit boundaries.

How did it come to this for the World Test Championship winners? Jonny Bairstow destroyed the cricket nation formerly known as New Zealand. He would do similar things in the following game where he made 162 at better than a run a ball and a 71 from only 44 deliveries. In his next Test against India he scored back-to-back hundreds both with strike rates over 75.

Bairstow is not a great batter. He has a huge flaw in his technique when it comes to facing full balls on his stumps, at one stage in his career averaging 13 to these balls. Overall, he averages less than 40. But when he plays an innings, you feel it.

The hype around Bazball did get out of hand. People forgot that England had beaten a weak South African team only 2–1 at home, that they gave up a series in New Zealand 1–1 that they should have won, and that Pakistan beat them by simply using two spinners on loop. They won a lot, but they lost a lot too. At home in the 2023 Ashes, they came back to get a 2–2 draw, and won early against India before losing 4–1. That was when people really started mocking Bazball.

But they did have some success with the style on Indian wickets. Rahul Dravid was India's coach when England turned up for a Test tour in 2024 with their Bazball style:

We were very calm initially because we had planned for Bazball. You were always saying, okay, if he's good enough to play these kinds of high-risk shots in these conditions against the quality of bowling we have, we'll take it. But in the back of your mind, you're thinking he can't do it.

But when Ollie Pope's shots start coming off, then you start thinking, man, what the hell is this? Is he that good? Is he going to be able to do this all the time? And that's where you just need to then hold your nerve.

And that's not easy because then you just get too frazzled. You start thinking everything's wrong.

That was the coach of a team that beat England easily, and yet in one innings from Ollie Pope they had doubt because there is an element of Bazball that means you need to kill it off. Pope and England are not perfect; they were using these tactics to get the most out of themselves, to change the plans of the opposition and cause mayhem.

While England being the pioneers of a new method was weird, the pious way they talked about it and how they were saving Test cricket got on people's nerves, to the point that people started saying what they were doing was nothing new. On one level, they are right; England did not invent attacking batting.

But attacking as a team-wide plan for all batters, that was a lot rarer. There was really only one team who noticeably scored quicker than everyone else.

Australia were an average-scoring team who dominated Test cricket in the 1990s but got a lot of draws. In 1999 – with Gilchrist's help – they decided to score quicker to get more results. For the next nine years, they were quicker than average; half a run per over quicker than any other team and a run quicker than the slowest in that period. This was a huge change.

However, Gilchrist was the only player with a strike rate over 65. The next best was tail-ender Shane Warne. It felt like a dramatic shift at that time, and it led to the then England captain, Michael Vaughan, pioneering the boundary rider fields.

What England did under Bazball was completely different. England were 1.3 runs per over quicker than the next fastest side (the Aussies) in the first two years of Bazball, while being almost two clear runs of the West Indies at the bottom. We had never seen anything like this.

In their first 14 months they managed to score 300 runs at more than five runs an over seven times; the great Australian side managed five runs an over once against Zimbabwe.

England had the most disruptive strategy in the game since the West Indies picked four fast men.

Clearly the game was heading in this direction. The bats got better, the batters hit more boundaries, scoring quicker in white-ball cricket was economically important and new shots were in vogue. Scoring faster in Tests was due.

Even before McCullum and Stokes joined forces, something interesting happened. In 2017, ODI averages were higher than the Test game. That had never happened before, and it led some to wonder if players shouldn't be attacking more in Tests. The only issue with this was that when white-ball specialists were picked for Tests they generally struggled. England's did not, and part of that was the all-in nature of it.

This wasn't choosing one attacking player and hoping he would come off. It was an all-out attack, safety in numbers. England won a lot of Tests doing it at the start, and then it slowed down.

When it worked, everyone said it was genius. When it didn't, it was seen as lucky.

Nothing tells this story better than Joe Root playing his reverse scoops off fast bowling. The England legend played this shot off Neil Wagner in the Leeds Test that followed Bairstow's innings at Nottingham in 2022. No one could believe a player of his talent and experience would play this shot that involved such risk and insanity. It was like watching the most well-adjusted adult you know move to Iceland to start a new music genre.

For Root, it was an equation. The left-arm seamer was angling across him, trying to get an edge to slips. Root could swing his arms freely at that ball, knowing missing it would cause little issue. If he helped it on its way, it was not only an easy boundary but would also bring a tactical or field change.

The following year, he tried the same shot to Wagner when they met in New Zealand. The field and angle were similar, but Root failed to make proper contact and was caught at slip, the position his shot was supposed to take out of the game. This time, the shot was wrong; the other time, it was right.

That is how attacking shots go. Virender Sehwag once remarked that getting caught at slip or on the cover boundary still meant the same thing: you were out. But even through England's success there was always the fear that it wouldn't work everywhere, that it would be found out, or limited, or fall down when needed.

That is generally what happens to attacking players. Except one.

Richard Hadlee is bowling, the ball is moving in the air, he is at home, and he's sent off Gordon Greenidge and Richie Richardson already. New Zealand's greatest ever player – and deadly seam bowler

– took six wickets in the first innings, West Indies are three wickets down in their second innings and still need 152 runs to get New Zealand to bat again. The game is over.

But in comes Viv Richards. There was a bit of a shootout element: the world's best batter and bowler standing at each end. Like John Wayne, Richards had an odd walk that on anyone else would have looked comical. But no one laughed at him because of moments like this.

As Hadlee comes in, Richards is chewing gum and almost grinning, like he knows what will happen next. In a way, he does. Hadlee is going to deliver a ball near off stump on a good length – that is what happens – and Richards swivels into a pull to dispatch the ball most would defend. It's arrogant and brutal; it bounces off the fence and back on to the field of play; '20 metres,' says the commentator, Peter Williams.

Hadlee self-corrects next ball to pitch up outside off stump, even though the last one really wasn't short. Richards is already on the front foot, it's almost a yorker in the end, but Richards digs it out and still finds another boundary straight down the ground.

Hadlee delivers the next ball to the top of off stump and just outside. Richards is in the same spot he was for the previous ball, but this time he drives through the covers, despite the line being more or less the same as before.

Hadlee clearly believes he needs to drop shorter and try something different. Richards is inside the line of it almost before it's out of the hand and it crashes away past the two boundary riders. In eight minutes of batting, including one over from Hadlee, Richards has six boundaries.

It doesn't last; New Zealand get him for 38 and go on to win the game. That was his highest score in only three Tests in New Zealand. There was no other side who ever found a way to slow him down. You might think that again we have an attacking player who struggled against the seaming or swinging balls. But in England he averaged 64.3, he was 44.4 in Asia and 47.5 in Australia. This all meant that he averaged more than 50 away. He could smash spin or pace; the mode of bowling had little impact on him.

The New Zealand Tests were also not peak Richards. He was past his best. For the first 45 matches of his career he averaged 60.2; for the rest of his career he was 43.9. His last three years had 19 Tests, one hundred and he averaged 36.2. And like many of the great Australian players, he never had to take on his own attack.

In 1976 he played 11 Tests and made 1710 runs, averaging 90. If he did that at anywhere near his career strike rate of 70.9, the fifth fastest ever, it's probably the best year of non-Bradman batting cricket's had.

And in that year, he faced Dennis Lillee, Jeff Thomson, Bishan Bedi, Bhagwat Chandrasekhar, Bob Willis and John Snow.

He made 8540 runs at 50.2. But that doesn't include the World Series Cricket Supertests: 1300 runs at 57.

He was at his best at No. 3, averaging 61.5, which is largely dragged down by moving down the order when he was older, because when a team took a wicket, it allowed him to come in and attack.

At Trent Bridge in 1976, the West Indies weren't the champion team they were about to become. They were still using the medium pace of Bernard Julien and Vanburn Holder. West Indies batted first, and Richards was in when Mike Hendrick removed Gordon Greenidge with the score on 36.

Richards' first boundary is a short ball that he reaches from way outside off and despatches to square leg anyway. It's followed by a tap of the wicket. It was one of the most common sights to see of Richards out in the middle. It seemed to have little to do with checking on the wicket; he simply wanted people to see that the last shot wasn't a big deal to him.

But Richards wasn't well known by England then. He'd made his debut in 1974, his only Test hundred was 192 not out in Delhi, and he'd struggled in the first men's ODI World Cup in England in 1975. He had almost 1000 runs in Tests this year, so the stories were there, but England hadn't bowled much to him. You can tell some of this by the fact that John Snow keeps bowling short to him. Richards smashes one through an ancient Brian Close at square leg, then another two through midwicket.

The England bowlers eventually pitch up. That brings about its own problems. As he did with Hadlee, he would walk right across the stumps and either play a classical off drive or smash it straight back past – or through – the bowler. Sometimes he would drag it further and go past mid-on. There were even times that the same ball that others would cover drive he'd flick to square leg.

As a child, his school cricket ground shared a fence with someone who wouldn't toss the ball back. So Richards and his brother were forced to score on the legside.

The power is what people remember about Richards, but the placement was also incredible. He would hit the ball very hard into whichever gap he wanted. The other thing lost in talk of his swagger and machismo is his technical ability to hit the same ball in multiple places. He could cut and pull, but also in front of square to both. If he needed to, he would hit the ball straight from the back foot. He could drive from point to square leg, often from the same ball and foot movement. And even if you were one step ahead of him and got the field exactly right, he went over them. This was a man unafraid of being caught, almost daring you to stop his shots.

England left-arm orthodox spinner 'Deadly' Derek Underwood bowled a sharp turning ball outside off stump, and Richards played a lofted cover drive for six. From a spinner. In a Test match. In 1976.

Eventually, Underwood would have a deep cover and long-off. Richards would take them on as well for another six.

Setting a field to Richards was deciding which player would be the quickest to pick up a ball from the fence.

When Tony Greig finally does catch one at long-off, the crowd run on to celebrate with him. Richards has made 232 from 313 balls. The West Indies will make it to 494.

Long-off at least gives you some time. The worst place to field in cricket was silly point to Viv Richards for a spinner. It was a war crime by the bowling captain to send anyone under the cap – it was rare to wear a helmet then. Your job was to get ready for a small edge on to the pad that would balloon up and then fling yourself forward for the catch. The reality was he was going to hit the ball hard at you and test your commitment to safety.

There was no good position to be in the field against him. Australian off-spinner Tim May delivers a beautifully flighted, drifting off-spinner to him at the WACA in 1988. Viv takes a small shimmy towards the ball and smashes back a straight drive over May's head. The ball slams into the fence like it's punching it in the face. The crowd get up to watch the ball and then all sit down in unison as if shaken by the experience of being that close to a rocket.

May stands still in the crease for a moment, then blinks, like someone who has seen his life flash before his eyes. Then he takes a big breath of air. Australian keeper Ian Healy watches in stunned silence – not his natural state. Captain Allan Border moves mid-on back to the fence. Not that it would help; there is no way a fielder not directly in the path of the ball would ever stop that. May takes one look back towards Viv before heading to his mark, then widens his eyes as far as he can and steps back into the fire for another delivery.

What is incredible about this exchange is that Richards is 14 years into his career, and his power is still scaring and scarring people. Tim May would have grown up watching him on TV or heading down the Adelaide Oval to see him play. In this period Richards was as famous in Australia as any homegrown player, yet being face to face with power, May still can't believe this is real.

A few seconds later the off-spinner comes back in and bowls a waist-high full toss that Richards gives a full swing. Anyone could hit this for six; it's a terrible ball. Not many players could make a bowler deliver something this horrible, but Viv Richards could.

As the ball flies over the WACA boundary, it feels like it has been whacked out of Perth. Maybe it landed in Fremantle. Because even The Doctor couldn't stop Viv.

9

PEAK

The sweet spot of a batter's career when their technical mastery matches their athleticism

'I think it was me getting to know myself a little bit better as a person that helped me.' – Rahul Dravid

I genuinely don't remember a massive amount about the pair because I wasn't there – I really wasn't there at all. I didn't feel like I was supposed to be on the team.

It was like I was keeping somebody else's place warm for them while they dodged Curtly Ambrose and Courtney Walsh. That was what it felt like. I didn't really take it to heart.

I wasn't walking out to bat with the kind of will behind me that I was going to go out there and make some runs, or I was going to get stuck in, or whatever it might be.

It was just I'm here. I'm walking out there, something might happen of some use, and more than likely it won't, and that was it.

It wasn't like I had given up. It wasn't that. It was just I couldn't find it within myself, or the belief in myself that I deserved to be there in the first place.

I wasn't playing well enough to be able to do something about it. The gods were going to look after me or not, and they decided "not today, Sunshine."

That is Mark Butcher, former England No. 3, talking about his first and only Test pair in 1998.

In the first Test of the series, at Sabina Park in Jamaica, England elected to bat first; perhaps the worst decision they had ever made.

Five minutes before the toss, Jack Russell gets sick. So Alec Stewart has to take the gloves. So they're missing a batter. And they decided to throw me in there at number three.

The first ball goes flying over Stewie's head, the next one rolls along the floor. I saw the whole thing, I was next in, so I was sat there watching it just going, "Oh no, you're kidding me." The pitch had ripples on it, like a wave that had set in ice. It was, in every way, the very opposite of a flat pitch.

In the first over, [Mike] Atherton had one almost take his head off. The next ball rolled along the ground twice, on the way to the keeper. Alec Stewart played forward to a ball that almost displaced his nipple. And the first ball of the third over, Atherton tried to get away from one that ended up being guided to gully.

At 4/1, after 13 dangerous balls, Mark Butcher walked in.

Neither Courtney nor Curtly had actually run in at any point in there because I think they knew that if they were really giving it their all, someone was going to get seriously hurt.

I had played against Walsh, he was playing for Gloucester. So he ambled in and just lolloped this ball down on a length and I just went back to play it. Expecting it somewhere around just below chest height. And this thing just kicked and flew twice the speed that it came out of his hand. Straight up my face. It was just bizarre.

I had plenty enough time to see it and enough time to go, "NOOOOOOOOO!" I faced one ball, and was out.

Shortly after, with England 17/3, the entire match was abandoned as the wicket was deemed unsafe.

Later, I was having a rum and coke by the pool and the scorer tapped me on the shoulder and said, "Your day's about to get a little bit worse."

Butcher found out that the records would stand, so his golden duck remained from an abandoned match. He was dropped from the following Test.

A few Tests later he would be chosen again, but this time to bat down the order. "Number six was fun, by the way. Oh, what a place to bat if that was all you did all your Test career, just bat at number six."

In that match he made 28 and 24 not out from a combined total of 207 balls. The unbeaten 24 helped win England their only Test of the series. He was promoted back to No. 3. By the sixth Test, England had to beat the West Indies to draw the series. At that time, Butcher was averaging 23.7. He had played nine tests and made no hundreds.

The West Indies was no place for a former all-rounder still learning how to be a specialist batter.

There's a sort of ferocity to the way they support the game. That kind of marries up with the ferocity of the way that they bowl. The way those guys bowl all the way.

I'll never forget about that trip in Barbados on an old coach ride. Tiny little narrow lanes and these guys are driving, no traffic anywhere, 80 miles an hour in these rickety old buses with police outriders. It's like everything is going to be done at the risk of your life in order to get to the ground and there's just no need.

But it was going past all the sort of old boys in the rum shacks and the fizzy drink stalls as you're driving past, and they'd obviously hear the sirens going and they'd know we were coming. So they'd all line up outside and they'd be standing out there doing the cutthroat signals.

Walsh is gonna get you, they're gonna kill you. For guys like me it was bloody terrifying. That was more frightening than actually batting. At least when you're out there batting, you've got some semblance of control of what's going on.

The one thing that Butcher didn't feel was the pressure, because he didn't think he should have been there anyway.

The expectations were so low, none of it felt very real, actually. I didn't feel like I was in the team. I felt like I was playing, but it wasn't really meant to be. The way that they'd shuffled the team around and they'd come upon this batting order by mistake almost.

This wicket at Antigua was wet, 'You could put your thumb in it.' At 27/1 he was out there batting.

Three balls. Two fizzed past the outside edge from short of back of the length and flew past me and then I nicked the next one and walked off. In my own head, I'm like, jeez, I'm nowhere here. I'm not really sure what I'm doing.

The bowler was Curtly Ambrose.

Curtly's the best bowler I've ever faced. And there are two reasons for that. One was because I wasn't very good. I didn't have the tools to be able to cope with it in Test match cricket. Again, I'd scored runs against him when he played for Northampton.

I'd felt like this wasn't a problem. What's anybody talking about? But again, he went up a notch for the West Indies.

I was too early in my career to be able to unlock the riddle, to be able to take care of myself well enough. And so the combination of the fact that he was obviously bloody great as well just meant that I found him impossible.

If he wanted to, I wouldn't be able to get away. I couldn't get down the other end. There was nothing that I could do to get him off me.

By the time we batted second innings, it was flat. Proper easy, like it's supposed to be. Like glass. But we're batting to save the game.

Butcher entered at 45/1. I asked him if he remembered the innings:

> No, I really don't. I think I must have played some sort of horrendous
> waft at something and nicked one to the keeper. [Ambrose was the
> bowler, Junior Murray completed the catch with the gloves.] I
> faced six balls. Managed to double up from the first innings.
>
> I didn't really feel like I belonged in Test cricket really.
>
> Not just in that side, but I just didn't know what I was doing
> enough. I hadn't learned enough lessons about what to do when
> you're not at your best to be able to survive. And making that pair
> is the biggest endorsement of that.

That lost man finally learned his craft. In 2001, at Leeds, he would
make 173 not out chasing 315 to beat an Australian team with Glenn
McGrath, Jason Gillespie, Brett Lee and Shane Warne. A big chase
against a great attack (albeit in a dead rubber) that is still remembered
as one of the more amazing hundreds of all time.

Butcher did not end with a great career. He was beautiful to watch
when he was good, but it took him a long time to learn the game.
Between the ages of 28 and 32, he averaged 41, making six of his
eight Test hundreds. In the first part of his career, he averaged 29.9.
Mark Waugh said of Butcher, 'When I played against him, I thought,
jeez, he's a good player.'

Simply put, Butcher was a Test player, but because of his talent –
and England's abject failure to find batters – he was promoted when
he was still figuring out how to bat at the highest level. The most
talented players are often promoted before they have all the required
technical and mental skills.

Australia had three incredibly talented batters in the 1990s;
all of them were successful in the 2000s. The best was Matthew
Hayden. It is impossible to explain how much bigger Hayden is
than normal batters. For generations, smaller batters dominated
for a few reasons – pitches often kept low, so being tall made that
difficult. Some experts, like Mark Nicholas, believe that it is easier
to be coordinated with shorter limbs. You needed to be nimble on
your feet, so being bigger naturally slowed you down. Hayden is
188cm, so above six foot tall, and then some. But he is massive in
every single way, just a Moreton Bay fig tree come to life.

His early first-class batting figures were also huge. After averaging 50 in his first two Shield seasons, he was picked for a tour to England. Despite crushing all the state bowlers in Australia, Hayden was a mess when playing Tests. He made a hundred in his third match, on a good wicket for spin bowlers against a West Indies team with none. But from the first seven matches, he averaged 21 and couldn't get back in the side. Australia had abundant talent in the opening position; Michael Slater had exploded in 1993 to make it harder for Hayden to find a spot. Matthew Elliott was also making a ton of runs for Victoria quite regularly, and when he got his chance, he played sublime Test knocks – when not running into Mark Waugh and injuring his knee.

'I remember someone telling me that he was in the gym trying to become an all-rounder because he had not found a way to break into the side,' said Kumar Sangakkara about Hayden.

Australia also had Mark Taylor, a player like Hayden who had destroyed Shield attacks as a young man, but he continued to play that way when he got into the Test side. For 16 Tests, he averaged more than 60. The rest of his career, he averaged 39.6. He was kept in the team largely because of his captaincy and a late-career surge that got him 334 not out in Pakistan. Australia stood by their captain, even in dire form, while keeping Elliott and Hayden out of the side.

The more interesting thing is that Taylor was in what are referred to as 'peak batting years'. Batters are at their best in cricket between the ages of 28 and 32.

The truth, according to cricket analyst Amol Desai, is more confusing: 'The typical batter peaks in their early 20s, while really good batters relative to the level of competition peak in their late 20s to early 30s and decline at a slower rate.'

The reason most batters peak at 22 is that it is the apex of their athleticism. But the players who peak around their late 20s are the greats. That is because they are adding technical knowledge well beyond a normal first-class batter to their game.

Desai says:

I focused on Test numbers for batters in positions one to six. And then I compared these batters with the same guys batting in first-class cricket and batters who were just first-class cricketers without any Tests.

Top batters continue improving and peak at a later age. By seven years! However, they are still on a decline beyond 30 years of age. The top batters have a plateau rather than a peak. Their peak is longer lasting (~3–5yrs). Top players perform better than the average player at their peak age by around four runs and then improve on that later in their career by an additional 3–4 runs per dismissal. They decline more gradually, thus widening the gap to the average player of the same age later in their career. They don't underperform the average active batter in the game until much later in their careers.

But perhaps his most interesting work is in how batters age against different bowling types.

Let's examine how ageing impacts performance against pace and spin and infer what we can from that. The premise is that facing pace and spin requires different primary skills and physiological mechanisms in terms of reaction time and coordination.

Against pace, where batting relies a bit more on reflexes, the decline starts early but the curve is flatter both on the improvement side and on the decline. Batting against spin is arguably slightly more of a cat and mouse game that has room for strategic growth, and batters improve as they learn to read quality spin at the highest level over the first few years. The steeper decline against spin may be a result of a decline in swift footwork with age.

Something else is interesting about Desai's work. When batters are young and have no knowledge, spin is an issue; as they get older, it becomes an issue again. Whereas the play against pace stays fairly level all the way through. Age always plays a part.

Between the ages of 28 and 32, 237 batters have made 1000 Test runs batting in positions one to six. Mark Taylor averages 37.2 in this period, the 59th highest. Many of the players with worse records than him are those who are considered to have failed, all-round talents or mid-tier players.

Taylor was a lot better than that, finishing with an average of 43 while opening the batting in a tough era. He played 20 Tests against the West Indies – almost a fifth of his total. In those he really struggled, averaging only 28 (though 39 when in the Caribbean over two tours). He made a lot of runs in England against the moving ball yet struggled in New Zealand and South Africa. He averaged almost 50 in Asia, but almost all of that was from Pakistan, and largely on the back of the 334 not out. This was a great player at the start of his career, who became a slightly better-than-par opener for the back half of his career.

His career arc is very similar to Andrew Strauss, who averaged 60 in his first year of Test cricket and only over 50 once more. He also had a lesser record because he went up against the best attack – Australia – for a fifth of his career but stuck around because he was leading a winning team.

Matthew Hayden came back to the Australian team just as he hit the age of 28. He made 4983 runs in his peak batting years, 57% of his total. Another change happened at that time. The 1990s were a tough batting era, where wickets fell at an average of 31.5. The 2000s were a great batting era, with an average of 34.1. If that doesn't sound like a lot, it really is. Except the 1940s (which was not a full decade due to the Second World War), it is the highest average per wicket ever in a decade. The jump-up was huge as well. Usually, decades are close in terms of averages, so this is one of the bigger changes.

It comes from three major factors: curators finally perfected covered wickets, bat technology took a step forward at this point, and ODI cricket (as well as Australia in Tests) showed that hitting boundaries and hustling for singles in a Test worked well. So, there was a boost on average and strike rate.

Enter a huge Queenslander with vicious intent in his prime, and bowlers got whacked. So much so that Steve Waugh started to say that Hayden would break the world record for the largest score in an innings. At the WACA, he slammed 38 fours and 11 sixes in his 380 from 437 balls. Kumar Sangakkara says of him:

> I think the strength he had was upstairs in the way he viewed himself in the game.
>
> He thought about, "Okay, I'm going to impose myself. I'm going to score runs here. I'm going to show these bowlers who's boss" and he had the game to do it. I mean, even with spin, I think what we sometimes miss is the brutality of how he batted.

We missed how much he thought about the game with spin being the ability to sweep and sweep and sweep for an Australian. [...] He really prided himself on anticipating what bowlers were trying to do. So you miss all of those nuances and subtleties when you just look at Hayden, taking a big stride down and hitting you back over the head at 150 miles per hour or counting down how many balls Shoaib Akhtar had left saying, "That's one, 15 to go."

The power, machismo and skill are all exceptional, but so was the intent. Hayden wanted to score fast. He struck at 60, which was incredibly fast for any opener not named Virender Sehwag. Hayden averaged 70 from 2001 to 2003, a number almost as big as the man.

There were holes in his game. Like other attacking openers (such as Sehwag and Warner), he struggled against lateral movement and didn't make runs in countries that had a lot of it. He averaged under 40 in England, South Africa and New Zealand. He also averaged 42.6 on the road, but an enormous 57.9 at home.

Yet, he averaged 50 in Asia. That includes his first tour to India where he made 549 runs at an average of more than a hundred. However, he never averaged more than 35 again on two other tours. He was a player with a huge impact when it worked. He had seven-plus years as a batter (with two years at the end when he was well beyond his best), and almost all of them were brutal. When I was doing a show with David 'Bumble' Lloyd for talkSPORT, picking our ideal XI, Bumble wanted Hayden as an opener.

But the biggest question on Hayden should be what he would have looked like if he had kept playing in his early 20s in the 1990s, which was a tougher era. Does Hayden only look great because we never saw enough of him struggling? Or would he have ended up with a more rounded game because he learned more than just dominating Shield and county attacks, which he was clearly too good for?

It wasn't just Hayden who got this treatment. Damien Martyn was seen as a future Australian captain until he was one of the many victims of South African seamer Fanie de Villiers in a tough SCG chase in 1994. Australia hadn't played South Africa in two decades. They were the last to do so after South Africa's readmission, and they got whipped.

After Shane Warne picked up 5-72, Australia needed only 117 to go 1–0 up in the series. Australia lost exciting opener Michael Slater before David Boon joined Mark Taylor for 109 minutes. They added 47. Boon was caught at short leg by South African opener Gary Kirsten – himself a fine bat. It's ironic because of how good Boon was when fielding in that position. As it was late, Australia sent in Tim May as the nightwatchman, who lasted a ball. It got worse when Taylor was out before stumps as well, meaning de Villiers had three wickets.

Starting at 63/4 on the last day, they needed only 54 runs. It was free entry, so the usual small crowd was boosted by a lot of people coming in to see the Aussies without having to pay. Allan Border lost his off stump almost straight away to Allan Donald. Mark Waugh was trapped straight in front, and Ian Healy didn't last long either. Shane Warne was run out to add to the disaster.

This meant that Martyn was left batting with tail-ender Craig McDermott. The two needed 42 runs; the chances of that looked low until McDermott started swinging some balls away. His runs got Australia to 110, only seven runs needed. Martyn had scored only six runs at this point from 58 balls. That is when Donald bowled a length ball outside off stump, and Martyn never moved his feet and tried to flay it through the covers.

At this point, little was known about Martyn other than his talent. His top score was a 74 he made in Auckland. Years later, a few teams would know a lot more about him, like England. Nasser Hussain said:

He was incredibly gifted. One of the sweetest timers of the ball I've ever seen. He'd be right up there with David Gower – my hero growing up. When I played against David, he used to stand at cover and think, oh, what's this timing all about?

Marto especially through the off side, especially between backward point and extra cover. He used to stay on his back foot. He wasn't a great mover of his feet. It's overrated foot movement, it's just balance. And he had great balance.

That is how Martyn would become known. But in early 1994, he was a kid who took 109 minutes to make six runs and didn't move his feet when getting out playing a risky shot through covers. Australia lost that Test.

Martyn would not play another match until after the millennium. At one stage, he was so angry and disillusioned with the game that he almost left to become a travel agent. Again, he would come back in that great batting era.

When he did, cricket saw some of the most aesthetically pleasing batting ever. He was fantastic away from home. He had weird quirks that lived on from that SCG match, like never enjoying the last innings, averaging a shocking 27. But he had a 40 mark on every continent he played on; 55 on Indian wickets and 40 on the English.

In his peak years, he ended up with an average of 50.7. Despite missing some Tests when he was dropped, he still had six top years, three of which were great. Even though it looks like a long career on paper, it wasn't.

Then you had Justin Langer, Martyn's left-handed teammate from Western Australia. A top-order player who played Tests from 1993 to 1997, but only eight in that period. He found form in 1998 before losing it the following year, but he had done enough to keep himself around the side for quite a while (including a double century at No. 3 against India at the SCG). But in 2001, when Michael Slater lost his spot, Australia tried Langer as opener.

In 65 Tests there, he would average 48 with 5000 runs. The list of players with better records when opening the batting with that many runs are: Sunil Gavaskar, Graeme Smith, Sehwag, Len Hutton, Jack Hobbs and Langer's batting partner, Hayden. And in his peak years, Langer also averaged 48.

You can see just how much this matters. All these players were incredible. Hayden and Martyn were attractive in different ways, and Langer was stoic and brave. He was hit in the head so often that it made Cricket Australia rethink its policy of head injuries, before concussions in sport were widely discussed.

All have way better averages simply because Australia could afford to pick other players – that country was producing such a deep pantry of batting talent. When these players came back, they did so in a great batting era and in their prime.

Let's compare that to a player who had a very different story: Martin Crowe. Because he came from New Zealand, he made his debut at 19. Early for any player – even a future great. He averaged 24 in the first three years of his career. But at 22, with all that experience behind him, he exploded. From the start of 1985, he scored 4842 runs at 51. That included dominating the Australians (home and away), making decent runs in England and averaging 45.3 against the West Indies.

Despite his body failing him far earlier than most greats, he averaged 49 in his peak years, which were sadly cut short by retirement. He didn't get the last couple of years in his mid-30s to continue his run because of his body. In his last five matches, he averaged only 14.7, a far cry from a six-year period where he was at 61. In that period, he was 60% better than players in his era and matches.

When you are picked matters as much as anything. Martin Crowe is still in New Zealand's top two batters of all time, but if you saw him play in his peak, he was No. 1.

What if you missed your peak for some reason? Like, what if a genocidal maniac tries to take over the world? That might sound weird, but that is what happened to Don Bradman. The great Australian played 52 Tests, and only nine of them were in his peak. Now, there are two ways to look at this. He averaged only 95.7 in those matches, and his entire career was peak, so maybe he just does that. But if he did rise like other players, he would have averaged not just above 100, but well over.

How to work that out is not easy. An article in the *Journal of Quantitative Analysis in Sports* titled 'Was Bradman Denied His Prime?', states: 'Time series clustering was used to show that, relatively, the impact of Australian legend Sir Donald Bradman's Test career as a batsman was most similar to West Indian Brian Lara in terms of career progression and not in terms of overall calibre.'

Essentially what they were looking for was a player with a similar career arc. While Lara never made as many runs per game, the pattern of his career was similar. As noted in the study, not many players have careers as long as Bradman:

The model fitting and clustering suggested that Bradman's prime may have been most likely to occur during the Second World War when international sport was disrupted. The study then imputed Don Bradman's likely performances during this period to estimate his batting average. Although the estimated average was calculated to be 105.41, this was not significantly different from his actual average of 99.94.

Before the war Bradman averaged 97.9. He then didn't play a Test from 20 August, 1938 until 9 November, 1946 and then played 16 Tests at 105.7. He was 38 years old when he came back to play Tests.

Bradman didn't just miss his peak; he missed his mid-30s as well. When you look at raw averages, it suggests the best year to bat in Tests is when you are 37. So does that make Amol Desai's research wrong, or are the peak years not from 28 to 32? The reason people make so many runs at the age of 37 is that only players who are great last until that age. So, you will find many articles written about how great batters are in their 30s in Tests. It is true, but it is not their peak – they are getting worse, just from a higher place.

Bob Simpson is a fascinating player when it comes to peaks and longevity. He made his debut when he was 21 years old, made his first hundred at 28 and played his final Test at 41. On the face of it, he had a very long career, but he played only 62 Tests. That is because he retired at the start of 1968 when he was only 31. When Australia lost their players to Kerry Packer's World Series Cricket, he made a return for two series, only to retire again at the age of 42. He played for 20 years and 62 Tests with an average of 46.8 while mostly being an opener – a great in any era.

Simpson was once the overseas pro at Bumble Lloyd's side in Lancashire:

He started off 0, 0, or two very low scores. And immediately, the spectators, of whom there were many, are on his back. To cut to the chase, he breaks the league record. He gets 1511 runs. He bowls fantastic leg breaks and caught pigeons. I'm just a kid. I would have been about 10, 12, or something like that. I can see him now catching unbelievable things at Accrington Cricket Club, and not in the slips. He became a wonderful slip fielder. But, you know, in the outfield, diving one-handed.

He opened the batting and he gets 300 at Old Trafford against a strange attack. It seemed to have nothing really. The attack was very samey, no pace, on a wonderful pitch. And so then, the art of batting. [...] Well, he got 300 and so the powers of concentration kick in. [...] Simpson was one of these with great powers of concentration.

Simpson's legacy is more than just batting; he was the person who made coaching at the international level an accepted pastime. But what about just as a batter?

How do you evaluate someone who retires in the middle of their prime years – this was more common in the amateur cricket outside England – comes back to play again against India and averages 54 at home against a quality spin attack. However, he then went to the West Indies and averaged 22 against the new kings of fast bowling. While Simpson didn't complete his peak, he scored 2656 runs at an average of 59 in those years. His last full year of Tests (the first time) was 1967, playing five, making two hundreds with an average of above 50. He was above that mark in each of the three previous years.

There is absolutely no doubt that Simpson cost himself a lot of runs by leaving the game so soon. He might always have made his average better by not leaving in his prime, and not playing on too long.

He had a largely messy career, struggling against two of the best pace attacks in the West Indies and South Africa. He had a sub-40 average in both. As an opener, when he lost the toss and was sent in, he averaged 25. On a flat track away from home, he was incredible with a 70 average, but in the live Tests he barely scored any runs at all. When he did make big scores, like his 311 against England (his first hundred), it was a high-scoring match. Similarly, his double hundred and twin centuries in one match were also from high-scoring matches. Those last two were in Pakistan and were important for Australia.

His average of 47 on its own is incredible. His ability to make a comeback after being out of the game for a decade and still make any runs is also good, especially as it took him so long to get good. After 29 Tests, he was averaging 36. He averaged 57 in his next 20, including the most runs ever in a Test year at the time. He then retired. So his career is 29 sub-par Tests, 20 incredible ones and 10 as a comeback in his 40s. What the hell do you do with such a record?

Simpson certainly had elements of greatness to mount a comeback in his 40s. That shows how great his talent was, and what we may have been robbed from in his 30s. As Kumar Sangakkara's father Kshema wrote, 'There are many batsmen who have been tagged as great, but I consider those who go on to make runs after they turn 35 and their reflexes start slowing as true legends.'

His son Kumar is the only player in history to make more than 2000 runs at an average of over 60 past the age of 35. Bradman falls short by only 97 runs. So, Kshema got his way, his son was on Don's level.

There is truth in what he says; that you can see from Amol Desai's work. However, not only are there expectations but players also deteriorate at different rates. One player may be peaking at 24–28, another 32–36. There is no one-size-fits-all.

Take Tom Graveney, who did not end with a great average. He played in a tough era, and the wickets he played on were even worse, with an average of 34.1 for the batters in the top six positions. But his career was weird. We know he wasn't perfect. He never averaged 40 on the road. He played well in Asia, but from limited chances. Against the two best attacks he went up against away from home – Australia and the West Indies – he never crossed the 40 mark. But like many English batters, he jumped all over the place in terms of position.

The most interesting part of his career is when he made his runs. The first part before he turned 28, he made runs at 40.4; during what should have been his peak, only 38; after 32, he went up to 52.1.

He last played Test cricket in 1969. In four matches, he averaged 44 in Pakistan and his final innings was a 75 at home against the West Indies. Looking at Kshema Sangakkara's theory, Graveney was certainly a great. He played in 31 matches when older than 35, and again he was above the magical 50 mark.

But Graveney did not make runs in Tests before turning 30. Four days after crossing the big three zero, he played in a Test that brought his career average down to 34.7. He averaged 50 after turning 30 and continued the run after turning 35. It wasn't like he was smashing the ball for Gloucestershire in county cricket either; his mark for them was 43.

Even after adjusting for tough wickets, the era and the longevity of his career, it is hard to make a case for Graveney as an all-time great. Yet, he was able to make runs when many of the best players ever were finished.

What about the players who started late? Vijay Hazare was another player who lost years to the Second World War, like Bradman, Len Hutton and West Indian No. 3 George Headley. The difference was that those players had already started, while it delayed the beginning of Hazare's career. In 1946, he made his Test debut. It meant that sadly he only played 30 Tests. Also, he probably didn't develop his game as quickly as he should have.

That he was talented is a given – he averaged 58.4 in first-class cricket, and 47.6 in Test cricket – but that record was largely on the back of the magnificent way he played in India. However, we know that he could have been great away. His debut Tests were in England in 1946. He played four and struggled, as you would expect from someone who had to wait so long for his debut. But he toured Australia in 1947–1948 and faced a top-quality bowling attack including Ray Lindwall, Keith Miller, Ernie Toshack, Colin McCool and Ian Johnson. On the entire tour, he averaged 47.6 against a team that would be soon known as 'The Invincibles'.

All summer he had got himself in but then almost immediately got out. Over three Tests, he was never dismissed for less than 10 but never made more than 18. Then he arrived in Adelaide, and it was a flat wicket where Australia put on 674. From a pressure situation, it was huge for Hazare, as he came in at 69/3. This meant his team were 605 runs behind. He took India past 300, with the tail making 116.

India were still 293 behind, so Australia asked them to follow on. Hazare was back out there way too soon with the score 33/3. No one else made more than 51, and he added 145 from 372 balls. They would be his only two hundreds outside of India. Even in the next Test, he added another 74 – again in the face of a massive Australian total.

So, his great average is from India, but we know it may have translated in England and Australia. The only place he really struggled was the West Indies. On a single tour in 1953, he passed 50 only once, but he averaged 69 at home and was clearly a high-quality player.

He did all of this in a serene and composed way. These were not innings by someone who was overawed. Hazare knew how to bat; the only thing that stopped him was a World War.

There is another incredible thing to look at. He made his debut in first-class cricket in 1934, and while it took him a few years to find his feet, he would have made his Test debut, had it been possible, in 1941. He played his last first-class match in 1967. He was still pretty good, making 68 against a touring West Indian line-up that included the legendary quicks, Charlie Griffith and Wes Hall. Sure, it was on

Indian wickets, but being 51 years old and facing those two is no one's idea of fun.

His Test career was short, but his impact on Indian batting was massive. Hazare's first-class average is spread over four different decades, which means you must take it seriously.

Perhaps the most famous late bloomer in Tests is Mike Hussey. So much so that there is a myth about him being overlooked because Australia were so good. That isn't true. Hussey made his first-class debut in the summer of 1994/95. When he was a well-established player for Western Australia, he was dropped. From 2000–01 to 2003–04, he averaged 36 in Shield cricket. He wasn't Vijay Hazare, kept from the game by a freak occurrence. He wasn't making runs consistently.

Australia had long looked for the next 10-year player (or 'once in a generation', as they put it), and Hussey was never on that list. He was an unfashionable player – no power, pretty but not the most eye-catching. People said his record was bloated by county cricket (in his poor period, it was). He also came from Western Australia in a time where you still had to make 10% more runs to be noticed.

When Hussey was chosen, he had finally become the player that county cricket had long seen, but he was in as an injury replacement and really a bridge player. Most of the batters in this book were chosen because of their potential to be stars, or at least plus players over a long period of time. Hussey came in as a backup opener and impressed so much that they found a spot for him in the middle order.

They clearly thought enough of him to bring him in, but no one in the world would have guessed what he did next. He averaged 84 from his first 20 Tests. He was supposed to be a bridge between generations; instead, he stuck around for a little more than seven years and scored 6235 runs at better than 50.

The two best bridge players are Rangana Herath and Clarrie Grimmett. Herath was picked from club cricket as a role player. When Muttiah Muralitharan left, Herath became a bridge player. By the end of his career, he was the second-greatest bowler his country had produced. Grimmett, who had played in New Zealand, New South Wales and Victoria before ending up in South Australia, wasn't even picked for Australia until he was 34. Even as good as his first-class record was, to think he would take 200 wickets and play for 11 years would have been a story H.G. Wells would have disregarded as fanciful.

When Hussey turned into a player of that level, it meant the narrative was that he should have always been picked. But Hussey wasn't a lost champion. If he had started playing in his early 20s, at best he would most likely have a lower average. He certainly would have been dropped, based on what happened in his domestic career.

Hussey even had a dip during his international career. In 2008 and 2009, he played a frankly ridiculous 27 Tests – five more than George Headley managed in a 24-year career. In the first of those matches, Hussey took his average up to 80.2. In the last match, it dropped to below 52. His mark in those years was 34, and he'd turned 33 in 2008.

So did this mean that Hussey was just ordinary, or he was naturally ageing out of his peak?

It gets more confusing, because Hussey averages 50.9 from 2010 onwards. In that period, he certainly became – like many Australian batters – a giant at home, and he struggled on the road. He averaged 40 away from home but almost all those runs were from two hundreds and a 90 in Sri Lanka. But those were against Herath and an assortment of other spinners on turning wickets. Also, the 90 was match-winning in a low-scoring innings.

There is no doubt that Hussey was a fantastic player from the ages of 27 to 37. But if he had played from his early 20s, like other players, his average would have been far lower. Would it have been so low that he wouldn't be here at all?

For many years, I referred to Hussey as the anomaly because his average never truly made sense. He eventually regressed to the mean but still ended up with a record that was worthy of praise.

If we surgically dissect his record, it becomes just as fascinating. He averages 41 away and more than 60 at home. He also averaged 69 against spin (which is special from a player who grew up on the WACA pitches), so he went at an average of 63 in Asia. That means it was 32 when not at home or Asia. The final interesting thing about him is that he played in an era when batters were smashing the ball everywhere. Batters in the top six positions averaged a huge 40 during his years (the fourth highest in my long list). You add in the fact he had a nine-year career, of which two were poor and two were all-timers. His record is all over the place.

How good would other players have been if they only played in their peak? But how many players not in Test cricket would come in and play at that level into their late 30s? Was Hussey the ultimate late bloomer?

The one player worth comparing him to is Graham Gooch. He averaged nine less than Hussey, but there are some caveats to this. Gooch was an opener who made his debut at 21 and finished at 41. Hussey made 22,783 first-class runs; Gooch practically doubled this at 44,846. When you look at their overall first-class averages (including Tests), Hussey averaged 52.1 and Gooch was not that far away at 49. We also have to factor in that Gooch opened far more – and in tougher conditions – especially in Tests. Gooch also played in a much tougher era – the top six average three runs fewer than in Hussey's.

Gooch needs to be looked at because he was mediocre at his peak, averaging 38.4. In fact, until he turned 35, he had 4337 runs at 37.7. He more than doubled the total after that and averaged 48.5. We know from Nasser Hussain that Gooch had incredible eyes. We know that he batted in an era when it wasn't just natural; he was thinking about his craft.

Hussain used Gooch as a role model:

The fact that Goochie got that 150 against the West Indies on that dodgy pitch, and the next day he was in at Chelmsford having throw downs and having a net, that I would pick up straight away.

Here is a bloke who doesn't just sit back and go, "I'm Graham Gooch, I got 150 yesterday, I'll have it, I'll take it easy for a week." Goochie kept things pretty simple.

A young Mark Waugh played with Gooch at Essex:

He played some great innings. His average is not as high as some of the other players ahead of him. But to me he was a fantastic player.

A real tough Test match batsman. He'd make tough runs against the West Indies, great bowling attacks. And then he'd have series where he was just out of touch and he couldn't make a run. But when he was playing well, he was as good a player as anybody, I think in any era.

He's just had great awareness about the game. I had so much respect for Graham when I was playing with him at Essex. He played the game aggressively as well. He was always looking to win the games.

Gooch was an interesting athlete in that he looked like someone cosplaying as a British general, rather than a great batter. His front elbow eagerly pointing back at the bowler, his white helmet without a grill to obscure the moustache, and his squatted stance that made his posterior stick out. His bat was held high in the air, a style that was rare then but has taken over the world since. But when he got going, he was incredible, like at Leeds in 1991, the 150 that Hussain mentioned. 'In the context of a particular game, I've never seen a better Test match innings than this one,' is how Richie Benaud presented the highlights.

The context was a low-scoring game; England made 198 in the first innings, with only England middle-order batter Robin Smith passing 50 before being run out. West Indies struggled even more, but late-career Viv Richards managed to score 73. Even then, West Indies ended up with a 25-run deficit. Gooch went in to bat under the grey Headingley sky, hoping to put on a lead. He did, almost on his own. Opener Mike Atherton and middle-order batter Graeme Hick both made six, but off a combined 53 balls. Allan Lamb and Robin Smith both lasted a ball, and Mark Ramprakash, on debut, added 27 from 2 hours and 22 minutes. Yet, when last of the recognised batters was gone, England had 116. The other five members had a combined total of 39.

All those batters were dismissed by Curtly Ambrose, who was an incredible bowler. The rest of the attack was spectacular. Malcolm Marshall and Courtney Walsh were also greats. And the *worst* bowler was perhaps the fastest quick of that era: Patrick Patterson. That was probably one of the best and fiercest attacks ever.

With Ramprakash's 27 on debut, England's joint-second top-scorer was Gooch's Essex teammate Derek Pringle on the same score. This was a tough pitch that required technical mastery against great bowlers, and Gooch was imperious. He was waiting for each rare mistake from a West Indian bowler and capitalising on it. His drives had his feet scuttling into position and an efficient curt push. When the ball was on his hip, he would turn it away like someone moving a box. But his pull shots were something else.

Patterson drops a ball slightly short and outside off. But Gooch is in a zone, and he rolls a powerful shot to square leg, like he is dismissing a naughty child from his desk. Later, from a similar ball – this time from Walsh – he leans back and drives it through point. The rest of his team couldn't get the ball off the square, while he was picking which boundary to hit decent balls to.

Perhaps his best shot came against Marshall's bowling. He was coming in on that famous angle. Any batter has seen it and knows that three things can happen: the ball moves in, the ball moves away, or the slippery bouncer that no one can duck. This ball is full; Gooch steps across to meet it on off stump and then with a straight bat drives it through mid-on. The only flourish is a slight kick of the back foot, like a Hollywood starlet kissing to show how passionate it is. But the moment the ball rolls off, he snaps back into floor manager role and goes back into his bubble.

When he passes 150, he has on a large jumper that looks like it's for someone else. His collar is up, but in the way a school kid does when he forgets to look at himself in the mirror. He does not look like a gladiator, or someone to be feared. He is a 37-year-old man who looks mortal, but who has just played at a level that few ever have. When the book *Masterly Batting: 100 Great Test Centuries* by Patrick Ferriday and Dave Wilson was released in 2013, this was their choice at No. 1.

Gooch was great by the end of his career, but he played a long time while still working his game out. He needed time to become the player that many others on this list were earlier. His pattern is repeated a lot.

Usman Khawaja and Rohit Sharma are two modern openers who showed their talent in the middle order when they were young, then moved to the top of the order and found their calling. But there is no real pattern in the older players. Pakistan had two at the same time: the late-blooming Misbah-ul-Haq and the forever great Younis Khan.

Of course, there are players who struggled once they turned 35; interestingly enough, two attacking openers in David Warner and Sanath Jayasuriya.

One of the most interesting players is Ricky Ponting, who averaged 37.2 after turning 35. Of the 63 batters with 1000 runs at that age, he was the seventh worst. Ponting admits in his autobiography that he played on too long.

The last few years really hit his overall average, but he was still a genuine great of batting, which is not up for debate – someone who was right beside Sachin Tendulkar and Brian Lara as the best in the world. No player ever has made more runs in their peak years than Ponting's 5313. Only Jacques Kallis and Michael Clarke have more than 5000, and only a dozen more have over 4000. Three men – Herbert Sutcliffe, Mike Hussey and West Indian Clyde Walcott – are the only ones with higher averages than him, but they only made 500 more runs combined than Ponting did. So, there is little doubt that Ponting had the greatest peak batting years ever, averaging 70.8 with 19 hundreds.

Unlike his Australian teammates, Ponting was in the Australian setup very young. He stayed there through the back end of the 1990s, even if he wasn't automatically in the team. There were obvious signs of talent, but over the first four years of his career he averaged 36.6 with two centuries. Then he went on an eight-year spree where he averaged more than 1000 runs per year, while having a mark of 65.4. He scored 700 more runs than Hayden in that period, while averaging three more than the next highest, Kallis.

Another player with an incredible peak was Rahul Dravid.

Comedian and cricket statistician, Andy Zaltzman, came up with a method looking at players' pinnacles a few years back that he called Peak 33. It was a simple enough measure, taking the 33 matches where players collected their most runs or wickets and then checking their averages. For batters, Bradman had the best record – of course – at 102.9, second was Viv Richards with 72.6 and third was Rahul Dravid on 72.4.

It took a long time for the Indian player to find that groove:

I played county cricket in 2000 when I was 26. I played three or four years of international cricket. It was actually a perfect time for me. I went to county cricket for six months, went in April, came away in September.

Played all the games, lived on my own. I think I just grew as a person […] a certain amount of obsession with the game […] made me work harder. It made me do a lot of things. Go outside of my comfort zone to develop certain skills. […]

Then from 2000, to I think 2007, I had probably my best run. […] I think it was me getting to know myself a little bit better as a person that helped me. […] I think that figuring out that I actually needed to be less intense. […] I needed to understand where I was actually tripping myself off at times by overthinking things and obsessing.

In his peak years, Rahul Dravid averaged 60.2. When you hear his story, you realise that while this is a cricket thing – athleticism mixing with knowledge – it is also about knowing who you are and understanding what works.

What happens when that never occurs or is disturbed? Jimmy Adams had an incredible start to Test cricket, and his debut was an important match as well. It was South Africa's first Test after re-admission, and the West Indies were behind. In the second innings, Adams was batting at No. 6 with his team only 37 runs in front. He was not out at the end, from three hours and 41 minutes at the crease, and made 79 not out. The West Indies now had 201 to defend, and their bowlers were inspired by a story that South Africa had already started planning their celebrations.

For the next four years he was extraordinary, averaging 60.6 over 23 Tests. He is most famous for his play of spin on Indian wickets, partly because of the runs but also because of the method. He was known as 'Padams' because of the way he would use his fast feet to come down the wicket, then thrust his pad towards the ball and move his bat like he was playing a shot. Usually that was an illusion, as the entire plan was to pad the ball away.

In the course of making two hundreds on Indian wickets against Anil Kumble and their slow left-armer Venkatapathy Raju, he batted for 860 minutes. In the three-Test series, he made 520 runs. But while that method and series was what he was remembered for, he did well in all sorts of places. He averaged 49 over three Tests in Australia, scored another hundred versus New Zealand, made runs versus England and that debut against South Africa. In four years, Adams had taken attention from his frequent batting partner Brian Lara.

Then it all stopped. There are many stories as to why. In 1995 against Somerset, Adams was batting in the late afternoon when the light was getting bad. Dutch speedster Andre van Troost was very fast, and later that season would be banned for intimidatory bowling. Mark Butcher once said he was the fastest he went up against. He had already dismissed Richie Richardson with a ball he left – and seemed to not see – that bowled him. Adams ducked into the ball that probably wasn't that short and ended with a broken cheekbone and missed the rest of the tour. In that summer, Adams was already struggling and when he did recover, he made a double hundred on the road in New Zealand against their fastest bowler, Danny Morrison.

England started convincing umpires, according to then coach Bumble Lloyd, that the pad-led style against spinners was not really a shot, so it was given out. Also there was a big revolution going on in cricket at this point as umpires were seeing TV technology to understand that spinners' deliveries were hitting the stumps a lot. However, his play against pace had also dropped.

In 1999, he was involved in an incident on a plane involving cutlery and a torn tendon in his hand. This is not an ideal injury for a batter, but by that stage his form dip was already well underway.

All of these are realistic reasons for the dip, but the man himself tells his own story:

This is in hindsight. But I think I ran into some what we'd call nowadays stress-related issues in 1995. Just burnout. Played too much cricket. […] The science tells us now that it's very difficult if you don't catch it early, which I didn't.

And basically it – mentally focusing, specifically – became very difficult for me after that. I didn't realise it at the time because we didn't have the information available. […]

I would be one Test into a series and I'd be, like, tired, just mentally drained. And I knew something was wrong, but didn't know what it was. Nobody knew any of this back in the day. There wasn't the advantage of being able to plan around it or anything like that.

Jimmy Adams looked like a great batter when he was young, but by the time he got to his supposed peak he was just surviving. He did the hard work, but never got to cash in.

10

AVERAGE

Overall average only tells us so much about a batter

'When I played against him, I thought, jeez,
he's a good player.' − Mark Waugh

Daryll Cullinan's batting is known as a punchline. Even a look at
him when he first made it to Test cricket brought about some weird
shapes. His elbow jutted towards the bowler like he'd read every
page of *The M.C.C. Cricket Coaching Book*. His posterior protruded
violently towards square leg with that odd symmetry of angle
between his thighs and back. Even his helmet had novelty oversized
plastic flaps on the side of his head.

The reason the world laughed at Daryll Cullinan was that he
became perhaps the most famous bunny in the world. Shane Warne
dismissed him 12 times across Tests and ODIs. Weirdly, only four
of those were in Tests, where Muttiah Muralitharan dismissed
him seven times. In Warne's 12 dismissals, seven were in single

figures – including four ducks. Essentially, Cullinan came out, Warne came on and Daryll went off. It started with a flipper that he couldn't pick, but in the end, Warne had a psychological hold over him. That word isn't used accidentally; Cullinan sought the help of a sports psychologist who taught him to play the ball, not the man. Sadly, Warne found out about this and asked Cullinan what colour the couch was.

If it were only the two greatest spinners of all time to torment Cullinan, that would be fine, but he also averaged 15 against Pakistan in five matches. It is clear his batting was not perfect, yet he's on my long list of the greatest batters of all time. It is also worth mentioning that he is perhaps the only batter to stop a first-class match because he hit a six into a pan cooking calamari outside the ground. (The game had to be stopped as the ball was so hot it needed to be cooled. Then it was too greasy anyway, so it was replaced. This is definitely the only known situation where calamari stopped play).

Cullinan was a childhood prodigy. At 16, he made his first-class debut. Only Zimbabwe's Graeme Hick was rated higher as young batter in this era. By the end of his second season, he'd played nine first-class matches, had not yet turned 18, and averaged 52. The next 10 seasons he averaged 37, and only once was over 40. For three straight years, there were no hundreds at all.

By the time he was being chosen for South Africa, the young boy wonder had become a seasoned pro. While he did not force his way into the national side, there was a spot available to him. As a No. 4, mostly in the 1990s, he would average 46. His overall average dips down to 44 when other batting spots are factored in.

It would have been higher, but in seven Tests versus Australia he averaged 12.7. That was Warne, who took him 12 times from 26 international matches (it happened in ODIs as well). His median score in the innings Warne dismissed him was 2.75.

Cullinan was also frequently dismissed by Anil Kumble and Muralitharan, which is part of being a middle-order batter in the 1990s. But Warne made it impossible for Cullinan to make any runs, meaning he was unplayable against the best team in cricket.

If you look at Cullinan's record without Australia and Warne, he averages 48.4. But that is not how cricket goes, and when judging the best players ever, we must be even harsher. There are great players who will not make my list of the 50 best, and Cullinan's mid-40s average is not great.

Ted Dexter writes that 'around the 50 mark is always passable, below 40 means that there is a fatal flaw somewhere.' The truth is a lot more complicated. An overall average tells you a lot, but there are huge gaps in this data. Cullinan batted in a very tough era: of the players we shortlisted, he was in the top 10 for the hardest era. During his career, the top six batters around the world averaged 37.8 but Cullinan more than topped that.

It gets worse. In the games Cullinan played in, the average of the top six batters was 32.1. This meant he played on wickets where no one was making runs. Playing with a great bowling attack can lower this, which Cullinan did. But in his games the opposition bowlers were decent which usually means the pitches he played on were in favour of bowlers.

So, overall average only tells us so much.

England's Eddie Paynter averaged 59.2 from his 20 Tests, including a double century against Australia, but his first-class average was only 42.4. A quality player, not a Test great.

As a modern example, Australian middle-order batter Adam Voges averaged 61.9 from his 20 Tests. He was also dropped with that number.

'When he started he was almost a bit of an all-rounder,' says teammate Chris Rogers, 'he bowled his kind of left-arm leggies and batted a bit in the middle order. I'm not sure anyone at the time was thinking he was going to go on and average almost 70 in Test cricket.'

Voges' record was in part because of him making 269, which had a weird moment when he was bowled but the umpire had given it as a no-ball. It turned out it was a legal delivery, but because the batter might have heard the call, the wicket was still not out.

Rogers says, 'He worked at becoming better and better all the time. When the opportunity came, he was probably at the peak of his powers. I think it was probably the perfect time for him to come in and play international cricket.'

So, Voges' record flatters him, and he was dropped at the first sign of weakness. No one would have him in their top list of Test batters.

When looking at the greatest players ever, there needs to be a cut-off mark: an average of 44 and 3000 runs to start with. But total runs and average only tell us so much.

There are other things worth looking at. Take Rogers with his teammates Shaun Marsh and Marcus North from Western Australia. All were clearly well above average in terms of talent, but what about their median scores? That lets us look at how consistent batters were. Marsh and North when set looked incredible, but they barely ever got into their innings. Rogers always seemed to be fighting his way through knocks but was incredibly consistent. Marsh's median score was 16 – incredibly low – yet North's was 10. On the other side, their domestic teammate Rogers was at 38. Rogers was consistent, and the other two were infrequently brilliant.

There were a few other factors worth looking into. An obvious one is sheer weight of runs. The problem with that is older players didn't play as many matches. England's No. 3 Jonathan Trott made 3835 runs in six years, and Australia's No. 4 Lindsay Hassett produced 3073 in 15, thanks to fewer matches and the Second World War. There is a need to factor in the number of years they played in as well.

Just looking at years or runs doesn't entirely tell us about quality. How many years were they great or even better than average? Kumar Sangakkara had 13 great years with the bat averaging more than 50; Saeed Anwar only had five.

What about batting positions? Because the original list was first full of middle-order players, by adding openers with slightly lower marks (42) it meant the men at the top made up two-sixths of the entire list, which makes sense.

Openers average 35.7, and positions three, four and five combine to average 39.4 No. 6 is seen to be the easiest position – there are a few great players who have batted a lot there. Usually, that is a position held for someone with a second skill – keeping, bowling, sometimes fielding. So, while No. 6s average 32.6, it is not because of how tough the position is, it is because of how many all-rounders have found that as their home.

The batters were only taken from those who were top six players; that was mostly done automatically because from No. 7 down, batting obviously drops off a fair bit. There is one exception: Adam Gilchrist. He was the king of the No. 7s, making 12 hundreds there. The next three highest run scorers at that position didn't have that combined. A lot of players have been in the comfy lower-middle batting spot, but no one else has 3000 runs at an average of above 39.1.

Gilchrist brings in another metric worth considering: strike rate. While he didn't invent the concept of a wicketkeeper batter, he was certainly the first nuclear weapon batting at No. 7. His strike rate was 81.9; the rest of the No. 7s combined were at 46.8.

Tests don't really require fast scoring all the time, but those few who score at a fast rate cause chaos for opposition bowlers and give their own side more time to get the 20 wickets. A batter who can score a hundred in a session on their own explodes plans and changes the trajectory of the match quickly. Not many batters do that, but those who can should get a bonus.

Where batters score is also important. While most standard Test players can make runs at home, finding players who can make runs when travelling is far harder.

Denis Compton was a fantastic player. In England he averaged over 60, and on the road he averaged 36.9. Most countries can find players who can make runs at home; the real trick is finding people who can score them away as well.

It's important to look at players by different kinds of locations. New Zealand, England and South Africa favour seam bowling, while Australia likes tall, fast quicks. India, Pakistan, Sri Lanka and Bangladesh obviously go for spin, while West Indies have a mixture of everything. By clumping these together, you get a good idea of batting strengths. It's a great way of looking at openers, as the main job is to handle the moving ball and nowhere does it dart around more than England, South Africa and New Zealand. Gordon Greenidge managed 2000 runs in these conditions at an average of 56.

Finally, it was the percentage of runs each player made for their team. There are some batters, as good as they were, who were essentially just in stacked orders. VVS Laxman and Damien Martyn were two players who were as elegant as any before or since, but they both contributed only 12% and 11% of their team runs, respectively. Brian Lara produced 18% as he carried West Indian batting almost single-handedly.

Everything is then put into a ratio against the other greatest batters ever. The idea of this is to find as much information as possible on each player, to know what they did at a level not usually discussed when talking about batters.

But for all the numbers, at times, there are factors that are just hard to consider without being subjective. If you are a great prospect for a bad team, chances are you will play early in your career, which means your overall average will not be as high as you learn the game.

Martin Crowe is a perfect case study here. New Zealand had struggled to find above-average talents with the bat. So at 19, Crowe was in the national team, despite the fact he hadn't made many first-class runs. Over his first three years, he averaged 24.1 in Tests. Then it all clicked, and for the rest of his career he averaged 48.7. We can't know if he needed those early games to be the player he was. But also, Crowe batted at No. 4, which was way higher than a young player would usually be eased in.

Compare that to Ricky Ponting, who also came into a quality Australian team young – though on the back of a lot of first-class runs. He only batted above No. 4 in three of his first 42 Tests. He batted down the order for so long that he has the 15th most runs ever scored at No. 6. However, even Ponting's record shows signs that his overall average is inaccurate. After 127 Tests, Ponting was averaging 57.2. From 2009 onwards, he averaged 37. In his book, Ponting admits he played on too long. Who was going to drop one of the legends of batting? It means that his record overall includes soft batting at the front, and a decline in his average when he should have retired.

It's not just about when you start either. Virat Kohli's average was about 55 before India started juicing up the local wickets for the spinners. No player in history would make consistent runs on those tracks. So the era you play in, and specifically the wickets you bat on, really matter.

Simon Katich has a fantastic record, especially after failing at the start of his career. One game in 2001 makes it look like a longer career, but he only played six years in total. He ended as a great makeshift opener with an average of 45. He was more of a solid player who played most of his matches during his peak, like a super-high-functioning role player.

His career ended prematurely because Australia were worried that their batting line-up was too old. He probably had another two decent years in him. But Katich also batted in the best batting era we could find. During his career, the batters in the top six averaged a staggering 40.7 runs each. It was probably the best batting era ever. The average in the matches he played in was 40.9. This makes his number look better than someone like Crowe, who played in an era where other batters averaged 37.1, and the wickets he went in on were tough, at 35.6.

Let me tell you about two fascinating teammates. Ted Dexter was a great batter, and he averaged 47.9. In 12 matches, he played with Peter May, who averaged 46.8. On first look you could make the argument they are pretty much as good as each other, or maybe Dexter is slightly ahead.

Ted Dexter batted in an era where the global top six mark was 37.6. That is pretty much a middle-of-the-road record. But May's era average was 34.1; the lowest of any great player I searched after the First World War.

It gets weirder because the match average for each player is vastly different as well, Dexter's is a very comfortable 38.7; May's is 30.5 – the lowest by two runs, under Daryll Cullinan's number.

The first thought must be, how on earth did May and Dexter end up with such different conditions and eras, if they overlapped? They played 12 Tests together in the late 1950s, which was a dead-ball era, hard to get wickets or score runs. Probably the direst cricket to watch ever. Dexter played in 12 Tests with May, and in those he averaged 36.3. When May was not in the side, Dexter averaged 50 in Tests.

From that alone it is obvious that May played in a terrible era, and even within that, he got a bunch of horrible wickets as well. Match averages can be deceiving, because Richie Richardson has a low match average record of 33.2, but that is because his bowling attack was great. May had some incredible bowlers in form when he played as well, but the bowlers he went up against also took a huge number of wickets per match. May was simply unlucky, and without that his record would look better than Dexter's.

There are other signs of this. May's Test numbers completely hold up when looking at his total first-class record of 27,592 runs, averaging 51, while Dexter made 21,150 runs but at the average of 40.7.

This is where it gets more confusing because Dexter's record is better away. It was 53.6 on the road, and outside of Australia he was over 40 everywhere he played. May was at 37.6 away, making the bulk of his runs at home: 63%.

Those first-class records I mentioned were mostly those players crushing at home. Is Dexter – who was an incredibly consistent performer no matter where he played – a better bat than May? Longevity or total runs haven't been factored into this either. In one case, two players overlap who still played very different kinds of careers.

Jack Hobbs started his career just as liquid manure was being stopped, when some bowlers still averaged well under 20, but he didn't have to go up against Jimmy Anderson checking out his every forward defence on his smartphone. Mahela Jayawardene made 9399 more runs in Asia than Don Bradman, who never played a Test there.

The other important thing is watching all these players – or at least getting eyewitness reports in some cases. A friend of mine is from Brisbane, but the cricketer he obsessed over was Pakistan's Zaheer Abbas. He was a player whose overall numbers looked good, but I never understood why people called him the Asian Bradman. He never made any runs in India, New Zealand or the West Indies, but was incredible in England and Australia.

But averaging 44 is not 99.94. So, what was it about him that sticks, that makes a random kid in Queensland love him or that makes people give him that nickname?

Zaheer stood at the crease tall, almost too tall, like he was trying to duck under a doorway but make it look like he wasn't. There wasn't anything sexy to view, he had glasses on and a bunch of hair tucked under his helmet.

You don't see any of it coming until you see the first moment he is given width. Then this nerd transforms into a superhero when he unfurls what suddenly feels like the world's longest bat into a drive that is at once languid and muscular through the off side. You're changed afterwards.

It is the same when you watch David Gower loft an off-spinner over cover, flick the ball over backward square leg, or really any shot. The way a batter scores has an impact as well. Once you start to pierce the off side with dramatic intent like Zaheer, or casually launch a ball too straight into the stands like Gower, the bowlers are impacted.

Mostly, it is about runs. Cullinan, Gower and Zaheer made them, others made more; some prettier, some in turgid defiance of aesthetic pleasure.

Runs are runs, and when Shane Warne is standing at the other end, you are happy to get them anyway you can. You are not battling your average, but the world's best bowlers.

To put together this book, I made it as simple as the great batters do; I took it one ball at a time. There is an art to batting, but the currency is runs.

11

TAXED

Some of the greatest batters have not always
been in the best place to make runs

*'You're facing the new ball and at least you've
got half a shot.'* – Barry Richards

Mark Richardson is running as fast as he can, wearing a tight
bodysuit with parts of his non-athletic body bulging and jiggling as
he hurdles a keg of beer.

He is doing this because he likes to challenge the slowest player from
the opposition to a race. This time, it is Australia's Darren Lehmann,
and the entire thing is being filmed. The New Zealander easily beats
the Aussie. Lehmann is a little shy with his running suit, so he pulls a
T-shirt over the top. Not Richardson. Every imperfection in his body
is shown in its non-conformist glory as he powers to victory.

Mark Richardson was always this bizarre. He started as a bowler.
His first-class debut was against India. He batted at 10 and took three

wickets in the match with his slow left-arm orthodox. Two of those victims were Kapil Dev and Sachin Tendulkar.

In his first 19 matches for two different Plunkett Shield teams and various development teams over three years, Richardson took only 22 wickets at 43. However, he averaged 21 with the bat, with 10 not outs and a high score of 34. He was kind of a nothing cricketer. His bowling was good enough to get Sachin out, but practically no one else, and he was handy at not being dismissed but not making runs.

He probably wasn't ideally suited to professional sport at that point.

So he just went off, missed the 1993/94 season, and returned the following year as a batter. He never really bowled that much again. In 1994/95, he turned up for Otago, batting at No. 4.

Almost five years after his first-class career began he is finally a batter, and he makes 122 from 311 balls batting at No. 4. He then bounces around the middle order a fair bit, makes a hundred against a touring West Indies side, and averages 37 as a middle-order batsman in four years.

But in 1998 he opens for the first time. He makes a duck in the first innings, and 162 not out from 402 balls in the second, so he is the player of the match. In his first 54 innings opening the batting he was outstanding. That included a touring double hundred against Sussex and a triple hundred in Zimbabwe. For nearly three years he is a stud, blocking and nudging balls and being as hard to dismiss as he was as a No. 10 all those years ago.

Finally, New Zealand let him open for them, almost 11 years into his first-class career, at the age of 29.

In 38 Tests he averages 45 and has the fourth-most runs of any Kiwi opener and the fourth-best average of anyone who has done it for them more than 10 times. If you believe that an opener's job is twofold: to score runs and face as many balls as possible, he is a giant of New Zealand opening. It took them 11 years to get him to the top of the order because of his weird career path.

Richardson was such a strange dude. He rarely made friends with his teammates and it's unclear how much he ever loved playing the game. He retired after four bad Tests, he was a bowler who became a batter, and it took him eight years of his professional career to do what he was actually best at. He went on to host home improvement shows before becoming the right-wing opinion guy on TV and radio.

Using Richardson as an example of anything would be unfair because he is his own man. But openers are weird. It is an odd choice to want to go out and bat for the first ball when you have no idea what the ball is going to do off the wicket.

There is also the fact that you are facing the ball when it is moving the most and is the hardest. Obviously, opening the batting helps some players; Australia's Matthew Elliott was asked to bat first drop, and he had so much energy that he was sparring with boxing gloves on before hitting the crease.

Some players, like Barry Richards, became openers by accident:

I initially went to number three when playing for Natal, but we were always three for one, two for one, three for one, four for one. So one of the South African selectors, Dereck Dowling said, "What's the point of coming in at two for one? You might as well go in from nought for nought and then start from there."

I wasn't all that keen on opening when I first started, but his logic made sense, and I thought I might as well go in there. You're facing the new ball and at least you've got half a shot. 'Cause the bowler hasn't got a wicket and you're out there against the new ball.

It is undoubtedly the hardest job of the specialist batting positions, while batting at No. 6 is the easiest. And it takes a special type of player.

A lot of openers have a level of patience that middle-order players do not. Mark Waugh talked about it just not being his game:

I could definitely not bat as long as or block as many balls as Alastair Cook, no way in the world. I would feel almost embarrassed if I was. Nothing against Alastair Cook, but if I was blocking the ball and not scoring, I probably couldn't cope with that, to be honest.

Cook's numbers don't scream greatness, but as an opener he averaged 45 at home and 46 away. Being that he was an English opener, even allowing for him batting in an easier era as a non-opener you would expect that mark to be closer to 50, maybe more. Weirdly though, for someone brought up on English wickets, he struggled in New Zealand and South Africa, averaging less than 30 in both. But he made up for that making runs in Asia, and while he was a sluggish player against spin, he was very effective.

He was the kind of opener who had very few shots and was completely okay with that. He never even dreamed of cover driving most games. He restricted his game as much as possible, which suited his personality just fine.

Players like Cook, Sunil Gavaskar and Geoff Boycott have a near-singular style of just staying in. They bat in a trance-like state that can last for days if it's not pierced by something miraculous.

While there are attacking and even more free-flowing openers, these are the kinds of players we think of at the top. They restrict their games in part to succeed most consistently, because opening is the most unfriendly of the batting jobs.

There are other things that hold back players when it comes to their overall records. Garfield Sobers averaged 86 runs per Test match but also bowled 38.7 overs per match. To put that into perspective, Jimmy Anderson delivered 35.5 overs each Test.

Let's use another example: Don Bradman scored 134 runs per Test at a strike rate of roughly 58. He faced around 228 balls each match. Sobers was directly involved in 232 balls when bowling and 132 when batting, meaning he bowled or faced 394 deliveries each match.

There is no doubt that Sobers could have been even greater with the bat if he'd simply not had the workload of a frontline bowler as well.

Looking at Sobers' record, it is clear he's not as consistent as other batters on his level. For instance, he never made runs in New Zealand (15.1) or Pakistan (32). However, he averaged 99.9 on Indian wickets, 45.3 in Australia and 53.5 in England, not to mention 66.8 at home. Being that New Zealand and Pakistan were two of the weaker teams, it is harder to see that as a failure but more as a blip. If he'd cashed in against them, who knows what his record could have been?

He also should have been a player who batted in the top order. He averaged 72 at No. 3 and 63.7 at four, however he spent most of his career at numbers five and six where he was still over 50, but not the same level. Part of the reason he had to move down the order was the workload. You cannot bowl 30 overs in an innings and then front up at first drop every game.

South African all-rounder Jacques Kallis had a similar dilemma. He was even more a natural No. 3 than Sobers, but he had one advantage. South Africa had multiple all-round options and he was never bowled like a frontline option. While he batted 174 balls per match, he delivered 121 – almost half of what Sobers did.

Kallis still had a bowling load, and it never seemingly dragged down his batting, though it must have. He averaged 50 when entering the game with the score under 20, which is an incredible effort for a player who was at No. 4. He never conquered English conditions (35.3) and against the best attack of his generation, Australia, he went at 41.1, which was fine but not incredible. He also struggled a lot against Sri Lanka – he grappled with Murali. It is still an extraordinary record, no matter how you tally it up.

He was like Boycott and Shivnarine Chanderpaul in playing in a bubble that always gave runs, but not always in the way the team wanted. Kumar Sangakkara explains:

His rhythm of batting was very similar throughout his career. But the Kallis way, it's the way to greatness, isn't it? How amazing was he? I don't know whether he doesn't get the same credit, perhaps maybe in the public eye, but I think when cricketers talk to each other, you mention Kallis. Everyone's in awe. And you speak about him with a lot of respect and appreciation for the great that he was.

Kallis was probably the first player to move from No. 3 to four, which has changed the landscape of batting. (Lara did, but he'd already batted at four a bit, too.) Until the 2000s, many cricket cultures assumed the best bat went in a first drop. With Lara and Tendulkar also batting in that spot, and Kallis making the move, most teams put their best at No. 4.

Most players in this list batted in their best spot. They were usually the greatest player in their team or had very specific skills. Sometimes they were unlucky, and you had to fit in where there was a slot, like VVS Laxman. And there are a lot of makeshift openers like Bob Simpson. But even then, it probably suited both of those players.

There is an interesting quirk that we see in one nation: England. Since the Second World War, cricket has been a little obsessed with the tyranny of the batting order. By that, I mean deciding what number a batter should come in, and not adjusting for the game. Take the great England side of the early 2010s. Number three was Jonathan Trott and four was Kevin Pietersen – very different styles of player. If England were 11/1, Trott is an automatic player to come in next, but what if the score was 200/1 in the 55th over? At that point you really want the broken bowling to be exploited before the new ball is taken in 25 overs time with Pietersen.

Older cricket teams would often change their line-up based on conditions, tiredness or any other worthy factor. It is a trait coming back in vogue through T20. But the England Test team of the 1950s and '60s had their own version.

Ken Barrington batted 40 times at three, 44 times at four and 31 times at five. Tom Graveney was also split between those spots a lot. Colin Cowdrey was another, and he also opened quite a bit as well. England's non-openers were all over the place in the order. You check old scorecards, and the batters change spots from match to match, seemingly without reason.

Keeping the batting order the same all the time or changing your top-order numbers on a whim doesn't make much sense. Barrington was a No. 3, but his batting style wasn't as suited to coming in later when the game had developed more. The problem was that Graveney was probably also a first drop, so they had a natural overlap there. But Cowdrey also batted 36 times in that spot during this era, despite his numbers being better suited to batting at five.

Cricket has made batting orders so much a part of batters' psyches, even if they should be more flexible. Moving them upsets their rhythm. One former player asked me what the difference was between batting at four and five, when talking about a potential change in the batting order. The simple answer is largely psychological, but also 11 overs. That is how often a wicket falls in Test cricket, including the tail. So it's really about every 12.5 overs.

A first drop is very likely to face the new ball every game. A second drop will face some of it on occasion. And a No. 5 should start most of their innings with at least one spinner on. They are different roles, so mixing them up regularly for no good reason is probably something that hurt players like Barrington, Cowdrey and Graveney. The fact that from Test to Test they didn't seem to know where they were batting makes them like a club cricketer turning up on a Saturday with no idea of their job.

People often talk about the added pressure of being a captain and how that has ruined many a batter. It is such a change in your career; you go from a specialist player to a coach and batter. But Amol Desai looked this up and found that Test captains average 15% more when they're in charge than when they're not.

That seemed wrong, so I looked at first-class captains. They average 7% more. This goes back to when the captain was a team manager, coach and salesman, and includes right up until now, when they have to lead in a 24-hour social media cycle.

A lot of this 7% or 15% jump makes sense. Most teams pick their best batters to be captain, and they get it when they are experienced. Most are probably between the ages of 28 and 32 when getting the job, so they are due more runs anyway. Overall, it seems that while captaincy has ruined some batters, many others have handled it perfectly well.

There is one other tough job in cricket: being a keeper batter. Until the Second World War, wicketkeeping was a specialist position; only one player averaged over 32 with the bat while keeping and that was Les Ames – a man who is often overlooked in the history of great all-rounders. In the years he played, all the other keepers combined an average of 20.3. Ames was 43.4. He was worth two other keepers with the bat. This was otherworldly and is barely talked about now. Before Ames, we had wicketkeeper and almost every year since we've had more keeper batters, until the modern period where there are no true wicketkeeping specialists.

Ames was a freak bat for a keeper but not elite compared to the Headley and Hammond era he was in.

The first great keeper batter was Clyde Walcott, who went at 40 when squatting behind the stumps and 65 when he gave up that job. In truth, we really don't know enough about Walcott's batting.

His first-class record is strong, so it is easy to give him the benefit of the doubt, but he needs it – he averaged 70 in the West Indies and only 40 on the road. And all those runs came from destroying a poor Indian attack. He also went at 66 against another poor New Zealand line-up. Sadly, 44 Tests in 12 years doesn't tell us much, but when he was on, nothing could stop him. He once hit 10 hundreds in 12 Tests.

Was he a Sangakkara-level batter or just someone who dined out on poor attacks and batting at home? I mention the Sri Lankan because he also averaged 40 keeping, 66 when not.

'Keeping helped me get on the side,' says Kumar Sangakkara, who was keeping and batting at No. 3 early in his career:

> That is physically challenging, even as a 22-year-old going through keeping in the heat, keeping in overseas conditions, it really saps energy, both mentally and physically. No matter how much I was enthused to go out and play well and really wanted to do well, there are certain things my body just wouldn't do.

When you study the numbers at Test level, few players have been keeper and non-keeper enough times to trust the data. But in first-class cricket, this happens a lot. Amol Desai looked at it once, and he couldn't see anything that suggested first-class keepers scored less without their second job.

But Tests are different: they are 20% longer. When you look at wicketkeepers compared to top-order players, there is a noticeable drop off in their averages in Test cricket when you get to the fourth innings.

Top six players have a 23% decrease from the first innings until the fourth. For wicketkeepers, it goes up to 26%, so there is a tax to keeping the gloves on.

Even for all that, not all players want to become specialist batters. 'When the selectors actually wanted me to give up my gloves, I was quite adamant that I shouldn't because I knew it was an insurance policy for me to stay in the side if I were doing badly with batting,' says Sangakkara.

'But what it forced me to do was take a new look at my batting and say, "All right, if this is all I have now, I've got it. I've got to be really good at this."'

Walcott, Sangakkara and Brendon McCullum all had a similar pattern of improving greatly when they only had one job to think about. At first glance, you believe that stopping keeping is what changes everything, but again, they become specialist batters when they are experienced and reaching their peaks. They were due more runs at this period anyway.

AB de Villiers doesn't start keeping regularly until six years into his career. As a specialist batter his average was 48.9; when keeping for 24 Tests in his prime it was 57.4.

There are also players whose keeping seems to give them a sense of freedom. Adam Gilchrist and Rishabh Pant played in a way that as specialist batters would have been tough.

In 2021 Pant was batting against England in Chennai when he decided to take on their left-arm orthodox bowler Jack Leach.

Older cricketers and fans hate it when spinners start with a long-on, but that is what England did; the same way they hate seam bowlers having a sweeper out. They believe the batters should earn it by stepping down the wicket and lofting the ball to the boundary. In Tests, that used to be seen as a risky shot. First leaving the crease where your specialist wicketkeeper would be behind the stumps waiting to pounce on your mistake. Then you had to clear mid-on, a mishit could get you caught and so would hitting hard but low.

So, a few things have changed. The wicketkeepers aren't as good now. Jos Buttler has four first-class stumpings in 110 innings while keeping. Picking keepers based on their batting skill has clearly affected the overall level of keeping.

Pant is not worried about there being a mid-on fielder. White-ball cricket has taught players that the only way a mid-on will catch you is if you cannot loft the ball right or hit it straight up in the air from a miscue. Most normal mishits will float well clear of any fielder in the circle. It's not just the big bats, but the way batters hit now. This isn't a high elbow punch through the line; these are full swings, often power hits. Players have been in the gym to get strong for this. They range hit for T20 and are used to seeing balls enter the stands.

Modern cricket is about the ball being in the air.

Spinners use the long-on at the start because they think the batter will still hit. Long-on is not a deterrent to many modern players.

Now, more players have that mindset; spinners don't see long-on as a defensive option; they see it as a catching position.

So, Leach starts with a man out and yet even with a fielder on the boundary, Pant sprints down the wicket to smash the ball over his head. It doesn't matter where the fielders are because Pant isn't trying to keep the ball inside the playing arena.

Pant had never faced Leach. He had only seen 11 balls in the innings so far, not one from Leach, and tried to hit him for six over a man on the boundary – unsuccessfully. Being a bit lucky and getting the ball in no man's land didn't stop how he played. The third ball he faced he danced down again. As the ball was straighter, he dragged it to midwicket for six.

England put out a deep midwicket, and he hit the next one there, too. Pant didn't seem to care and again went all in on attack, nearly being caught by that very same fielder.

This would slow down even some of the game's most attacking players, but Pant has a licence, so he keeps going.

Next over he went back to long-on, and the following one he's at it again. He was almost caught again, but who cares because soon he has five sixes from Leach; four of them were directly over the head of the boundary rider.

There is one more thing: he did all this from or near the footmarks. You can see that on more than one occasion, when the ball landed, puffs of dust popped up.

Traditionally batters try not to hit out of the footmarks because seamers have big heavy feet, and they ruin the flatness of the pitch. And yet, that is partly why Pant was batting as he was. He thought he could completely take Leach out of the attack, perhaps before one hit a pebble, rolled along the ground and bowled him.

India had a plan to attack Leach, and Pant was part of it. He was allowed to fail, but he went that hard because he had a sense of freedom you only get with a second job.

Bowling all-rounders often have great strike rates as well. Pant can just go. If you take the gloves off him, he may slow down, or at least change who he is as a batter. While we don't always count keepers as all-rounders, we should.

That is how Jimmy Adams talks about Zimbabwe's Andy Flower. He captained, he kept and he batted at No. 5. He had no rest at all;

he was in the middle for most of the game, making decisions. It must be the biggest load any cricketer has had.

'Flower once said to me, anything you do off the field sort of makes you feel a bit better when you step over the line,' says Nasser Hussain.

Flower had three frontline jobs, all of which he did well enough to be a player for a major team.

As a coach, Flower was the same. Jimmy Adams describes him:

In our dressing room we saw him as a modern-day great because of what he was doing in a weak team. Simple as that he averaged over 50 in Tests playing in the weakest team in international cricket.

He was doing it against India and against Pakistan. They played England. So it was as if he was playing Bangladesh and whoever, as they might say, for Zimbabwe. He rocked them up against everybody.

Flowers' record is weird, because Zimbabwe were a new team. So he has one match against Australia (though he was rated so highly that he was an overseas player for South Australia). He also only managed two Tests in each of England and the West Indies. In total, it was 42 matches over a decade. That included five matches against South Africa – a great attack in his era – where he made two hundreds and averaged 70.7. At Harare in 2001, South Africa made 600 in the first innings. Zimbabwe added 286, were asked to follow on, making 397. Out of 677 runs, Flower made 341 of them, and was only dismissed once.

The team he played the most was Pakistan – who also had a great attack – going at 44.3 over his 14 matches. Sri Lanka was also a common opponent, meaning he had to go up against Murali; 38.9 was the result.

One reason he is remembered so much is his average on Indian wickets: 117 is not easy to ignore. He was also robbed of the last few years of his career because he decided to protest against Robert Mugabe's murderous regime in his country at a World Cup. That meant he would never play for Zimbabwe again. He was a great player right until the end, averaging 70 in his last two county seasons.

'I wouldn't put him on the level of Lara or Tendulkar,' says Jimmy Adams. 'But he's on a level just below, especially for the fact that he's always under pressure. No disrespect to his brother and a few others, but he was carrying that line-up.'

Flower batted at five. Perhaps he would've been better suited at four, but the load he carried as a keeper meant five was the better option. It didn't matter, the median score when he came out to bat was 65/3. Michael Clarke and Steve Waugh spent most of their careers batting at number five in great Australian teams. Clarke's median entry was 114/3, and 113/3 for Waugh. Almost double what Flower had.

He was a No. 4, even a five. Often fighting a fire from the top order's struggles, he was lionhearted and awfully consistent.

Flower's first match against the West Indies was in Port of Spain. The hosts were bowled out for 187. Zimbabwe would get a first innings lead, despite being 27/3, and only one batter passed 50. That is because Flower made 113, despite the bowling attack having Curtly Ambrose and Courtney Walsh.

In the second innings, Flower failed. Because of that, Zimbabwe ended up 36 runs short of their chase, which was only 99.

When he batted well, they were in matches; when he failed, they lost. He averaged 43.1 runs in losing causes. Of players who made 2000 runs in losses, no one ever averaged more.

Who knows what Andy Flower could have been in a stronger team, coming in later, resting from the gloves, allowing others to captain? Through all that, and even fighting a dictator at home, Andy Flower went at 51.5 in Test cricket.

It was one of the weirdest careers in cricket, yet Flower barely seemed to notice, just focusing on the next ball, no matter what gloves he was wearing.

12

MOTIVATION

What makes the greatest run scorers keep going?

'There are times when Brian gets bored.
Sachin never got bored. Ever.'
— Jimmy Adams

A young player looks at the car park and sees a legend getting out of his vehicle. It is an hour after the match started, but that is okay; he said he would be running late. He is already in his whites, but his trainers are undone. He comes out to stand at first slip and tells the coach to run on a couple of pastries for him, eating one and keeping the other in his pocket. When an edge comes, he steps out of the way, looking at the younger second slip, 'It's your job to dive and catch it.'

Later he would be batting, and the opposition would put on their worst bowlers, part-timers and the once in a year dregs. He would get bored, step past one, ask when the team's other star was batting and tell everyone he would be back tomorrow when needed.

Then some days, the opposition would do something to annoy him, and he would score 150 or 200 in a flash.

That young player was Kumar Sangakkara; the legend was Aravinda de Silva. That was all from a Sangakkara story about his former teammate from Nondescripts Cricket Club, and you could hear the hero worship come out.

But Sangakkara averaged 57.4 in Tests, while Aravinda just a little under 43. So, what was the difference that made the former one of the greatest players ever, and the latter an infrequent genius?

Aravinda was incredibly talented. In 1991, he went to New Zealand for a Test series. In the first Test, he was batting on day one after 12 wickets had fallen for 216 runs. He made 267 with 40 boundaries. In that series, he made 493 runs at an average of 98 from just three Tests. Aravinda could flay the ball through point, he'd pull you into the crowd if you went short, and his work against the spinners was incredible.

There is a lot said about Sanath Jayasuriya and Muttiah Muralitharan winning the 1996 World Cup. But in the semi-final, Aravinda did something incredible. In four balls, Sri Lanka had lost their openers, both caught at third man on the boundary. It was barely believable.

Aravinda was 12 years into a 20-year career, and just finding peak. For years, he had been the batter carrying a weaker side on his own. But Sri Lanka were finally a great side, and that allowed their star to play the way that mattered to him.

The normal thing to do would be to rebuild when you're two down for one run. De Silva attacked. It did not slow him down, even when they lost their third wicket. When he receives a length ball way outside off stump, he moves across and flicks it to the legside with power. Like the ball and the bowler had made a mistake, not that he had just turned a ball many players would hit to backward point to one smashing into the square leg boundary.

Eventually, Anil Kumble would bowl him, but by then he was 66 from 47 balls. India never even got close to their total.

A few days later in the World Cup final, Shane Warne overpitches outside off stump, and Aravinda goes on to the back foot to play a straight bat square drive to a huge ripping leg-spinner. He splits two fielders set to stop it. The entire shot is preposterous, an affront to the coaching manuals.

Again, he did this after Sri Lanka lost their two openers cheaply. Towards the end of his innings, he walked across the stumps to play a leg glance to the vacant fine leg. It doesn't look like a special shot, but the number of times he moved across and tickled from the middle of his bat made it one of his biggest weapons. He could flay you through off, heave you over midwicket, or tickle you wherever he wanted. In this game, he was in complete control of a bowling line-up containing Warne and McGrath. He was chasing Australia's 241, and he would make 107 (unbeaten) of them.

This was not a normal level batter, but on average he looks that way. So, what is the difference between him and Sangakkara? They are both Sri Lankan, and their eras even overlap. But Aravinda was playing in a developing team that was learning how to be good at international level. The real difference is motivation; Aravinda de Silva needed something external to fire him up – a collapse, a big game, a tough wicket, a sledge, whatever it was, and he would activate his genius. Sangakkara says:

I think he and Brian [Lara] were very similar in personality. They needed to be really inspired and motivated to give their best. Until he went to Kent, I think in the mid-nineties, he didn't really understand what it meant to be consistently good or great. I think there were times when he was just bored, or he wasn't really motivated inside.

Lara is worth talking about here, but first let's look at the evolution of the world run-scoring record.

Charles Bannerman opened the batting in the first Test and faced cricket's inaugural delivery on 15 March, 1877. On day two, injured and barely able to hold the bat, he would retire hurt for 165. Australia made 245 – this is still a record for the highest percentage (67.3%) of runs in the team's total in a completed Test innings. Despite what this suggests, Bannerman was not great. He would play only two more Tests. In first-class cricket, he averaged 21.6. It was a tougher era, but that is still very low.

Fifteen Tests later, Billy Murdoch made 211 for Australia against England at the Oval in 1884. He was a better player, who managed to represent both England and Australia.

In the 78th Test at the SCG, Tip Foster made 287 for England on debut. He was a great player from a huge cricket family. He would captain England in football and cricket. Through to 1912, he would average 41.8 in first-class cricket. A huge number for that time; he also made 22 hundreds and almost 10,000 runs.

Tip's score was in 1903, but it wasn't until 1930 that it was bettered by the first triple hundred. Andy Sandham's 325 for England against the West Indies at Sabina Park came in Test No. 193. The Surrey player only managed 18 Tests, averaging 39 in them, but he was a giant in first-class cricket, scoring 41,284 runs at 44.8.

That was the last time the record was held by anyone near mortal. Bradman made 334 versus England in the Ashes at Headingley. That Test was No. 196 in 1930. Test 226, Wally Hammond made 336 not out versus New Zealand at Eden Park in 1933. Len Hutton took it in the 266th Test at the Oval five years later by making 364 in England's 903 against Australia in the Ashes. Then Garfield Sobers came on at Sabina Park (again) to make 365 not out against Pakistan in 1958.

Every single one of these innings was incredible. Bannerman's with a busted hand and no support, Murdoch's huge total in an era not known for them; Foster's came just as batting got easy, but that is a huge total for before the Second World War. Sandham took it one step forward just as batters were working out how to make big scores. Then it took Bradman, Hammond, Hutton and Sobers to add to these scores.

So, what does it take to do this twice?

Brian Lara is playing England in 1994, 36 years after Sobers has broken the record. It is St John's in Antigua, The Rec, a ground where the crowd is on top of the visitors. For two days, Lara went at the same pace, dissecting England on the small friendly surface. Once Lara saw the wicket was perfect for batting, he realised the chance of a result was low, and he chased a different one: the World Record.

It took him three days. The first two were easy – well, for him. That was just batting, he'd already made a massive double hundred against the Australians at the SCG. The problem was sleeping before the third day with the entire world expecting him to break the record. At 4a.m., he woke up with nerves. He stood in front of the mirror, practising his shots. As the sun came up, he went for nine holes of golf to try to occupy his time.

When he finally arrived at the ground, the slow outfield meant his shots smashed towards the boundaries did not reach them and he had to leg the runs. A 19-year-old Shivnarine Chanderpaul, in his debut series, was at the other end helping him to the mark. When Lara got to 347, he got completely stuck for 20 minutes. England's warhorse Angus Fraser beat the bat twice. 'I don't suppose I can call you a lucky bleeder when you've got 347?' Fraser told Lara.

The camera was on Sobers as much as Lara, as he was kept on the boundary edge like a proud parent, waiting for his record to fall. When England's beanpole Andy Caddick overpitched, Lara drove him through the covers to go equal with Sobers.

England captain Mike Atherton brought the field up to try to force a mistake from Lara. England quick Chris Lewis was bowling to him, and their spinner Phil Tufnell told him to make Lara work for it. But Lewis decided to bowl a short ball. Lara was expecting that, and he smashed the pull shot to break the record.

The already volatile ground exploded as people ran out into the middle. There were police there to stop them, but they came on too. 'The whole place was rocking,' Fraser said. 'There were people climbing over the fences and running on to the field doing cartwheels and headstands.'

That record held until 10 October, 2003, when Matthew Hayden smashed 380 against Zimbabwe at the WACA. Hayden's was the 1661st Test, Lara's had been the 1259th and Sobers did it in the 450th. So, it took Lara 809 matches to go past Sobers, and Hayden 402 matches to take the record away.

On 12 April, 2004, 185 days and 35 Tests later, Lara took his record back again. There had not been a gap this small since Murdoch outscored Bannerman.

What Lara needed, more than anything else, was motivation. In 1994, it was the search for the record, that many people in the Caribbean thought he was born to break. At the non-striker's end that day was Jimmy Adams:

There are times when Brian gets bored. Sachin never got bored. Ever.

I know for a fact that Brian is driven by a record. If it's there, he's going after it. So once Mattie Hayden went ahead of him, whenever that was somewhere in Brian's mind, and you're coming back to Antigua (where he broke the record the first time). I can't remember what kind of form he had at the time, but he had a template from ten years before.

Get a start, you'll go at a rate of four runs an over for a day, which will give you a hundred and plenty runs in a day. About two days you'll have three something, and then if you're about two days and a bit, you know. It's a dead wicket, so if 500 plays 500, nobody can say that he gave up a chance to win a Test.

Brian would not have been ignorant of any of that information.

What Adams is really talking about is the spark, that is what Lara needs. Once it seems that he can do something special, he found levels that few batters ever got near:

> Different animal. I mean, the normal Brian Lara was fantastic. But, when you get a driven Brian Lara, then yeah, try and get him out early. There are times when it is just people who provide the motivation. McGrath has a crack at him in a Test match and then he plays the best Test match innings of all time.

The innings that Adams is talking about is when Australia set the West Indies 308 at Bridgetown in 1999, and the West Indies fell to 105/5. That doesn't seem to matter to Lara. Three runs later, he gets a ball at off stump. He runs down and flicks it over midwicket. The bowler is Stuart MacGill, who with all his talent and experience decides to toss the next hard spun leg break outside off stump to stop Lara hitting over the legside. It doesn't work, and even though the ball is well outside off, it goes to the same boundary.

Australia's captain Steve Waugh has seen enough; he moves a fielder to deep midwicket.

Lara scoops the next ball down the ground for two, and the following ball he gets inside a straighter ball and taps it to fine leg for another boundary – 14 runs in four balls, with his team in all sorts of trouble.

A few hours later, Jason Gillespie gets smashed through the covers. The West Indies chase 308 with nine wickets down. Lara is unbeaten on 153; the second top score is Adams with 38.

Australia would end up with a rule of not talking to Lara when playing him. Unfortunately, no one told Pakistan's leg-spinner

Danish Kaneria at Multan in 2006. In fact, it was the opposite; his captain Inzamam-ul-Haq admitted to the press that he encouraged it: 'I was the captain of the side, so I went over to Danish and told him to tease Lara a bit more. I felt that Lara was angry so we might make him throw away his wicket.'

The spinner flighted up a ball outside leg stump, and for a moment Lara thinks about coming down and smashing it away. He realises very late it is a wrong 'un, so he quickly switches to defending the ball from the middle of the bat.

Kaneria says, 'Well played, Brian.' Lara looks shocked, and replies 'OK sir.'

Next ball, Kaneria tries the same delivery – a wrong 'un outside leg stump, and Lara jumps back deep into his crease and pulls the ball for six. Almost as the ball leaves the bat, he turns his back on where it's heading to look back at the bowler. The next delivery, Kaneria delivers full and wide, and Lara sprints down the wicket to slap a straight six. The next ball is straighter, but with fielders out on the legside Lara plays it inside out against the spin over long-off for another six. The final ball is not important because no matter what was coming, Lara had already run down. Kaneria panics and fires it quick and full down leg, and Lara picks up another boundary, despite many fielders out on the legside to stop them.

The sledge was followed by 22 runs in four balls, moving him from 70 to 92. Lara would be dismissed by Kaneria for 216.

Adams said, 'Like, here he was just doing his normal little great Brian Lara thing and Danish Kaneria decides to give him some lip and it's like, Danish, no, man. No, no. There is another level.'

Shivnarine Chanderpaul was in that same match. By the 2000s, West Indies managed to have two of the greatest batters of all time in what was still a sub-par batting line-up overall. Other than his crab-like technique, Chanderpaul is often accused of being selfish.

But the patron saint of self-serving batters was England opener Geoffrey Boycott. This is what Ian Chappell said:

Boycott is the most selfish player I've ever come across.
   Boycott was a good player, um, but he wasn't someone who kept me awake at night because he didn't score quickly, and he

was a very predictable player. If you bowled the ball in a certain place, you pretty well knew where he was going to hit it. So you could always place a field for him. And I always felt that if Boycott made a big score, there was every chance that we could make a big score because he would never do it quickly.

And it generally meant that the pitch was pretty good. I didn't think that Boycott was scared of fast bowling. But I thought that he was well and truly scared of failure.

Greg Chappell tells a story about Geoffrey Boycott when England were facing the Australian mystery spinner, John Gleeson. Basil D'Oliveira was his partner, and the debonair middle-order player started to score off Gleeson for the first time. He went down at the end of the over to tell Boycott that he could pick him now.

'I worked it out in the second Test,' Boycott replied. 'But don't tell those buggers in the dressing room.'

Now, that story is disputed, but it has stuck because of who Boycott was. His Yorkshire teammate Don Wilson once said, 'He thinks of nobody else in the world.'

Boycott is an extreme example, but many other batters have been referred to as selfish. If you search sites like Quora or Reddit where online fans talk about the game, you can find almost any famous batter in a Google search of: 'is [insert player name here] selfish'? The website *CricTracker* has a list of the most selfish players ever: Tendulkar, Lara, Boycott, Gavaskar, Dhoni and the Steves (Waugh and Smith) are all on the list. The only specialist bowler is Hadlee. So, either the two jobs are seen differently or there is selfishness built into batting.

Jonathan Trott was called selfish early in his career by his teammate Ashley Giles. Trott's international career was short, but he still played a huge number of Tests because that's what England do. Despite his career dropping off after Mitchell Johnson got to him, he still averaged 44. In England that was nearly 50, but Trott did bat in an easier era. He was most known for batting in the kind of bubble that was so all-encompassing that he often didn't notice the world around him. The sort of person who would mark his guard as the rest of the players left for tea. That is how Trott made runs, which helped his team.

From a socialist viewpoint, your runs should be for the greater good, but the capitalist thinking is: the more runs you accrue, the better your team is.

This brings me to one of the least spectacular innings ever played. In 2008, South Africa toured Bangladesh for two Tests. In the first match, Bangladesh fought hard in a low-scoring match; after the first innings they had a lead of 22. They set South Africa 205, which the hosts chased successfully with five wickets down.

The next match was very different. South Africa batted first, and Neil McKenzie and Graeme Smith opened. McKenzie was a solid opener, and while he had tried hard, he was averaging 32 in Tests eight years into his career. Rather than his batting, he was most known for quirks like taping cricket bats to dressing room ceilings.

In 2018, McKenzie told *ESPNcricinfo*:

> When you are OCD, it is all about numbers and feeling right. In cricket, we play in an uncontrollable environment. ... I tried to control the outcome by giving myself more of an edge, or luck, with the superstition.

But on day one of that Test at Chattogram, he was in control. McKenzie would make 169 not out, which was his highest score. He would go on to add more the following day and end with 226. That was 106 more than he had ever made before, and this innings would kickstart his career. In the next few months, he would make two more hundreds in India and England. His knock was only part of the story, because at stumps on day one, his opening partner Smith was also not out.

Smith was a muscular opener who never saw a ball he didn't want to turn to the legside for one. He is a player whose captaincy has outshone his batting. But he was an incredible run scorer with an average of 12 more away than at home. The reason he did not end up over the magical 50 mark was that he struggled at home, averaging 41.5. He was a spree run scorer, struggling against India and Australia, but when he played in England he would average 67; he was over 50 in New Zealand as well. This was not a man motivated by runs; he was about legacy.

At the age of 10, Smith had a list of his goals on his parents' fridge. The main one was to captain his country.

The way he did that was remarkable, and it came from perhaps his biggest failure. He was left out of the team for the 2003 World Cup at home. So as a loud 'fuck you', he demanded the captaincy of Western Province against South Africa in a warm-up match. A bold move for someone his age.

What was supposed to be an intra-South African friendly practice match turned very serious when Smith demanded that his players take it seriously and bring down the national team.

Smith and South African captain Shaun Pollock had a disagreement over the fielding restrictions and how the national team weren't adhering to them. Here was a player in and out of the national team standing in the face of Pollock, a legend and captain. For a young player, this could have gone horribly wrong. There was a high chance the senior team would smash his side, and he'd look like a fool.

Western Province won by seven wickets with almost 20 overs to spare. That's not a contest. And that is how Smith is known, as a leader. Because of that, sometimes people forget just how good a batter he was, but he was a great player in certain circumstances, and one of them was this day (or days).

His wicket on day two was the first Bangladesh would take with the score at 415. Smith made 232 of those from 277 balls. The partnership is the world record for the first wicket. After making his double hundred, McKenzie was dismissed with the score on 515, and that is when Kallis came in. At this stage in their history, Bangladesh had never scored 500 in a Test innings.

Yet Kallis would come in with the score on this huge total, see a small collapse and decide that the best way to bat was to slowly knock the ball around. There was no urgency or intent, he was not trying to put pressure back on or bat in a way to get them to declare sooner. Kallis batted for nearly two and a half hours. He would face 120 balls, hit no boundaries and make 39 not out.

Was it selfish? Was it just a run-scoring legend doing what he always did, putting a score on the board? Kallis would play T20 in the same way, almost oblivious to the world around him, just the next ball.

This is what helped him become the incredible player he was. In 1997, he was still a project. He hadn't made any runs, but the idea of a seam bowling all-rounder who can bat in the top four was too tempting, so South Africa kept trying him. At the MCG, he was batting in an improbable chase of 381 over 122 overs. The problem was that he would be going up against Glenn McGrath. But perhaps more importantly for the last innings, it was Shane Warne, on his home pitch.

The ball would fizz and bounce past Kallis' edge so often, yet it never seemed to occur to him that it was an issue. That bubble that he remained in allowed him as a young and unproven man to believe in himself so much that the world's best spinner at home ripping deliveries past him didn't matter. Was Kallis selfish at times? Probably. But many batters are.

Cricket is a weird sport. It is a team game but played in a way that needs individuals to star on their own. Cricket also has two very distinctive playing styles. Australian cricket had very much a collective team style. But the England method was split through class, and because it was a professional game, a lot of batters were more worried about their next contract than winning in Derby.

'There's a lot of players who [...] we call the not out boys,' says Barry Richards:

They're just looking for averages. And there were a lot of them in county cricket, and I can understand why. They're trying to get 150 not out against the universities in the first game.

Knowing that at the end of the year, if they average 40, they're likely to get another contract. But they've got 150 not out against the schoolboys, as they call them. And they were pretty much a schoolboy attack. I played against them my first year of county cricket, and I never played against them again.

Despite Australia's dominance, the English style has influenced most cricket cultures. So, around the world, batters do what they need to for their next contract or to remain in the side, not always to win the match.

In limited overs cricket, this has become obvious as batting has got far more aggressive. Things like slowing down for your hundred stick out. But there is something else that shows cricket's selfish and team dynamic the best. You can see it in the semi-final of the 2020 World Cup, because Meg Lanning is furious. She's swiping her bat and her body tenses up. The Australian women are struggling. The pitch slowed them down at the end, so their total was low.

At the death, South African quick Shabnim Ismail bowled the 19th over for only five. And with one ball to go of Ayabonga Khaka's over, they've only got five runs. The final one is a low straight full toss, and Lanning drags to leg, straight at the sweeper. She pushes hard for two, only to see there is no chance of her making it back safely, and Nicola Carey seems to call no to confirm it.

Lanning's anger is probably not at the lack of a second, but that she got a full toss and found the sweeper. But she should be mad at the running. Even though there was no chance of a run, a fumble was possible. And that is what Khaka did. But Australia couldn't take advantage as they weren't running. Why on the last ball of the innings would they not continue to run until they were out?

When the Australians bowled, with two balls left, South Africa needed 12 runs to win. Had they stolen one on that Khaka fumble, it would have already been game over. But South Africa still had a chance. Australia won by five runs, and it wasn't an issue.

Not running until the end has been an issue before. It occurred in a Pakistan Super League game, when Islamabad played Karachi early in the season in 2015. On strike for the last ball was quick bowler Mohammad Sami. He hit one to England's Ravi Bopara at deep midwicket. It was a simple bit of fielding on the bounce, which should have been a run out, as the tail-enders had decided to run two, and it was never on.

Because of their cavalier attitudes to their wickets, Bopara felt the pressure, and he fumbled because they were turning for two regardless. In the end, they didn't just steal an extra run, but two. Bopara fumbled, and because the two batters were just running until the end, they would end up with three runs. Islamabad United would end up winning by two runs.

The Australian coach Dean Jones was in charge of Islamabad, and he would use this example to tell everyone to run until the end of every first innings.

Yet most players still don't run until they are out on the last ball of the first innings. For an article in *The Cricketer* magazine, I tracked a period from 2017 to 2020 in men's T20 cricket. There were 1548 balls bowled to complete the first innings of a match. Of those, 353 were boundaries and 163 non-run out wickets. That's 1032 deliveries with a run out chance, and it includes 137 run outs. So every 7.5 balls a batter is run out off the last live ball.

Of course, there are last balls where a batter has gotten home and the bails have been dislodged moments later. But even adding another 137 chances on, that's still 73% of the time where the opportunity is there. Teams dive in the field, batters put their throats on the line with scoops, cricketers play through injuries, yet we regularly see teams not even try for the last run. They just give it up.

This conversation entered the mainstream through an incident with the England men's T20 side, because England batter Dawid Malan was accused of being selfish by his captain Eoin Morgan for not running on the last ball of a T20 in the first innings.

Malan is a late bloomer whose Test career didn't bite, and was desperate for a T20 career in his 30s. Against New Zealand, he smashes a hundred from 48 balls, and for the last ball, he's at the non-striker's end. Sam Billings misses one, it goes through to the keeper, and Malan says no.

Eoin Morgan said after the game, 'If we get guys that are not running off the last ball of the game because they want to get a not out, there's something to address.' England – the team that ticks all its boxes with its army of nerdy analysts and Morgan's details obsession – saw that as a missed opportunity even though they scored 241 and would win by 76 runs.

When Malan was left out of T20Is in South Africa for Joe Denly, his fans kept pointing to his average as a reason he should be in the side. At that stage, Malan's T20I average was 52. If he'd been run out attempting that bye, it would have dropped to 47. That probably wouldn't change the argument, but two run outs early in your career on that last ball could dent the overall mark. What England know is that averages just don't mean as much in T20 as other formats, but we've grown up with them, and there's no widely used superior metric ready to replace them.

Many batters in T20 as late as 2020 would happily open the batting and look for high run totals, often ignoring coaches' and captains' guidance to bat quicker. The IPL still has an award for the most runs, the orange cap, which is talked about during the tournament.

Even the greats are affected. Tim Wigmore writes for *ESPNcricinfo*:

Consider Sachin Tendulkar's 100th international century. He took 125 balls to reach 94. Then, just as he should have been accelerating, Tendulkar started batting with all the intent of a sloth. He took 13 balls to get his next six runs – a remarkable go-slow, considering that this was from the 40th to 44th overs, and India were only two wickets down. Tendulkar then sped up, scoring 14 off his last nine balls, but it was too late to lift India up to a match-winning total. They lost the ODI to Bangladesh.

In Test cricket, batters are judged by their averages. That is the number people focus on and discuss. So it feels weird to turn around and call some batters selfish for batting for runs and not for the team.

That is the dichotomy of the individual pursuit of runs, and the team looking to win. There are no correct answers.

But the players we call selfish often have other motives as well.

The West Indian team would often play indoor cricket in their massive hotel rooms when touring India. It would just be a game with one hand, one bounce with a tennis ball. But there was one batter who would argue every single time about whether the fielder had really picked the ball up before the second bounce. Even in a joke game, with no stakes and no one keeping score, Chanderpaul loved to bat. Jimmy Adams explains:

I thought I was competitive but he was on a different level. It felt like, to me, it was more about crease occupation than selfishness. It wasn't like he was chasing numbers, he was just trying to stay out there as long as possible. I genuinely believe that what gave Shiv the biggest high was to get to the point where he owned a bowling attack. After two hours, I own you.

You will not get me out unless I want to get out. And then his love of batting kicked in. He just loves to bat.

On 10 April, 2003 in Guyana, his homeland, Chanderpaul showed something else. Chanderpaul walked out to join Lara with the score on 47/4 as Australia were all over them. Early on Australian seamer Andy Bichel bowled back of a length and Chanderpaul punched the ball off his back foot past mid-on. An extraordinary shot. Sadly, soon after, Lara was out and the score was 53/5.

Australian quick Brett Lee was brought back on to clean the innings up fast, but Chanderpaul smashed a pull off him and kept going at Bichel as well. Left-arm wrist spinner Brad Hogg came back on to spin the ball away from the bat, and Chanderpaul cut him so brutally, the ball smashed into the fence and bounced back onto the field.

Waugh brought on MacGill; the leg-spinner flighted one outside off stump and Chanderpaul's slog swept it for six. That was his fifty, from 37 balls.

Waugh had to take his spinners off, so he brought back Jason Gillespie. That did not stop anything as a short ball was despatched. At the other end, MacGill was again attacked against the spin through the covers. Ridley Jacobs went up to hug him, the crowd erupted, and the dressing room went wild. Chanderpaul made his hundred from 69 balls; the third-fastest ever at that time.

Even all these years later, it is as high as sixth.

Chanderpaul would make 30 Test hundreds, but only 10 of them were at a strike rate of over 50. This one was 138, his next quickest was 75 when setting a declaration total against Bangladesh.

'The odd one-day game was when he decided to go ballistic,' says Adams. 'So, I always felt that there was another element to him or another level to his batting where he could have gone beyond occupation to total domination. But we'll never know. We'll never know. And that is more tied in with his psyche and his history.'

Steve Waugh, the captain in that game, was another player who swallowed his attacking instincts in the middle order. He put the hook shot away so he could stay in longer. He went from an attacking all-rounder to a middle-order wizard.

People who batted at Nos. five and six like Waugh during their careers were not out 9.7% of the time. Waugh wasn't dismissed in 17.6% of his innings, almost twice the rate of other players. Part of this was just because he was one of the best lower-middle-order players ever, but it was also his style of putting a huge price on his wicket. But he often got the most criticism for batting with the tail and allowing them the strike.

Waugh would argue that this was a way to get them to take their batting more seriously, and he also played some great partnerships with the tail. Others suggested this was a way to get more not outs in Waugh's – very public – campaign to end with a 50-run average.

The odd thing about that theory is that Waugh was incredibly competitive. 'Steve was so combative, up for a fight,' says Nasser Hussain. 'The knock he played at the Oval on one leg. Or when we had him in trouble that time, Mark Taylor won the toss and batted on a damp one. The tougher the situation, the more he revelled in that.'

Waugh was motivated by trying to end as a great, but that moved him to make innings that other players couldn't. There is an interesting nature vs nurture battle that we can look at within the Waugh family. Steve and his twin Mark were both clearly incredibly athletic. Both starred in other sports as kids and could also bowl. Mark Waugh was arguably one of the greatest fielders of all time as well.

But there is no doubt that when they batted, they were very different. Steve broke into the side as an all-rounder thanks to his clever swing bowling, and really struggled being an attacking middle-order player. Mark came into the side at the expense of Dean Jones – who would finish with a better batting average – because he could bowl. At first medium pace and then off-spin.

There was nothing Mark couldn't do on the cricket field. He played his entire career like someone who knew that at any moment he could do something no one else could. He batted the same when he made his debut as he did in his last match.

The nature was similar, the nurture was similar. Yet Steve Waugh averaged 51, and Mark Waugh 41.8.

Was the difference as simple as motivation? Mark wanted to leave a good-looking corpse, and Steve wanted to be remembered as a legend.

I once wrote an article for *ESPNcricinfo* about Kumar Sangakkara and Mahela Jayawardene being even closer than the Waugh brothers, despite not sharing a womb. But, again, they were very different. Mahela is a fierce competitor but Kumar is on another level.

In 2015, his father, Kshema, told *The Indian Express*: 'For the world, Kumar was this venerated technician. But in my opinion, he never reached that level.' It is an extraordinary thing to say about one of the best batters the game has seen. He also added:

For me, Don Bradman was the ultimate batsman. He scored a century once in every three innings. If you truly consider yourself to be a world-class batsman, you should be able to do that. Kumar did well, don't get me wrong. But did he achieve his true potential? I don't think so.

Sangakkara grew up in a house where being Don Bradman was the only option. Despite being easily one of the greatest 20 – if not higher – batters of all time, he failed to live up to his expectation. This pushed him to a level of production that few players have had before.

When asked about the batter he wanted to be, Sangakkara said Brian Lara, 'was great at everything except perhaps the thirst to be consistent.'

Barry Richards said:

I couldn't keep clubbing baby seals, which is what Brian Lara does rather well. Lara and Bradman. They absolutely loved making as many runs as possible. You look at Sachin Tendulkar. He loved being in the middle as long as possible. You look at Lara, and he's decided he's the Bradman of his era. He wants to just get big scores and be remembered for big scores, not for winning games or whatever. He wants big scores.

Let's say Richards is right. Does that matter? Lara's inspiration was to play great innings – sometimes for records, sometimes to win matches. He needed that.

Richards had his own issues as someone who was stuck in first-class cricket because of South Africa's isolation from Tests. Many players I talked to had Richards as one of the best five batters they saw. 'I would put him as one of the greatest of all time,' says Bumble.

Bob White, an opponent of Richards in county cricket, said:

> He was just always in the right place at the right time. He never seemed to be out of position when he was hitting the ball. You couldn't find the length or whatever to make him hurry.
>
> The first time I saw him play was on the television, Hampshire played Yorkshire. He had a very cramped stance when he was playing, and he was facing Fred Trueman. But once he went into his stroke, it was magnificent, beautiful. Fred was still at his peak then. And I thought, well, this chap can play if he can do this to Trueman. He was only a young lad.

White couldn't remember what game it was, but the first match where Richards went up against Yorkshire was at Harrogate. Hampshire were bowled out for 122, and Richards made 70 of them. It may have been a John Player 40-over game a couple of years later where Hampshire batted first, and they made 215 with the second-highest score being 18. Richards made 155 not out. You look at his scorecards and they feel like a kid made them up for his favourite player.

When he made 207 for the World XI against the Australian XI in World Series Cricket in Perth, there is a moment when Dennis Lillee overpitches outside off stump. The normal shot is to get on the front foot and punch it through the gap. Richards goes back instead and plays a straight bat cover drive along the ground to the fence. It's in essence the Caribbean style of shot, but there is something else here: the control, straightness of blade and mastery of one of the best bowlers in the world. Barry Richards was built differently.

In that innings, Gordon Greenidge and Viv Richards made hundreds as well. Usually when those two great players went large, that was the story. But not that day. Part of the reason Barry Richards went so hard was because this was like a Test to him, and he hadn't played one in a decade.

At lunch on day one, the Australian XI were in trouble. Greenidge was firing, with 51 from 98 balls. But Barry Richards had outscored him with 60 from just 87. Both men got their hundreds, but despite Greenidge's fierce cuts, Richards beat him there by 30 balls. So, after Greenidge picked up an injury and went off, that meant the two Richards were at the crease.

Years later, the Aussie pace bowler Max Walker would say, 'The papers were asking who the best batsman of the world was. Richards or Richards? Black or white? Barry had already got a hundred when Viv got out there and we knew we were not going to get Viv for much less than 200.'

Barry loved batting with Viv. It reminded him of the early partnerships he'd had with Graeme Pollock. There was a difference, though. 'Graeme was always keen for a single at the end of the over. So, Graeme would try to hit five fours and a single every over. Viv on the other hand tried to hit all six balls for fours.'

This day it was Barry who went hard, scoring 93 to Viv's 41. Ray Bright, Australia's long-suffering left-arm orthodox spinner, was straight batted over the legside. It should have been a slog, but Barry was so correct that his hooks to leg were still grammatically correct.

Barry Richards hit 28 fours and four sixes in his 207. After 60 overs, the score was 369/1.

Many had Barry as high as Viv, some even higher. This was a batter robbed from cricket by a racist regime. Who knows what he could have done if he was motivated?

I've got over 150 scores over 50, which is twice as many as Graeme Hick, who's got a hundred hundreds. So if I just converted, let's say a third of them, into hundreds that would take me to 130 hundreds which I could easily have done, I promise you. If I'd really batted for not outs like boys, I could have averaged maybe close to 70 if you'd really wanted to pay attention to averages. The first 50 is much harder than the second 50 and I would lose interest in games if there was nothing there [...] I'd done the hard part. The challenge was gone.

It would sound like a boast, but Richards did get bored playing at a lower level. When talking about how a second-tier Sri Lankan side, well before they became a quality team, was one of the rebel tours to South Africa, he says, 'When Sri Lanka came with a team that were, at best, a club side, I couldn't play against them.'

Richards the batter was stuck in a loop of playing lesser cricketers. We have some stats of him at the higher level, four Tests against Australia, where he passed 50 four times in seven innings and averaged 72.6. In five Supertests, like the one we discussed earlier in the World Series Cricket days, he made 554 runs in eight innings, with two more hundreds and the same amount of fifties. It's a small sample size and who knows what he would have ended with? But the nine times he played at the higher level, he averaged 75.8. Many cricket experts think that was a far better representation of what he could do compared to his first-class average of *only* 54.

The question is at a certain point, whatever the motivation is, if it makes you end with more runs, isn't that largely the point of batting?

Think of the Waugh brothers again. Steve completely evolved his style from an attacking all-rounder to a middle-order rock. Mark was artistic; Steve was militaristic.

Because of their styles, and ultimately their careers, we start to assign different characteristics to each player. Nasser Hussain said:

Steve Waugh the tough nuggety fighter, great for a crisis, but you don't get the runs that Steve Waugh got without an incredible amount of talent and ability.

Mark Waugh, the other way around, so naturally gifted. He is an elegant timer of the ball and a brilliant player of spin, but he occasionally gives his wicket away or whatever. It was far from the truth. You know, not everything comes naturally to Mark. Mark had to work hard at everything. He was more natural than Steve.

'My first-class record, obviously, I had really good numbers,' says Mark Waugh. In Tests, he would average 41.8; in the rest of first-class cricket, it was 58:

Test match cricket I probably should have averaged three or four more points higher if I was really hungry when I was on top. And that's something I probably should have been better at but I was more concerned about getting the team into a good position and winning the games most of the time.

Was it as simple as Mark Waugh not needing to do as much when playing for Australia, because he had Glenn McGrath and Shane Warne behind him with the ball? The attacks weren't quite at that level for Essex and New South Wales, but Steve Waugh had the same bowling attacks for Australia.

He was a very different player, but not on all fronts, as Mark points out:

> I think we're just motivated by winning, really, and playing the game in an aggressive manner. That's the way we were brought up throughout our club cricket at Bankstown, and then with New South Wales. And the best way to win is to score runs probably quickly and try and dominate the bowling attack.

Most people would say that these two were motivated in a different way, yet they don't see it that way – they were both trying to win. But that came out different. Steve put a huge price on his wicket and punished the mistakes. Mark seemed to try to create mistakes by playing in an attacking manner.

Years ago, I was in conversation with Australian opener Ed Cowan, and I mentioned that Mark Cosgrove, an Australian cult hero who never fulfilled his incredible potential other than a few ODIs, was more naturally talented than him. He pulled me up straight away and changed the way I looked at batting talent.

When Hussain is saying that Mark Waugh is more natural than his brother, he means in picking up the ball, his footwork and ultimately his timing. The gifts we see as more 'man-made' are patience, work ethic, professionalism, fitness, smarts and motivation.

Cowan's point was that these are natural talents as well. Alastair Cook was born patient, Virat Kohli was born with a work ethic. We see these as things that any player can do, if they try hard enough, but it isn't true. Motivation is another one.

Barry Richards talked me through his triple century for South Australia, 'I got 300 […] that was because we […] didn't have that many runs […] we only got 500 [575/9]. I got 350 of that. So we needed those runs to win.'

Don Bradman didn't need a sledge, tough pitch, collapse or record to be motivated. He was like that every day, and it made him the best batter ever. Bradman was a huge fan of Richards, 'He could play speed and spin with equal ability,' he told Roland Perry for his book *Bradman's Best*, 'an exceptional talent, unfulfilled in Test history'.

They were different, and what drove them was not the same. Most players will say they played to win, but even within that there are differences. Looking at Allan Border, Mark Waugh said, 'he hated losing.' Others have a near-pathological need to win, but there are those who love to leave a good-looking corpse out on the field. Some are motivated by personal slights that only they remember.

England's Jonny Bairstow was not a great batter but played innings as good as many of the best in this book. When writing about him for *The Guardian* about his 100th Test, his former coach Mark Ramprakash wrote:

> There was a game in Sri Lanka in 2018 that I have mentioned before where he and Stuart Broad came into the side and he heard Mike Atherton refer to it as "The B Team" – obviously Mike was referring to the fact their names both begin with a B, but Jonny saw it as an insult and was livid. He scored a century on day one.

The bit Ramprakash might have missed is that Bairstow gave fiery statements at his haters, even though no one knew publicly why he was angry at all. Ramprakash himself was a fierce competitor who struggled to make runs in Tests, but never struggled for motivation.

Not all players had that inner drive. In 2008 at Lord's, AB de Villiers was batting with Ashwell Prince. Prince was a batter at Test level, a left-hander who batted at the top of the order, and struggled to get the best out of himself through sheer will. They had put on a decent partnership. Both were set. De Villiers had not been worried much by England's bowling and looked ready for a big total, but he flicked the ball mindlessly, needlessly and hopelessly in the air, and was caught at mid-on. Prince fought hard and batted very well with the tail to score a hundred. But AB's mistake meant that South Africa had to follow on.

According to South Africa coach Mickey Arthur's book, *Taking the Mickey*, Graeme Smith had been forced to go out and bat by England again. After stumps, Smith and Arthur confronted AB. Smith told AB he wasn't doing justice to his talent or justifying his place in the team and Arthur explained what taking responsibility meant.

This is how de Villiers remembers the incident:

> When we got back to the hotel, I got in the lift and that's when Graeme unleashed a little bit. A couple of harsh words really to make me understand the importance of me getting out in that situation.
>
> I didn't take it very well at the time, I didn't feel like I deserved the criticism. I felt I was being attacked. Later, looking back, I realised that was a very important moment and I needed some harsh words to just wake up a bit.

The next Test, AB walked out at Headingley with South Africa on 143/4, 60 behind England's 203. Prince was batting with him again and made a hundred, but AB made 174.

His average was under 40 in both Tests and ODIs before the Headingley Test. After, he averaged over 60 in both.

Whatever switch Arthur and Smith found, it completely changed everything. He was transformed from a beautiful failure to a beast of batting.

What about another wicketkeeper, the West Indian Denesh Ramdin? After making his second Test hundred at Edgbaston, he unfurled a piece of paper that said, 'yea Viv, talk nah', aimed at the great Mr Richards, who had 20 more hundreds than the angry gloveman. Nasser Hussain pointing at the number on his back when making an ODI hundred at Lord's is another obvious time when a player was motivated by something off the field.

The greatest players are usually motivated all the time – that is the difference. Not on a flat pitch or a spiteful one, not when their team needs them or there are cheap runs on offer, but every single time.

To listen to Sangakkara, Aravinda da Silva was more talented than him. He was, in his own words, 'a hacker' when he first came to Test cricket. He also chose Lara as a better player:

> Whenever there was a challenge thrown at him, he just had that ability to step up and take you down. I watched him score 680 runs in three Tests against us in Sri Lanka with Murali, Vaas, all of them in top form, and a series where him having scored 680 runs by himself, the West Indies lost 3–0.

In terms of overall record, there is not much between the two. Sangakkara did play 73% of his matches in Asia, but when he travelled, he averaged 47. It is also worth remembering that his average is split a little because he started as a keeper, where he averaged a very good 40. As a specialist batter, it was 66. He clearly played in a great era, but so did a lot of good players. They didn't make the kind of runs he did.

He averaged 61 in Asia, but 36 on Indian wickets, yet it would be hard to not see him as one of the best players of spin ever, especially considering the amount of turn in Sri Lanka. He never played in a four-Test series, which goes both ways; he never got to cash in when he was on top and he also never got worked over by bowlers. He stayed at No. 3 when most players of his quality moved to four in that era.

One issue for his top five case is how little he plays anywhere. Only in England does he play more than eight Tests. His averages in England and South Africa are 41 and 36 respectively. He wasn't tested enough to know if these are solid; the same as his average of 60 in Australia.

But we know what he could do there. In the 2015 ODI World Cup, he made 541 runs from his seven matches, with four hundreds in a row. It was actually five in seven, as he made another one against New Zealand just before. So across two nations, five teams, at the end of his career, Sangakkara made New Zealand, Bangladesh, Australia, England and Scotland look like amateurs. He would average more than 100, at better than a run a ball. And yet, he has – it is barely believable – batted better in Australia.

A week after Australia had smashed Sri Lanka by an innings and 40 runs in the first match on the back of a massive first innings total, they were playing at Hobart in 2007. Again, Australia made 500 in the first innings. When Sri Lanka made only 246, they were well out of the game, so Australia set them 507 to win. In 3.3 overs, Sangakkara had to come to the crease against Brett Lee, Stuart Clark, Mitchell Johnson and Stuart MacGill. It was Lee who hit him in the back of the neck, and MacGill was spinning the ball out of the rough. At 229/3, he brought up his hundred and he felt as secure as you could be at the crease. If a 500-run chase was possible, it felt like this was the one. But Sri Lanka lost three wickets close together and a couple more from the tail. Now they needed 217 with two wickets left. The game should have been over.

There is a moment where Clark – one of the most accurate, skilful bowlers – hits a length just outside off stump. Sangakkara with the straight bat guides it to backward point with ease. Soon after he backs away, Clark sees him and delivers a full wide one. Sangakkara was miles from the ball, and he still middled it to backward point. Clark went just outside off again; this time it was lifted over the off side, twice off the front foot, another from the back. Mitchell Johnson came on, and with the square and cover boundary locked up, he slashed him finer instead.

Australia had another problem. At this point, their leg-spinner was almost unbowlable because of the earlier assaults from Sangakkara, who treated him with disdain. With bowling outside off stump not working, they decided on just bombing him with short balls, while Lasith Malinga watched on from the non-striker's end.

He did the same to Brett Lee, but with the quick coming around the wicket and chasing him, he still got it away to the off-side rope. He did that twice, but the second one was incredible. Lee went for his throat, Sangakkara backed away, the ball got large on him and he still middled it over backward point for another boundary. Lee was not playing though, he smashed the middle of the wicket, and the left-hander jumped to the off side and flicked this one to fine leg for another boundary. All three Australian quicks kept going short; Sangakkara kept finding the rope.

Until Clark puts in one more. Because of his lack of pace, Sangakkara is through the shot early, and the ball hits him and balloons to gully. The Australians celebrate while the batter fumes and walks off, looking back at the umpire Rudi Koertzen. One replay and it is clear why; the ball was nowhere near the bat or gloves – it hit his shoulder. Sri Lanka would go on to lose by 96 runs but that score was the ninth-biggest fourth-innings total in a loss. Marvan Atapattu made 80, he was second top scorer. Sangakkara was given out incorrectly for 192.

When I asked Sangakkara about motivation, he said:

I hated this kind of positive reinforcements about your last best innings. [...] You can't recreate the past. Because every day is different. [...]

The same pitch, the same bowlers, the same environment, everything. There are always nuances and subtleties that change. You could have slept a little bit too long, the ball might have been better, and then the pitch would have deteriorated or changed. I allowed myself the time rather than fighting to recreate the past to understand, okay, well, this is it today, how do I now get through the tough times and how do I end up scoring runs?

I actually started putting a lot more value on runs scored and being effective, and understanding how to change that up in an innings.

So I would have periods where I would buckle down. I had periods where I would take a lot more risks. I had periods of acceleration throughout my innings. [...] change is absolutely inevitable and it's a must as long as you change with a plan and with a view to improvement. [...] You just have to be open that every day is a new day and you're batting anew.

If you watched Sangakkara, you know what he is trying to explain here, and he has a very different motivation than many of the other greats. Every single day, he was trying to create the best chance to make runs. It sounds silly because of how obvious it is, but even the batters have egos, self-doubt, personal pride, technical flaws and mental lapses that cause them to fail. Kumar was motivated by trying to overcome all those things every time.

When he says, 'Don't try to protect the reputation or legacy or kind of a career', he is letting you know that he managed to shelve all his normal human flaws at the crease, and create a perfect innings each and every time.

Aravinda de Silva needed to be motivated to be great, Kumar Sangakkara's motivation was to be great every time.

13

MACHIAVELLI

Some batters are supervillains

'Sometimes when you're young, you do stupid things.' – Barry Richards

There is one target, and the batter is obsessed with it. He has his eyes on finishing a bowler with one big blow. While most of the time he would look to find a gap – and it's part of what makes him a great player – right now he wants to hit the ball directly at a fielder. But not just any player, one in particular: the bowler. The moment he gets a chance, he is going to run down the wicket and hit the ball as hard as he can, straight back at the bowler.

It doesn't make sense. Usually, if you are hitting the ball hard, you are looking for a gap or lofting the ball. You want to get a boundary. But this batter does not want any runs from this ball; he wants contact with the bowler, not just anywhere but specifically in one part of the body.

West Indian legend George Headley is the batter, and any spinner could be the bowler. Headley sees the game in a different way than normal players. He believes that if he runs down the wicket and smashes the ball back to the bowler, he can damage their fingers.

He is playing a shot not for runs now but for runs later. One or two big blows on the digits of a spinner means they may not be able to get the purchase they want from the ball, or even bowl at all. Headley is trying to take the bowling unit down.

If that was the only story about him thinking about cricket on a metaphysical level, it would be enough. But Headley knew his plan worked better against spinners, so what would he need to do to take down the seamers? He decided to tire them out, but not in the Alastair Cook way of blocking the ball for days until they are exhausted. Headley would try to hit the ball to either side of where the quicks were. He wanted them doing extra running in the field, so they would have less energy for him.

Years later, teams like Australia would try to tackle this problem. Putting your bowlers at fine leg, deep square, or even mid-on or mid-off means that they will do more running than other fielders. Australian coach John Buchanan toyed with the idea of moving Jason Gillespie and Glenn McGrath into catching positions.

There are reasons this doesn't work. Most of the specialist catchers in cricket are batters because there is a link between the skills needed in each position. While you occasionally get specialist bowlers who can catch well in the slips or gully, it is rare, and trying to make someone do it late in their career doesn't work. The other thing is that bowlers are used to being in the lower pressure spots, and many like it as a break between bowling.

Headley was thinking about these things 70 years before Australian sport science started to get involved.

Some players just see the sport differently. In the Ranji Trophy semi-final of 1981/82, Bombay (now Mumbai) were in a lot of trouble. In fact, they were pretty much done. Bombay had managed 271 in the first innings, and Karnataka recovered from 195/5 to end up with a 199-run lead. But the real problem was that their innings finished on the final day. And in the Ranji semi-finals, a first innings lead is enough to proceed to the big match.

Karnataka didn't just want to win on first innings, though; they had a chance of beating Bombay – the best team in Ranji history – by an innings. And the wicket was spinning sideways. So they went for the kill with their left-arm orthodox bowlers. The occasional Indian spinner Raghuram Bhat had taken eight wickets in the first innings.

Because of this, Sunil Gavaskar decided to promote Suru Nayak, an all-rounder, up the order to No. 3. He was Bombay's only left-hander. It didn't work and he made only nine. By this point, the wicket was really turning, and Bhat was a high-quality bowler. He only played two Tests but took 374 wickets at 22 in first-class cricket.

Gavaskar kept sliding down the order. Part of this was because of conversations he was having with Sharad Diwadkar, the team manager. Diwadkar was horrified at what Gavaskar was proposing. But the little master had his way, and he went out to bat against Bhat's left-arm spin.

Instead of his normal right-hand stance, Gavaskar batted left-handed. Not a switch hit or reverse sweep; he stood there as if he was a left-hander. When he faced the off-spinner at the other end, he would bat right-handed. He simply believed that he would not be able to stay in batting as a rightie with Bhat ragging the ball away from him so much, so he decided to flip over.

Gavaskar told *Open*, the Indian magazine: 'I thought that the way to counter that was by playing left-handed where the ball would turn and bounce but hit the body harmlessly (without the risk of getting out leg before wicket).'

It worked. He batted for ages, blocking out at one end left-handed and conventionally at the other. Bhat got frustrated, as he recalled to *Wisden* years later: 'I tried all my tricks – the faster one, armer, chinaman, yorker. I bowled round the wicket, over the wicket, and used the bowling crease, but Gavaskar played with confidence.'

Bombay had fallen to 176/9, 23 short of the innings-defeat mark, when No. 11 Ravindra Thakkar walked out to join Gavaskar. They pushed the score to 200/9, ending the chance of an innings defeat before Gavaskar shook hands with the Karnataka captain Gundappa Viswanath (Gavaskar's brother-in-law and a great batter himself).

As Abhishek Mukherjee writes in *Wisden*, 'A "veteran writer" accused him of being "above Indian cricket at the time and would do as he pleased," adding that the reasons for his batting left-handed "went beyond cricket".' This sounds like the first time someone played a forward defence. Allegedly someone yelled out, 'it's just not cricket'.

Gavaskar said later, 'If the match was in the balance, I certainly would not have batted left-handed.' As they were just trying to draw the match, it helped Gavaskar because he was not trying to score.

The ability to bat the other way is incredible, even if Gavaskar didn't think it mattered.

Players of his level can do incredible things. Barry Richards once faced a county bowler with only the edge of his bat. Richards now talks it down:

I did it in one county game, just for a bit because there was nothing on the game. Only for one over, and that was it. I bet you can't play it with the side of the bat. Okay, what's the bet? And it was for dinner. But it's a stupid thing to do. That's a bit of disrespect for the bowler. Sometimes when you're young, you do stupid things.

Richards is an incredibly confident person, and you see athletes like him or NBA player Larry Bird using things like this to extend their dominance. Bird once told everyone he would play left-handed in a game when he usually shot with his right. He dropped 47 points. Richards was like Bird, in that he got bored and had to make things harder. But he also knew that stories that you couldn't get him out with the side of the bat probably helped build his legend.

Kevin Pietersen was smashing Sri Lanka at the small P. Sara Oval in Colombo in 2012, when he decided to start switch hitting. It was a blazing hot day, and there was an element of him trying to score quickly before tiredness got the better of him. We also know that Pietersen loved to play the switch hit as a way of opening up the field as part of his game theory batting.

To slow Pietersen down – who was vibing – Tillakaratne Dilshan bowled his part-time off-spin outside leg stump to bowl defensively with a legside field. He didn't have to, he was still finding boundaries on the legside when he viciously played a fine sweep and almost took out Mahela Jayawardene at leg slip, or when he belted a pull shot into the crowd. Even when Sri Lanka put a fielder out for the switch and reverse shots he was playing, he kept hitting them.

Yes, it was hot, and he wanted to dominate. But also, Pietersen wanted to show that he could play any shot he wanted. Left- or right-handed. The genius allowed the dominance.

That is different from Javed Miandad, who has perhaps done more for modern batting than any other player. As a limited overs batter, he started two major fads that still survive today. The first was hitting the ball in the pocket, simply finding a gap on the field where you could pick up two. That wasn't how ODI cricket was played – it was either singles or boundaries – but Miandad would manoeuvre the field around by placing the ball perfectly and taking twos. The Australian team were inspired by this method, and they changed ODI cricket with his style. Dean Jones writes about Miandad being the inspiration for his placement and running between the wickets in his book, *One-Day Magic*.

The second thing he did in ODIs was hit over cover. If you listen to commentary before 2015, anytime a player hit a ball over cover – especially for six – there were gasps.

At a WBBL game in 2018, India's all-rounder Harmanpreet Kaur hit a six over cover from an off-spinner at the SCG. In IPL 2024, tail-ender Karn Sharma hit Mitchell Starc over cover for six. In modern cricket, some teams even have three fielders on the off side to stop the tactic because players have become too good at finding that gap. It was the last place in front of the wicket that was never protected. Miandad did that, and his technical brilliance allowed him to hit normal deliveries with a perfect lofted cover drive, often bringing his two styles together and just chipping it for two.

Those are the things that Miandad would do that others would eventually replicate. There was something else that they could not. When Miandad faced spinners, he would attack them mercilessly and spread the field, then he would get frustrated that it was harder to score quickly. So he would bat in a scratchy way, often going as far as nicking the ball onto his pad to try and bring the field back in. How much of this is his former teammates adding some tax on their stories? We can't be sure. But one thing that is for certain is that Miandad would often intentionally bat in a rough way so that the opposition would change their fields, and to lull the bowler into his trap.

Miandad was a nightmare to bowl at for many reasons. Richard Hadlee said that the biggest issue with bowling to Miandad was he never stood in the same position, which meant your normal length meant little as he batted forward or back in the crease. In Tests, bowlers usually have a well-grooved length that suits their bowling. Miandad wouldn't allow for that.

This is a trick that some batters will use once or twice in an innings, often early on to upset a bowler. Miandad could do it for hours. Bowlers obviously noticed and would get their point or square leg fielder to tell them where he was standing. But even great seamers struggle to land the ball 40cm differently for every delivery. There was no time they could just run in and bowl their best ball, as Miandad would have changed that length on them.

While he didn't invent this method, he mastered the art and was also part of its spread. In modern times, we even had situations like when England batter Keaton Jennings was warned off because he was so far down the wicket on the danger area of the pitch when taking guard.

After 2020, many players were messing up bowlers' lengths. As the Wobbleball became the predominant delivery in Tests, the bowlers became more predictable with their lengths – and crucially, fuller. So, batters around the world started facing some balls from closer to the bowler to make their good bail-trimming length into something they could drive. Not every delivery, of course; even the players who did it a lot would only do it around 25% of the time. But it was enough to put bowlers off.

In a similar style to Miandad, Joe Root would go from down the wicket on one ball to deep into his crease the next.

His England teammates used another method: the Bazball shuffle. There are stories of Denis Compton running down the wicket as the bowler hits their delivery stride. But it really got more famous in the 1980s when players like Dean Jones would do it in ODIs. The difference was that when modern England used this method, it was not always to smash a boundary, but often just to defend or flick the now-overpitched ball away for a run or two.

Ben Stokes and Jos Buttler had been doing it for a while before, but their coach Brendon McCullum was also famous for this method. England had many players trying this at the same time, in what was clearly a plan to upset the lengths of bowlers. It was Miandad – with a Dean Jones twist.

These kinds of ideas, while needing pioneers like Miandad, are pretty standard. But batters have tried more extreme ideas. Zimbabwean Tatenda Taibu used to cut off the top part of his bat handle to make batting easier. When he was young, Hanif Mohammad would shave one half of tennis balls to make them swing violently. He also used a cork ball on concrete. These two things made him handle the fast and moving ball better when he got to Tests.

John Wright has made more runs opening the batting for New Zealand than anyone else. Before Tom Latham, he had almost double the runs of the next on the list. One time he batted so well, he came off the ground and glued his gloves onto the bat handle so that he could replicate the grip from then on.

In the 2007 World Cup final, Adam Gilchrist put a squash ball in his glove so that he wouldn't use his bottom hand too much while batting – 149 from 104 balls followed.

Batters often use weird techniques at times as well. Towards the end of his county career for Surrey, Mark Ramprakash would face left-arm pace bowlers by standing in a position to play an off drive, closed off, as he believed he could play across his front pad when the ball was straight. Australia's George Bailey batted with a similar – albeit even more ridiculous – stance in limited overs cricket when facing fast bowlers. The fact that either of these players had success doing this shows just how talented they both were.

Australian Sid Barnes played 13 Tests and averaged 63 in them. His first-class mark was 54.1. He didn't play more Tests due to the Second World War and because he was too outlandish for the Australian cricket board at the time. He actually had a lawsuit to prove in court that they had not chosen him because of how he was perceived by them. He made cricket selectors take the stand. But he also did weird things in games, such as betting fast bowlers that they couldn't bowl him. Forcing them to bowl faster and straighter, while he picked up easy runs from them because of how good he was against those deliveries.

What about the more conventional problem solvers? In a masterclass with Nasser Hussain on Sky in 2017, Virat Kohli explained the thought processes that went behind his batting. What struck Hussain about the interaction was how brilliant he was as a problem solver, and how much he thought about his own game.

'As a conventional player [...] it is very important to second guess the bowler from their body language. [...] If he is not that confident, he will probably bowl a good half-volley,' said Kohli. He nominates four areas: 'point, covers, straight down the ground, and the on side from midwicket [...] to square-ish midwicket'. When the ball is in the right area, his body already follows because it is in his muscle memory.

While asked about chasing, Kohli replied:

It is an opportunity for me to see the scoreboard, and do something special, and do something that's in my control mentally. [...] I read body language. When players start panicking with a couple of boundaries, that's when you hit the go.

Sometimes you must work out how to play a new form of bowling, like Martin Crowe did when touring Pakistan in 1990. He was beyond his best by this point physically, but still a genius thinker of the sport. Pakistan's reverse swing had gone from one or two bowlers to the entire team, and the Kiwi batters were having all sorts of trouble. Crowe made the decision to play reverse swing purely as inswing.

That doesn't sound revolutionary, as most reverse will swing in. But there is a reason reverse swing is so hard to play, and it goes back to how batters handle fast bowling. Even if you know a quick is reversing the ball, as they come up, it still looks like they are holding it to swing away. In that moment, a part of your brain starts to process that, and then the batter has to recalibrate what is happening as the ball goes the other way. It is why it is more dangerous than normal inswing, because the first instinct is that it might move away. It's also often why it looks like late swing (although some people do believe it swings differently to conventional swing, which almost may make it appear later).

What Crowe did was train himself to play inswing while the ball looked like it was going the other way. In the middle of a match, against the greats Wasim Akram and Waqar Younis, at 90mph, he rewired his brain based on a hunch. When they did swing the reverse away, he missed it, because he was playing inside the line. That also didn't bother him. He was fully in on this theory and able to switch it on or off when needed.

That is the other thing that a player like Crowe can do. Just decide to try something they haven't done before, go against their normal style and make it work in a game.

Perhaps the best player at changing mid-innings is Steve Smith. He told the ABC after a hundred against India in 2024, 'I pretty much change how I bat every different game depending on the surface and what I want to play like.' You may think that most batters do that, but what he was talking about was so much more. 'Today I kind of went back to a double trigger. I started batting outside the leg stump, probably two inches and going across perhaps a little bit further than I would have liked at the start of my innings. I was keeping my leg outside, so I was able to get my bat down on the path that I wanted.' The reason why he was making these changes was that he was going up against Jasprit Bumrah, who in this era has been a nearly unsolvable bowler. Smith was sick and tired of being caught lbw by the Indian's lower bounce. 'I've probably been bringing my left leg across a little bit too far on a couple of occasions when doing the double trigger. And I just can't quite jam the bat down on the ones that skid a little bit.' Smith is making small changes from ball to ball that other great batters would have to practise for weeks in the nets. Yet he can perform a mid-innings autopsy while facing Jasprit Bumrah and make a hundred.

Rahul Dravid talks about Sachin Tendulkar's ability to do that, 'I wouldn't just change in mid innings, but Sachin could do it in mid innings. Suddenly he felt, "Oh I'll keep my bat down now. No, I'll keep it up. No, I'll make an initial shuffle slightly different."'

The most noticeable change Tendulkar made was when batting at Sydney in 2004 and deciding not to cover drive for an innings. Like Crowe, he is going against his muscle memory. If the ball is wide and full, it is incredibly hard not to naturally play a shot he has done thousands of times before.

Australian captain Steve Waugh watched on in amazement that a player could make that decision and stick to it.

Tendulkar faced 436 balls in that innings and didn't play one. Even when he brought up his double hundred, he kept it up. The cover drive was removed from his vocabulary entirely. But he was also an incredible preparer for batting. He knew his contests against Shane Warne would be epic in 1998, so he took his training to another level.

In his autobiography, *Playing It My Way*, he explains how he prepared for the Australian leg-spinner. Essentially, he was worried about the drift, and so he would open up his stance to hit him to mid-wicket: 'I hardly stepped out to him all series and, more often than not, kept hitting him towards midwicket with a horizontal bat whenever he tried to extract extra spin from the leg stump or slightly outside.'

That is the normal bit; what he did next was dig up wickets outside leg stump in the nets, and then get all the leg-spinners he could find to bowl around the wicket into the rough. There was no way to replicate Warne's physicality or rotations on the ball. But the rough outside leg could at least give Tendulkar more time facing from that angle – which outside of Warne was rarely used by leggies.

The opening Test was in Chennai, and Warne bowled beautifully in the first innings, taking the edge of Tendulkar's bat to have him caught at slip. Australia had a 71-run lead at the halfway point. When Sachin arrived for the second time, Australia went with Warne again. Tendulkar used his feet to hit a boundary and to control him; Warne went to that trusted around the wicket method. While the leg-spinner could get wickets that way, it was really about slowing the batter down and giving him an angle that no one ever sees.

But Tendulkar had been waiting for this. He came down the wicket and lofted one over cover to start with, and it didn't stop there. There is one time where Warne decided to bowl around the wicket into the rough. He talks about it in his book *No Spin*:

> He slogged the third ball into the stands at midwicket for six and just carried on from there, ... After a few overs of this, Tub (Australian captain Mark Taylor) asked what I thought. "I think we're f★★★ed," I replied.

That kind of preparation has a long history in cricket. The 'sticky dog' pitch is caused by rain, and then usually sun afterwards. It makes the ball jump up vertically, and it can be dangerous. It turns ordinary bowlers into Joel Garner bowling with a breeze at his back. So, you don't really want to encourage them. But Victor Trumper went the other way.

As a young player he was looking for ways to improve as a batter, so he asked if the SCG curators could specially prepare sticky dog wickets for him. On a very hot afternoon, they flooded the wicket, and Trumper went out to practise on them. You can only assume this meant he got hit a lot. Whether he was training his body to take the pain or finding a technique that worked, he got a lot better at facing this kind of bowling.

At the MCG in 1904, there was a Test match where the wicket was even more sticky than usual. England had been 279/4, before none of their bottom six batters made it to double figures and they were all out for 315. Australia then had to bat on the same pitch. The third-highest scorer was Reggie Duff with 10, and Bert Hopkins added 18 as Australia made only 122. Trumper scored 74. At one point during the innings, England gave up on Trumper altogether. Bowling wide outside off stump. Even on one of the most spiteful wickets ever, there was no point bowling to him.

That is how people felt about Brian Lara. His genius was so obvious that you could see it in the way he walked out to the wicket. But his main skill was placement. It did not matter where the ball was, it mattered where he wanted to hit it.

Australian quick Brett Lee said to *ESPNcricinfo* that if he bowled a full ball on off stump, Sachin Tendulkar would hit down the ground:

So I could bowl six balls on the top of off stump and he would drive me down the ground with the same shot. Brian Lara I could bowl six balls on off stump, and he could hit me six different directions.

This is called hitting around the clock. It is something Barry Richards would do when bored, and it's well known that some players just have the ability to place the ball exactly where they want. But Lee was the second-fastest bowler in the world, and Lara was treating him like he was a county trundler in a declaration innings.

In his house as a child, Lara would play a game with his brother where they would try to hit a golf ball with a stick between objects. Potted plants, outdoor furniture, whatever they could find. The entire game was about hand-eye coordination and then placement. They would play this kids' game for hours on end. Lara said of this:

The minute you hit the plant, that is no runs. And I think I developed that desire to get value for my shots every time that I played. For me, I had this mental picture where, when I walked out to bat, I knew where everybody was. If I wanted to get a single, to get off the mark or if I wanted to take advantage of a bowler and score boundaries, I knew where every single player was. You play that game of chess where you have the captain moving players into certain positions to create other gaps for you, so I was in full flow.

Jimmy Adams said:

Find footage of a Test match in England on the '95 tour. He scores 100 at nothing. Ding dong. And look at the field they set for him. I promise you, between slip and cover point, they have like eight fielders. It felt like there were three people on the third man boundary.

And they couldn't stop him. They couldn't stop him.

'Wherever Michael Atherton has put fielders, Brian Lara has completely ignored them,' says David Gower on commentary. This is Lara making a hundred at Trent Bridge in 1995. Atherton had a gully, point and cover point to stop him. Lara went finer, despite the fact it was a perfect length ball on off stump. It was a back foot guide from a full ball from the middle of the bat to third for another boundary. The wagon wheel shows 16 boundaries; two to mid-on and a couple more behind square on the legside. The other 12 start at third, and every 10 metres, there is another a little straighter. A dozen off-side boundaries, and never the same one twice, like he was trying to hit a different part of the boundary each time.

Wagon wheels have been drawn for over 100 years for batters. Never has one been drawn so perfectly to show where a captain had placed the field. You could see every field change in where the boundaries were hit. Atherton stuck a fielder on the off side and Lara hit it next to them. Atherton moved them near the entire side there and Lara still found the gap.

And they couldn't stop him. They couldn't stop him.

14

THE LIST

Ranking the greatest Test batters

'The first 50 is the toughest.' – Abhinav Mukund

'What would Gilly do?' This phrase changed and saved my life.

In my teenage years, everything started falling apart for me. The decisions I made were either self-destructive or just out of fear. After leaving school early, I had more than 20 jobs. None were any good or really meant for me. Eventually, I worked in a call centre, with a steady income at least, but my work and life were eating me from the inside.

Around this time, a change or the end would have to come. Cricket was the one thing that did give me joy – mostly Adam Gilchrist, who was finding his peak as I lost all my form.

Watching him bat was what I thought Tests should be: an explosion of colours and music all happening at once. And there was jeopardy there. You knew he was about to fail; no one could do what he was without that. But that is what made it spectacular: the tension.

What was most amazing about Gilchrist was not the sixes, fours or even his dismissals. It was the moment after a mistake. He would swing wildly at a ball outside off stump, miss it and then shrug it off. The mistakes were part of it. Sometimes the ball goes over the rope and sometimes it finds a pair of hands. There will always be more balls. This is not the only one.

Crucially, the last ball wasn't as important as the next one.

I started thinking about my life like an Adam Gilchrist innings – not slogging but taking big swings. When some of them didn't work, it wouldn't stop me from taking the next one because I invented my own phrase: 'What would Gilly do?'

This may not seem like information you need in a book like this, but there is a reason it's part of the story. Because no matter how important Adam Gilchrist is to me personally, when I made this list of the 50 greatest Test batters, the great Australian wicketkeeper did not make it.

Saving my life only got him to No. 51.

Perhaps all the players who didn't quite make the list are really 51, spiritually. It's an arbitrary cut-off. Maybe there are only 32 all-time greatest, or maybe there are 74. Of course, every single part of this is subjective so it's okay if you wanted Gilchrist higher – I did.

Gilchrist's strike rate is a huge boost for his inclusion, and he is the only No. 7 I even considered. But he played in a great batting era and did so as a fully formed player, without ever having to learn his own game at Test level. And he had the comfiest entry point in Tests ever. When Gilchrist came to the crease, Australia had a median score of 241/5. That's like being carried to the crease on a sofa by your mates.

That is how harsh I had to be on players because the list of the greats of batting was longer than 50. Mike Hussey had an incredible argument, but like Gilchrist played in a batting era and then also didn't have to struggle like other players did when they were picked younger. He still had a hugely strong case, but only made runs in Asia and Australia (though, it was a massive amount). The third modern Australian not to make it was David Warner. The amount of runs he made and the rate they came at were huge, but he didn't make runs overseas, and he just never handled it when the bowlers took over in the second part of his career. Michael Clarke averaged less than 40 on the road in a period where that was about par. Australian middle-order batter Doug Walters has a similar record to Clarke with more power and faster scoring, but he struggled so much away and batted down the order.

Bill Lawry and Bob Simpson have good numbers, and at various times I had each in the top 50. Eventually, though, there were other players I wanted more. It is hard to overlook players with these kinds of records. In fact, because of the high averages on Australian wickets, lots of Aussies have huge records. But not opener Bill Ponsford, who averaged more than 60 in England, but played only 29 matches. Stan McCabe has incredible numbers batting in the middle order, but when you slice them, he made 784 (28% of his career total) runs in seven drawn Tests, averaging more than double his record in result Tests.

You could add in more Australians: Sid Barnes, plus openers Arthur Morris and Bill Woodfull as well. Morris would probably make it onto the list if it wasn't for Alec Bedser who dismissed him in almost 24% of his innings in Tests. All were fantastic players, but none quite pushed out anyone else from this list.

You could include VVS Laxman just for a couple of innings alone, but again, others did more overall.

The Vijays – Merchant and Hazare – both had good claims. Hazare was fantastic, but his limited runs on the road were the issue, and in a 30-Test career, he had one hilariously bad tour of the West Indies that tanks his record. Merchant's first-class average of 71.6 was incredible and he certainly made runs on English pitches the few times he toured. He is like Martin Donnelly and Stewie Dempster from New Zealand – they just didn't play enough Tests.

Barry Richards was the other one. If this was simply the greatest batters of all time, he and Merchant probably make the list. But neither played enough. Richards played only four Tests when he was still young. He had another five Supertests around a decade later. In those nine matches he averaged 75.8. His first-class record is also astonishing. Looking at footage of his best knocks, he certainly looks next level. Players from all generations had him in their top five batters ever, despite the lack of Test runs. He should be higher, purely on talent, but I have nine matches of information to use, and you can't say someone was a great Test batter from four official games.

South Africa had another two fantastic players in Dudley Nourse and Bruce Mitchell. Nourse was a fantastic batter whose career was split by the war. When I dived deep, I realised that while he made Test runs in England, he never made any in first-class matches. With a more rounded record, he could have been a top 50 player, but with only 34 matches I couldn't be sure. Mitchell also had the war in the middle of his career. He did make the most of his runs in draws, which downgraded him, and he was not quite as good on the road (and never against Australia). Mitchell was unlucky to miss out. My metrics love him, and I often looked more fondly on the great players on both sides of the war. Ultimately, his first-class record is far lower than in Tests, and he only played two teams (three, if you count a couple of Tests against New Zealand), starring against England and really struggling against the Aussies.

Another dour South African is Gary Kirsten, opening the batting and averaging almost 50 away from home. However, he averaged around 38-43 in most of the years. His consistency was a marvel, but he really had no top end. He made a lot of runs in draws, and when South Africa lost he went at 22.5. He was clearly a classy batter, but by the end of the series he struggled. It was like bowlers could work him out over a period.

While researching this book, I fell in love with Peter May's batting, watching almost every clip from YouTube, but he struggled away from home. The former editor of *Wisden*, John Woodcock, told Mike Atherton that Denis Compton was the best England batter he saw, but he averaged 37 on the road. I love how attacking he was, but I do think there is a romanticism about him that includes being a star in a war-torn country, a great athlete and his general swagger.

Not choosing David Gower made the doves cry, especially as he was such a good bat when travelling. However, his problem was getting starts and never going on. He was also destroyed by the West Indies at home (weirdly, not when touring) and was just okay in India. But he just got squeezed out. Also, how do you work out the overall quality of Basil D'Oliveira, who we only saw when he was in his late 30s.

Talking of old fellas, Graham Gooch was unlucky not to make it. The second half of his career was epic, and he had a huge amount of his runs against the great West Indies attack, but he still didn't average 40 when batting away. When England won, he almost averaged 60;

about a third up on his normal record and way more than in draws. He was also on English wickets against great bowling line-ups in a tough batting era. He did all this for 17 years during a terrible time for English cricket. But the truth is, the more layers you peel off any great batter's record, the harder it gets to be sure of anything.

There are so many great batters not on my list, many not mentioned here. If you ask me in two years' time, I could easily frame things differently and play with the order again. In fact, I feel like I'll be moving and updating this list for the rest of my life. It's already taken up a few years.

While I have allocated a number to each player, in truth I've put players into tiers and every batter has a range. So, while I might have a player at a certain number, I could make the argument they could be higher or lower fairly easily.

Like many batters told me during this book, 'the first 50 is the toughest'.

Tier 50–45: Just

Mohammad Yousuf might be dizzy from the number of times he was in and out of this list. He was a beautiful player, but he struggled in Sri Lanka, India, Australia and South Africa. However, he was fantastic on English and New Zealand wickets. He did spend a lot of his career batting at No. 5, tucked in behind Saeed Anwar (who was unlucky to miss out), Inzamam-ul-Haq and Younis Khan. He was probably just below great when travelling overall, but from 2000 to 2009 he never averaged under 40 in a year, and teams really had no idea how to get him out. He also has the most runs ever in a year, 1788.

Clyde Walcott and Everton Weekes are two-thirds of the three Ws from Barbados, and these two have very odd records, with big holes when on the road and against better sides. However, they still made massive runs when they got in, including against the good sides at home. Walcott could have averaged more had he not kept as well, probably. Both average more than 55, so people generally have them higher on these kinds of lists. But there are some issues with their records. Weekes' record is so damn crazy; he was one of the best players ever in the first innings, where he averaged 76, and that kept going down until it was only 28 in the fourth. He made no runs in losses but was spectacular in wins and draws. In England and Australia combined (the best attacks he played), he went at 30. Walcott's record has many of the same issues when playing good teams when travelling. And he kept.

Neil Harvey never lived up to how awesome he was as a young player, and that stops him from being way higher on this list. He was a true batting artist who struggled against England, but he certainly destroyed other teams. He averaged more than 50 on the road, and unlike most Australians, more than at home. He was incredible against spin and in South Africa, and some use his record against what was a poorer team there against him. I went deep on Harvey and while I found things I didn't like (he struggled against bowling attacks that averaged under 30), he was incredible against Hugh Tayfield, who was an off-spinner who should have troubled him. The great West Indian offie Sonny Ramadhin also struggled with the quick feet. I can't go through the complete records because no one has them, but it seems like Harvey was so good against off-spin that it overcomes many of his other issues.

Of the three Ws, the West Indian captain, leader and all-rounder Frank Worrell was the best everywhere. He didn't just score at home or against the poorer teams; he averaged 47 in England as well. Even if his overall mark is under 50, his numbers look more robust than Walcott or Weekes. He also never batted more than 23 times in any position. With a proper spot in the order, he's a better player. And he was already great. With his high backlift and lightning feet, his batting has been overlooked by the historical importance of his statesmanship.

Another West Indian gets in here too. Rohan Kanhai had a huge career but because he didn't average 50, people have forgotten him. He went at 61 in Asia and 58 in wins, with 48 in draws. So it wasn't flat-pitch batting that did it for him. He averaged 40-plus in all places – a steady consistent player across a long career. I had him as 15% better than the top-order batters in the matches he was in, but when I looked at the guys he batted with and against, he was outperforming great players with the bat. I think he is one of the most overlooked players of all. His work up the order was overshadowed by Garfield Sobers and Clive Lloyd, but he was a great No. 3 that allowed the others to thrive and crucially play their way.

Tier 44–43: Drop ins

This is the tier where I picked two guys who were the hardest to work out.

Born in India, but representing England, KS Ranjitsinhji played only 15 Tests over six years (the fewest on my list). He would have been in more, but he often was overlooked for racist reasons when teams were chosen by local venues, and his skin colour and ethnicity didn't play well in all parts of the UK. But he averaged 45 in an extremely tough era and his first-class record is even stronger. It is hard to make a case for him as a guaranteed top 50 player, but his numbers are obscene for his period. Ranji was 55% better than his era's top order and 40% better in matches. Those numbers put together with the reports on him really suggest greatness.

I know that Victor Trumper scored at a rate that would be fast now, in a time when these things did not happen. He was also the best sticky dog wicket player, and he really opened up what batters could do. His average is not impressive by today's standards, but it was in his era, and when paired with his ability to strike boundaries and handle the worst wickets, there is no doubt he's one of the best. His teammate Clem Hill was one of the first great left-handers and is unlucky not to be on my final list.

Tier 42–37: Ethereal and the magic feet

This tier has a lot of guys who are fantastic against spin, or just make batting look easy.

Kevin Pietersen's ability to win a match in a session and the fear the opposition had for him played a huge part. He batted in a great period and in a very good team, but clearly was an outlier in terms of talent and impact. He's contentious at times, but hey, as someone once said, that's just the way he plays.

Hashim Amla on the road was great against the best teams, but often struggled against the poorer ones. When he was on form, he made batting look liquid. He batted in a great era, but South Africa is always tough, so his numbers really do hold up.

Martin Crowe was a friend of mine, and I would have loved to find a way to push him higher. He worked out reverse swing and went at 45 against the West Indies in their prime. His peak was glorious, but he never matched it with runs. His era was one of the tougher ones, and New Zealand wickets are low scoring on top of that.

Mahela Jayawardene was an almost perfect player of spin, but outside of Asia there was not a continent he averaged over 41. His batting was a combination of your nicest dream and technical mastery.

Andy Flower was dour and wasn't tested at the highest level enough. However, he averaged well over 50 for Essex. I ultimately don't know where he should end up, but his class is not up for debate. He averaged 54 in Asia and 43 in losses. There are some issues, like he played only three Tests against West Indies and Australia – the best two attacks of his era. Pakistan he was fantastic against, and he's famous for how he played on Indian wickets. He did all this as a keeper as well. Thanks to the black arm protests (where he stood up against Zimbabwe president Robert Mugabe), he probably ended his career early. In the last two years of county cricket he averaged 70. It might be the toughest record to truly judge – a keeper who captained with almost no support in a losing team, ending his career early without ever playing against the best players.

Inzamam-ul-Haq averaged over 50 in the first three innings of Tests; he was a grizzly bear who could ice skate. Australian and South African pitches slowed him down, but he was class in most places. Made two hundreds back-to-back in the West Indies seven years apart; Curtly Ambrose and Courtney Walsh bowled at him in both.

For me, there is a clear separation between this tier and the next one. This is where the players really start to hit another level.

Tier 36–33: Heavy hitting and the new ball

Clive Lloyd's overall average is lower than some, but that is deceptive. He averaged pretty much the same at home and away. He was brilliant in Australia and India, and good on English decks. That shows his incredible flexibility. He was another player who didn't cash in on the poorer attacks of his time.

South African giant Graeme Pollock is another hard-to-work-out player; he just didn't play a lot of cricket. He would smash balls from a good length with his long levers and was not someone who moved his feet much. But he also picked gaps in the ring like he brought his protractor to the crease. Many people of his era have him as a top 10 batter, but he doesn't have the kind of cheerleading that Barry Richards received. He made a lot of runs at home but still went at almost 50 away. He wasn't tested at all against top-quality spin. I pushed him down because his Test average is a lot higher than his first-class numbers. However, many people would claim he is a top five candidate on talent, and a full career probably has him a lot higher.

Matthew Hayden and Virender Sehwag both get a boost because of their strike rates. They obviously had places where their style didn't work, but when they did, they won Tests. They changed games so quickly and gave captains the 'ick' before each game.

Tier 32–30: Kane and the middle order

Kane Williamson looks so in charge of his movements when batting, like he's a 16-year-old having a net against the under-12s. His overall Test average is unreal, but it's built against weaker sides. He struggles against Australia, India and England, and in South Africa. Those are the best attacks he's gone up against. He's made some great knocks on luminescent green wickets at home. He's incredible at making runs, but not against the best teams. He's still mid-career, so this may not be his final resting spot.

Steve Waugh and Shivnarine Chanderpaul were both greats of the middle order, but when their teams needed them to bat higher, they didn't. It is hard to ignore that on a list of players who batted in harder positions. Both were incredibly hard to get out once that ball was soft, and had hardcore mental attitudes that made them want to face one more ball.

Tier 29–26: The openers

Somehow, I ended with an opening cluster here. Alastair Cook was a player who won series. He was incredibly limited – perhaps the most of any other player on here. But he negated the new ball and averaged more than 44 in seven locations. His playing of spin, while less sexy than stained Y-Fronts, was very effective.

Gordon Greenidge played the moving ball well and made a lot of runs on Indian wickets. His last few years brought down his overall average. But teams feared him, and unlike the other attacking openers, he had a technique that worked in all conditions. He was at his best limping in a fourth innings, that's quite the epitaph.

Like Lloyd, Graeme Smith's batting was overshadowed by his captaincy. Also, he was not pretty. His ability to drag the ball across the line every delivery is not what sells tickets. He was a massive man who loved the nudge. But he was a beast when travelling, averaging a shocking 13 runs more. The reason he is not higher is simply that he didn't make more runs at home, or quite conquer Australia or India. It doesn't matter how ugly he was, this guy made a lot of runs.

Now I get to the man who kind of knighted himself, Geoffrey Boycott. Sure he was selfish, but Boycott averaged 54 in wins and 52 in draws. He won matches with his batting, even if he burned a few partners along the way. The Tony Greig accusations of Boycott dodging the fastest bowlers seems quite overdone. Outside of a blip in New Zealand, his consistency in different locations was matched only by the fact he said the same thing on repeat when commentating for years.

Tier 25–22: They make batting look good

Here I have Virat Kohli, AB de Villiers and Javed Miandad. Younis Khan wasn't at this aesthetic level but had some very pretty shots.

This as your middle order should sell a billion tickets on artistry alone. Kohli has one of the best records by an Asian batter in Australia and South Africa, but he averages 33 and 36 in England and New Zealand. He is still playing, and had a form dip for a few years, but in 2023 he had a mini comeback followed by a terrible 2024. The Wobbleball and India making their wickets toxic to batting really changed why he ended up here. But his peak was just supernatural. His career slump coincided with writing this book, so it is still raw for some people.

AB de Villiers averaged more than 40 in every country where he played more than five innings. They made him keep, and he has the highest average of any gloveman ever. He batted in a great era, and down the order behind Amla, Smith and Kallis, so he had a good ride. However, in South Africa, there is no good time to bat, and he was fantastic against true fast bowling.

Miandad was obviously a genius who saw a blank canvas and still painted outside the lines. There is no doubt a lot of his work was built on playing spin and batting at home. But he also handled the lateral movement of New Zealand and England well. He struggled against the West Indies, but played them in their peak.

Younis really never got to play much at home, but would that have mattered? He went at 59 at home, 49 away and 55 in UAE for his neutral matches. No cricketer has had a career like this before, and hopefully none ever will again. He averaged 50 in Australia and England, struggled in South Africa and weirdly the West Indies (who were terrible during his career), and was surely one of the best players of spin ever. If you can make runs in Australia, New Zealand and England, you can play pace as well.

Tier 21–19: Aussie captains

Three Australian captains come up next. Allan Border became known for leadership. He went to the Caribbean and averaged 53 against the most feared bowling line-up ever. That wasn't surprising because Border on the road was warrior-like. He averaged 56.6 away, the fifth-best mark of any major batter. But the difference is he did it when lots of teams had great bowling and the wickets were friendly to them, and he went at 10 more than at home – the opposite of most Australian players. Outside of failing in South Africa – when he was older than an oak tree – he scored runs everywhere. Fought for every last one of them too. He was nowhere near the most talented on this list, but certainly close to the toughest.

People have forgotten how great Greg Chappell was. He wasn't a great commentator and his reign as Indian coach meant his legacy got a downgrade, but he averaged 70 in wins, which is mind-blowing. His ability to score on the legside, from any length, meant setting a field to him was almost impossible. His two issues that keep him from top 15 are that he wasn't great in England, (though still decent), and he only ever played four Tests in Asia. His overall average is 53.9, but at his peak, he went off to play with Kerry Packer's World Series Cricket: 14 matches, 1415 runs, at 56.6 from the Supertests there as well, just further enhancing his record. He had a great record against spin, but those numbers are not in Asia. He did play against the great West Indian team only once, and made a hundred and a 70, after which he really struggled.

Ricky Ponting was one of the greatest players of pace bowling ever, and he ended up a very good player of spin (when not on Indian wickets). In an era of Tendulkar and Lara, he was in that conversation. He didn't have the longevity or early start of those guys, but at his peak he was right there. He also stayed at No. 3 when the other greats took the slightly easier spot at four. It wasn't because he wanted the harder job, but simply put, he looked to change the game, which was easier to do up the order.

Tier 18–14: God and the machines

George Headley is another player who could just go anywhere on this list. His Test average is epic, but he played only 22 matches (making 10 hundreds). The Second World War robbed us of the chance to see how great he was. That he was brilliant is not even really a question. He averaged 94.9 when playing for Jamaica and 64.4 when playing tour matches for the West Indians. So, his average of 60.8 holds up in a way that someone like South Africa's Bruce Mitchell's does not. He only played Australia in five matches, and his average of 37 there is a concern, but he made two hundreds against them. In the first hundred, he made 102 in a total of 193; the second top score was 21. His second hundred was later that tour when the West Indies batted first and he made a hundred with Freddie Martin, while no one made more than 60 for the rest of the Test. And it was the first win of the series for the West Indies. Including the first-class games, he did well on the tour. It would be easier if he played more, but this still feels like a good spot for him. He had a two-eyed stance, played really late and if you bowled short, he ended you. He was a run machine.

Then I have two English players from vastly different eras. Ken Barrington averaged 50 at home and 69 on the road, which is incredible. But if you look at his record outside of Tests, he averaged

43 in first-class cricket. None of that should detract from the fact he scored more than 6000 runs in Tests going at 58.7. There are other weird things that stop him from being a top 10 player. One of them is the fact that he didn't play a lot of great bowling attacks. He averaged 69 in Australia, which sounds great, but they had a gentler attack then. He averaged 34 against the West Indies, who had Garfield Sobers, Charlie Griffith, Lance Gibbs and Wes Hall. But he did well against South Africa. He played on great batting pitches, which explains his incredible average, but he scored 53% more runs than other top six batters on them. A lot of people suggest Barrington was boring; I'm not sure he should apologise for making this many runs though.

Next I have W.G. Grace. If Test cricket was around from 1866 to 1876, he would have an argument for being in the top four of all time – maybe in the conversation for first. Instead he was the best batter of the 1880s, and not by a little bit. If you look at raw averages, he just looks good, going at 36. But in the matches he played in, he was 78% better than other top-order batters. For context, the only person with a better ratio than him for a long period of time is Bradman. However, it is only from 11 Tests. I did compare him to Arthur Shrewsbury senior and Billy Murdoch, who had similar numbers. But the more you dive in, it is quite clear that while they were both great in Tests, their version of that is nowhere near Grace's. The fact that Shrewsbury had an 11-year career and Murdoch's first-class numbers are not great, suggests Grace was still the best bat in Tests – and not by a little.

The 1880s was also the decade he stopped taking cricket as seriously and put time into his doctor's surgery. So his debut in Tests is when he was past his best and had other things on his mind, yet he dominated. When he turned 42 at the start of the 1890s, he averaged 29 that decade, playing his last Test a month before he turned 51. To be a par top-order batter into your 50s is crazy. What am I even talking about here? You could make a case for him to be as high as No. 9, but also his record in the 1890s is lower, so you could slip him down. On a list of greatest ever batters, he is probably No. 2. But this is about Tests, and so we've got him high in the range as it is.

The big fella could play.

Rahul Dravid averaged 53 away and 51 at home. For one of the best players of spin ever to be that good away, it's something spectacular. Especially as he played on great surfaces at home and had a good portion of his career in a non-batting era. He averaged 42 in Australia (though McGrath and Warne were not in the side for some of it) but struggled in Sri Lanka and South Africa. But if you look at this by continent, he is otherworldly – 40 in Africa is his lowest, then it's 65 in the West Indies, 69 in the UK, 51.2 in Asia and 48.3 in Australia/New Zealand. He batted at No. 3 when he probably would have done better at four if Tendulkar didn't exist. He would need better numbers against the Aussies and South Africans to be in the top 10. You know you are good when your 4.25-inch-wide cricket bat is compared to a wall.

Then you have Joe Root, a great player of spin. He also averages more than 40 against every Test nation outside of the four Tests against Bangladesh and Ireland. His record against Australia is the only question mark. For a while, the lack of conversion caused him some problems, which is why he doesn't average higher. But the deeper you go into his record, the more he's conquered almost everywhere. Smith and Kohli have both had dips over the last couple of years. If Root has a similarly poor run, he could move down. Of the modern players, he made the biggest move during the writing of this book. Part of that was form, but also his increased strike rate. It speaks very highly of him that he was willing to play the team game when his side wanted him to try to be more aggressive under Bazball. When he makes runs, England win, and he averages 64. He is probably the highest player on this list to regularly reverse scoop in Tests.

Tier 13–11: Fringe top 10

This is the group where all players have a solid case for the top 10 of all time, and you could probably argue the cases of some of them.

Herbert Sutcliffe was overshadowed by his own batting partner, averaging 50 in every innings of the match. He was also a gun when he was sent in by the opposition with three hundreds in six matches. He has a similar issue to Barrington; he averages so much more in Tests (60.7) compared to the rest of first-class (51.2), that you start to worry that his Test record is more a lucky selection. He might also have played at a time when it made his Test batting look better. England were the best team in the world then, and they certainly had the best bowling line-up. Australia split three Ashes with them, but mostly had good spin bowling. If Sutcliffe had an issue with pace, it may have been hard to tell, but he did average 41 against a weak, but often fast, West Indies line-up. When you dig further there were a lot of the fastest bowlers of his era who seemed to trouble him (Mohammad Nissar, Tim Wall, George Francis, Herman Griffith and Manny Martindale). That is enough for him to just miss out on the top 10. This is the point where I really start nit-picking greatness.

Kumar Sangakkara played 73% of his matches in Asia. But when he did travel away from Asia, he managed to average 47. In fact, he averaged more than 43 against all nine Test-playing nations. He played in a great era, but did have to keep during some of it. He wasn't tested enough in Australia, but played one of the best innings ever there and averaged 60. He went at 41 in England, 35 in South Africa and 36 in India. But his overall mark is still mid 50s when touring. The England one does feel like a blip, because when he went back to play for Surrey after his international career, he played 33 matches and averaged 63. He did all of this, and his father will still be disappointed he wasn't second on this list.

A lot of people will focus on Wally Hammond cashing in on a bad New Zealand side. He did. But he still averages 54 without those matches. I know he struggled with the short ball, but it wasn't delivered a lot in his era. West Indies bowled that to him a lot, and he averaged 35 against them, and 25 in the Caribbean. However, he went at 62 in Australia with the extra bounce. His away average is 66, if you take out New Zealand, it is still 58. The West Indies is the question mark, but he clearly was a delight to watch.

Tier 10–4: Legends

Jacques Kallis wasn't box office, but he had a technical purity that is often ignored. His ability to make runs everywhere is what gets him this high. His only blip is England, but he was brilliant against the lateral movement everywhere else. He averaged 41 against Australia – that's good, but not great. He also struggled against Sri Lanka; Murali got him six times out of 10 Tests. But he was incredible in games when no one made runs. He was also a great player of spin, especially in Asia. If you look at it from a pitch extremes point of view, he averaged 55.6 in Asia, 48.2 in Australia, and 53.6 in South Africa, England and New Zealand combined (that drops to 42.8 without his home wickets). That means he was a plus or great batter when the ball spins, bounces or seams. This isn't a normal player. Sometimes I wonder if coach Bob Woolmer invented him in a lab.

Because of his batting position, Garfield Sobers' numbers didn't pop as much as you'd think on my metrics. But when he did bat up the order, he was better. Unlike other players who chose to bat lower, Sobers was batting down so he could bowl Jimmy Anderson level overs, and he could also take a Test away in an hour. If he and Kallis have similar numbers overall, the rate at which they affected games was miles apart. It would take Kallis a day to beat you, while Sobers did it in an hour. He didn't make runs against New Zealand, but that feels like a blip as they were a poor side then, and he handles the moving ball brilliantly in England. He went at 60 against England and more than 80 against India and Pakistan. Australia was 43, but when over there, it was 46.3. That also doesn't include Sobers' 254 against the Australians when playing for the World XI. Not making runs in New Zealand and Pakistan does tarnish his overall record, but there is no doubt he was a great player who could do nearly anything he wanted to with the bat in hand.

One thing not talked about a lot with Viv Richards is he wasn't at the same level in the second part of his career. After 45 matches he averaged 60.2, while it was 44 for the rest of his career. Part of that was that he played on too long, like Miandad and Ponting. Despite being arguably the greatest player of pace ever, he averaged 44 in Asia. The biggest question over Viv's high spot is likely the fact he never faced the best bowlers because they were in his team. Pakistan were the best attack he had to face, and he averaged 42 home and away. Another West Indian who couldn't work out New Zealand but had a strong record everywhere. His averages don't scream top 10. But when you add the fact he was the second-quickest scorer ever among the top six batters, that changes things. The pressure he put on bowling line-ups, and the rate at which he swung the game for the West Indies was worth a lot of runs off his overall mark. He still averaged more than 50 in an era when almost no one did that. But he was more than a number; he was a one-man batting attack.

The one thing that is wrong about Sunil Gavaskar's legacy is that he was the man who stood up to the mighty West Indian attack. When they fully assembled in the Caribbean, he played them in six Tests and averaged 30. However, almost everything else about him is undervalued. He averaged 51 in Australia, and more than 40 in England and New Zealand combined. That is bounce and movement, on top of the fact he was probably the best player of spin ever. He did average 38.5 in result matches, while 65 in draws, but he averaged more away than at home. He was the first guy to score 10,000 runs and he had a 16-year career. If he had a weakness, it would be that he struggled in the first innings of matches (I see this more in his record on Australian, English and New Zealand wickets). He made runs everywhere against all sorts. And to be an opener who averaged 50 in his era, and batted for that long (in terms of individual innings and career) is a marvel. A stubborn, complete warrior.

There was a time when Steve Smith looked like he was fighting for a spot in the top three all time – maybe as high as No. 2. But he's had a dip, and a weird late-career decision to become an opener. It was basically impossible to get Smith out on a flat wicket before Jofra Archer hit him with a bouncer. That, and the Wobbleball era, did bring him back to normal greatness. He still averages 85 in draws. He was always terrible in the fourth innings (until almost winning a game for Australia at the start of 2024, while opening the batting in a chase). He goes at more than 44 against every team (except two Tests against Bangladesh), and averages more than 40 in every nation (except Bangladesh again). He played against India, South Africa, England and New Zealand when they all had great attacks, and averaged 56 against them overall. On the road, it was 52. To average more than 50 away from home against the best bowling attacks of your generation, to have no blips or bubbles in your career, and still achieve high 50s, despite the second part of his career coming in a great bowling era, is obscene. Steve Smith hates watching cricket, so he tries to bat as long as possible. He nailed it, and for a while it looked like he might clock batting.

Brian Lara was the first man to make 400 in a Test and 500 in a first-class match. He is the only man to have held the world record twice in Tests. Yet, I think most of those records don't give you the complete picture. He has the second-highest average of any players in lost matches (minimum 2000 runs). His only real failure was against India, when he averaged less than 35. Against everyone else, he was 41 and above. He went up against the great Australian attack at 51. He batted in a tough era. When the pitches got better towards the end of his career from 2000 onwards, he averaged 54, despite being beyond his prime. He is a plus on every single metric I have. He was one of the best players of spin ever and great against pace. Only Bradman scored a larger percentage of his team's runs than Lara. He was style, he was grace but he was also runs.

Bryan Stott was one of Len Hutton's teammates who I hunted down. We spent an hour talking about how great the Yorkshire opener was. He talked about timing, how orthodox he was, and how it simply was that he didn't make mistakes. For each ball, he would reset, start again and diffuse another bomb calmly.

Something I love about Hutton is that he was a great player in the fifth Test of a series. That is when he had time to work out a bowling attack and went at 85 in those matches. Hutton played before and after the war, missed some crucial years and didn't make as many runs as he should have. In Tests it was 6971 with an average of 56.7; in first-class, 40,140 at 55.5. He did all this opening the batting, which is what elevates him. Unlike most of the batters on this list, he didn't cash in against the poorer attacks. The best bowling he faced was from Australia, South Africa and the West Indies; home and away he was above 50 against all those teams. He broke the world record with 364 when he was 22, but then didn't play a Test from the ages of 24 to 29, thanks to the war. Oh, and during his time out of the game, he injured his arm in training exercises and it was shortened by an inch or two. This meant that when he came back to cricket, he had to do so using a slightly different technique. So, at the age of 30, having missed some of his peak and with a shorter arm, he played 66 more Tests, scoring 5626 runs at an average of 54.6 while opening the batting. Colin Cowdrey said:

> He was always in balance. When he played forward his head, his left knee and front toe were always in perfect, text-book position. Nothing seemed more certain than the fact he would go on making hundreds... I became a total disciple of the way he played.

There is no doubt Hutton was not as pretty as others, but we like runs. And I don't know if there is a better description than when Cowdrey called him a 'fabulous automaton.'

Top 3: In another timeline

That gets me to the top three. The problem with this as an intellectual process is that in most cases when you are looking for the top 50 of something, everyone wants to know who is No. 1. Here, we all know who it is going to be.

So I looked at this differently. Independent of Don Bradman, could Jack Hobbs or Sachin Tendulkar have claims of being the greatest Test batter?

Hobbs' career is epic. The man made so many first-class hundreds, people still argue whether it is 197 or 199. He started Test cricket in 1908, and in 1929 (his penultimate year) he averaged 57. He had 13 high-quality years and 11 of them were great. And that is with a world war in the middle of it all. He is in the conversation for number one because he averaged over 56 across 22 years in two incredibly different eras, when no one had ever batted at a level even close to that. Before the First World War, no one had ever averaged 50 and he was at 57, more than 10 higher than his closest competitor, Warren Bardsley. At that stage, his ratio was nearly as good as Bradman's.

After the war until his retirement, he was good but not the same. The world caught up. Patsy Hendren, Bill Ponsford, Bill Woodfull, George Headley, Wally Hammond and Sutcliffe all arrive, as well as Don Bradman. At that stage, Hobbs is one of the elite players, not the obvious standout. Sutcliffe plays 25 Tests with Hobbs, he averages 77.3, while Hobbs is still great at the other end, at 58.2. But if you are the best player of all time, you shouldn't be dominated by your understudy for that many matches, even if you are no longer in your prime.

R. C. Robertson-Glasgow wrote in his book *Cricket Prints* about how he bowled to Hobbs:

He had strength of thigh and forearm far above the average, a strength which was concealed in the art of method and grace of movement. His footwork was, as nearly as is humanly possible, perfect... All his strokes, that is, all the strokes in the game, were equally strong and easy; they were of an even perfection...

Others talked of the incredible relaxed pose he had at the crease, everything in balance and sync.

There is the issue of bowling attacks. Hobbs' problem is that he could face only one great bowling attack during his career: Australia. England was the other. His record against South Africa shows how much they struggled with the ball. Aubrey Faulkner was truly the only regular world-class bowler they had during that period, and he was beyond his best for some of Hobbs' career. Cyril Vincent was a fine left-arm orthodox bowler and Jimmy Blanckenberg tried very hard, but neither were stars. Hobbs' numbers more than hold up against Australia, averaging 54.3 in total, and then even slightly more when touring, but those numbers are not Bradmanesque.

The biggest issue for Hobbs' case is first-class cricket. Until the Second World War many people would suggest it was as strong, if not stronger than Tests. Hobbs before the First World War really struggled in first-class cricket to be anywhere near as dominant as in Tests. In England from 1905 he averaged 26, 41, 37, 37, 41, 37.5, 33 and 42. By 1913, he would have averaged 50 and 59. Even when you take out his Test numbers, he still averaged 50.1 in first-class cricket over his career, but that is a long way short of his Test number.

What bumps him back up?

Hobbs played more than enough Tests, and showed he was a clear level above everyone before Bradman. Once you factor in the 197 or 199 first-class hundreds, he gets another boost. He missed key years when he was by far the best batter in the world to a war as well. And in terms of first-class numbers when he was beyond his peak, from 1924 to 1930, he made 16,616 runs at 58.5 and 66 hundreds.

He had as many years as Bradman did, but his peaks weren't as great. If he'd kept scoring at the same levels of pre-war better than everyone else, he'd have a case for being the No. 1. Instead, No. 2 is as high as he can get.

Let's look at Sachin's case. I think it is stronger for the No. 1 position than Hobbs.

The one tricky issue for Tendulkar is that during a large part of his career, his entire team could make runs. I know they had other great batters – two are on this list, others are not far away. That is probably a bigger issue for his numbers at home, but since he scored more runs on the road, I am not too bothered. No one else has ever had as many great years as Sachin (12) and no one has ever had as many plus years (18). India did not have to worry about the No. 4 position from

1989 to 2013. Bradman and Hobbs were robbed of years because of the wars; but even then, Tendulkar played for longer. That is because he made his Test debut at 16.

The only other player with more than 15 Tests in their teenage years as a top six batter is Bangladesh's Mohammad Ashraful, who averaged 22. Tendulkar entered his 20s with 1405 runs at 46.8. That is a higher mark than some players on this list of greats ever achieved.

After turning 35, he made the third-most runs ever: 4139 at an average of 49.9. You could argue that his numbers as a teenager and an old man are still great. There was not a single time over this incredibly long career when he was not great. Not to say he didn't have bad years – six times he struggled. So, he just had the 18 years when you had an above-average player for your nation.

In 10 different countries, he averaged more than 40. Five of them were over 50; New Zealand, the West Indies and South Africa were over 45. These were things that Hobbs and Bradman never had to worry about, especially learning how to play different teams in new locations. Tendulkar was tested over nearly a quarter of a century in two very different eras in a way no other batter ever has.

With a normal batter, you can work out which were the best attacks they faced fairly easily. With Tendulkar, it is almost impossible because he played for so long. The West Indies in 1997 was a tough tour, he averaged 57 there. That attack included Ian Bishop, Courtney Walsh and Curtly Ambrose. In five Tests, the latter never dismissed him.

South Africa was his other great challenge, and he averaged 46.4 when touring there. Shaun Pollock (nephew of Graeme) gave him some issues. But mostly he handled himself well against Allan Donald, Makhaya Ntini and Dale Steyn. Tendulkar was not quite as good in Pakistan, another great attack for the years he was playing there, but he went at 40.2, facing Abdul Qadir, Imran Khan, Waqar Younis, Shoaib Akhtar and Wasim Akram.

He played 20 Tests in Australia against the team that was by far the most dominant and longest lasting of all the good sides he had to play against. In 1991/92, Australia was still assembling. In 2003/04, they were without Warne and McGrath. So, even if I take those two series out, he still goes at 50 when touring Australia. So that completely holds up. He was clearly one of the better players of spin and pace simultaneously, which is a massive plus.

There are some things that slightly downgrade him, like batting at No. 4 when Hobbs and Bradman were higher. But he made runs everywhere, against all bowling types, post- and pre-Hawkeye, in an amateur system that turned professional, and he had to do it all being the most famous person in India.

Hobbs and Bradman were famous, but they were from smaller countries. Tendulkar had to live with fame daily in a way no cricketer had before. The pressure on him each innings was unrivalled. It is perhaps why batting became the only thing he seemed to care about. And he was freaking awesome at it, even as his life was not his own anymore.

But was he better than Bradman? No.

If you wanted to make a range of possibilities for Tendulkar, I think you could have him as high as No. 1 just because of his longevity, consistency and travel around the world. But you cannot replicate Bradman's runs, impact on games or how much better he was than his peers.

The argument against Bradman you hear the most now is that he played against postmen and plumbers. He did. So did everyone else in his era. None of them averaged 70.

The best bowler for much of Bradman's career was Clarrie Grimmett, Australia's (New Zealand-born) leg-spinner. He bowled so slow that most modern batters would reach every single ball of his on the full. But when he played, he took 216 wickets in 37 Tests at an average of 24.

Bradman ruled an era of the game that was easier than Tendulkar's. But it's because he batted the way he did the game would have players like Tendulkar.

As of July 2024, there are 334 players with more than 2000 Test runs. That is a lot of people, most of whom made it because of their batting talent. And there are no bad players on this list. Sure, a couple of bowlers slipped in, and there's no doubt some guys were given incredible goes by selectors. But to make 2000 Test runs is something special, and Bradman averages almost 40% better than second place.

There were only two top teams in Bradman's era, and he didn't have to face Grimmett, Ray Lindwall, Keith Miller and Bill O'Reilly because they were on his side (although he did face them in first-class cricket and smacked them). India and New Zealand were struggling in his era. West Indies and South Africa were slightly better, but it was England who had a professional setup for 100 years before Bradman, yet he managed to average almost 90 against them.

Australia is historically a great place to bat – something I have tried to account for here, but Bradman was better away. By that, I mean England because that is the only place he ever batted in a Test outside home. So there are no holes in this resumé, even when noting how limited his experience would be compared to a modern player with 52 Tests. How would he have gone on Indian and Sri Lankan wickets? Would the South Africa or West Indies attacks have bothered him away? These are all valid questions. But he was so good at what he was allowed to do, I can only assume he'd still have destroyed them all.

I wish Don Bradman had been tested against more left-arm seam, four fast bowlers trying to knock his head off, data analysis, video critiques, taller bowlers, faster bowlers, Asian wickets, the Wobbleball, DRS and reverse swing. But I also wish he had played as a professional on covered wickets, with juicier bats and proper protective equipment.

Outside of being a prisoner of the time he played, Bradman's other issue is sticky wickets, which he hated. And Bodyline. Take the pitches first. I think this strengthens Bradman's claim, as he was essentially a player from the future sent to destroy batting-friendly surfaces. The old method of wickets was never part of his plan.

What about Bodyline, where Bradman failed but still averaged 50 (albeit some of those runs were not against that method of attack)? It proves he was human, but if his failures are as good as everyone else's greatness it is hard to hold it against him. It kind of proves he was at least part alien or God.

I spent months looking for anything that would change the fact that Bradman was the greatest Test batter who ever lived. There was no evidence of it. For more than 70 years, people have been playing for second place.

15

THE BALL

157.5 grams of perfectly balanced wood and leather

'Cricket's oldest ball is not a trophy of the bowlers,
but a victim of the batters.' – Jarrod Kimber

English willow is the tree people talk about in cricket, but the Portuguese Cork Oak, or *Quercus suber*, is just as important. This is what's used for the cork in cricket balls. The tree is delivered in sheets to cricket ball manufacturers, who then grind it down in a giant hopper and put it in a mould until it's the size of a table tennis ball. There is often rubber used in this phase. Dukes – who have been making balls since 1760 – import theirs from Malaysia as they believe they are of the best quality. It is the inner core.

Modern Kookaburra balls have a plastic reinforcement to strengthen the outer core from within. This has more cork and sometimes leather glued together to give the ball its density and shape. The ball is then placed in a clamp and wound incredibly tightly with five layers of yarn. It is finer than wool but has no elasticity, allowing the ball to bounce evenly.

The leather must be of the highest quality available. It needs strength and flexibility. Too much of one and not enough of the other makes for a poor ball. When the right cowhide is found, it needs to be dyed using a colour called 'Test Match red'.

After 48 hours of drying, it is sliced into precise shapes to assemble on the ball. Other leather is often glued inside to ensure it stays in perfect shape. The ball is put back into a clamp and both sides come together so that the four pieces of leather of a Test ball can intersect. The skill of this cannot be understated. Hand-stitched cricket ball making is considered by Heritage Crafts to be a 'locally extinct' craft, no longer practised in the UK.

It takes a seasoned professional 45 minutes just to finish the stitching with the linen to bring the ball together. The best cricket balls are usually completely handmade with between 72 and 80 stitches of linen. They need to be flawless. This skill is often passed down through families – two, three or even four generations of people who make perfect cricket balls. It takes 6–12 months even to be good enough to make club balls. Doing it all the time can affect people's eyesight, such is the precision required.

Once this was done in the south of England, around Kent and Sussex. India's Meerut and Pakistan's Sialkot are now some of the biggest hubs.

With the ball stitched up, it is then put back in another mould and shaped to ensure it is perfectly balanced. A cricket ball needs both yin and yang. The ball must be checked to ensure it is no less than 155.9 and no more than 160 grams. The last part of the manufacturing process is adding a nitrocellulose lacquer with a spray that keeps the leather strong and allows the ball to shine. Each ball will be checked to ensure it is perfectly spherical.

It is then stamped, wrapped in paper and put in a box to be sent to whoever has bought it. Most Test balls are bought by the local ground, because they are used for regular first-class matches and Tests.

Before the match, they will be checked by umpires and match referees. Then the bowlers of each team will pick out the ones they like. Some bowlers go for feel in the hand, others the look of the seam and many just think the reddest ones are best.

The ball is then marked, and the umpire is tasked with taking it out on the ground. When the bowling team is on the field, they pass the ball, which ends up with the fast bowler after double-checking their bowling mark and performing any last stretches.

After all this time, the ball is ready to fulfil its destiny.

The oldest-known cricket ball is at Lord's in their museum. William Ward batted for three days in 1820 and scored 278 runs. One of his ball victims survived. The red is gone, the ball is scratched and flat spots are there from Ward's huge bat landing on it so many times. So cricket's oldest ball is not a trophy of the bowlers, but a victim of the batters.

Ward was facing under-arm bowling with a huge plank of wood. Grace added footwork when facing over-arm, and the art of batting was born.

W.G. Grace isn't remembered because of his famous beard and belly. Grace is remembered because of the runs he scored. But what is more remarkable is how he scored them, inventing a balletic art form.

From there, others added to it. From Ranji's leg glance, Trumper's legside play, and the Mohammad brothers and their reverses to Dilshan and Marillier opening up the final part of the ground. The Australians added the running, Miandad found empty pockets and Viv Richards showed us the impact of power.

From a time when the most important shot was the forward defence to the go-to move of clearing the front leg in T20 cricket, the best players can do both. AB de Villiers faced 228 balls at Cape Town and another 220 in Adelaide, both against Australia. He never passed 43 runs in those knocks. He also made 43 against India from 297 at Delhi to try to draw another match.

That was in 2015. That same year, in an ODI, he faced 44 balls against the West Indies and made 149 runs.

De Villiers can reverse sweep Lasith Malinga in a T20 match or block out Ravichandran Ashwin and Ravindra Jadeja for 354 minutes. You give him the canvas, and his ability to mimic what has come before blends into whatever your side needs that day.

He is not a batting pioneer; he is what has come before him in excelsis.

The bowler has the ball in his hand, 76 stitches, and the nitrocellulose lacquer makes the Test Match red glow in the murky mid-morning light. He tosses it from hand to hand, scheming, breathing, and then finally it rests in his fingers. Not straight, but the linen of the seam is angled towards the first slip. A relaxed first step, but the urgency and pace grows. The ball is jerked around, up and down on the run in, cocked in the wrist – firmly, but not tight. It is brutal, mechanical and sleek. Each step leaves a footprint, a history of the act of violence that is to come.

Then, a leap. Up and forward. Followed by a ba-doom sound. Back foot first, then front, violently crashing into the heavily pressed turf. The war cry of the carnage that is about to come. The human catapult unfurls the ball, it is not pushed by the fingers. It travels too fast to be contained by them any longer.

The ball hums from the revolutions that are imparted by the motion. The bowler doesn't hear them as he collapses on himself like he's been punctured by an arrow. The batter hears nothing else.

This is the first of 480 occasions where it will be flung down; if it is lucky, it will hit the stumps one every 344.8 times. And that is what it wants. What else is the point of being a ball? You want to break through past the batriarchy that controls, bashes and destroys you, skipping past the security guards of pads and onto those stumps.

Three vertical sticks with two small alarms on the three pieces of common ash – 71.1cm high, with a maximum diameter of 3.49cm. A big point at one end that penetrates the ground. Just five random bits of wood. Alone they are nothing, but together they are the holy grail of cricket.

I think of all of this as I thud into the ground, my seam slicing into the surface, taking with it a blade of grass as a souvenir. I feel the jolt of the cold, moist, rolled grass and the savagery of the deceleration. Now I am on a new path as I adjust my line toward the stumps. All I need is one mistake: the batter overcommits, loses their balance, swings their willow late or crooked. Just anything. A rush of blood to the head, and I can achieve my destiny.

But the bat is under the head, in perfect synchronisation with the foot, and I crash into the middle of the blade: 5cm from the edge, 15cm from the curved toe. I feel myself compressing on impact as I am hammered, but not straight, as the blade was opened at the last moment to steer me. I bounce repeatedly over the coarse square between cover and point. The fielders both see me; I barely get a wave as I fly by. They slowly turn to chase rather than stop; they know it is futile.

I now roll through the lusher grass in the outfield for seconds until I slap the padded boundary triangle, where I am flipped up and then hit a metal sponsor's logo and fall embarrassingly onto the ground. The sun flicks through the morning clouds to show that I'm wedged behind TV wires while the cameras are on the batter. He is shown as a hero for dispatching me while scratching at the ground like a bored rooster as I wait alone for someone to come over and pick me up.

I am 157.5 grams of perfectly balanced wood and leather, crafted by a leader in the field to British Standard BS 5993, which specifies my precise construction details, dimensions, quality, and performance. I am perfect, created with love and care from animals and trees. I have 479 more deliveries in which to achieve my destiny to bowl a Test batter. They win this one, but they will feel my wrath.

They always do.

THE TOP 50

Ranking	Player	Country	Range
50	Mohammad Yousuf	Pakistan	46–60
49	Clyde Walcott	West Indies	45–58
48	Everton Weekes	West Indies	45–58
47	Neil Harvey	Australia	40–55
46	Frank Worrell	West Indies	45–55
45	Rohan Kanhai	West Indies	45–55
44	KS Ranjitsinhji	England	38–60
43	Victor Trumper	Australia	40–60
42	Kevin Pietersen	England	40–60
41	Hashim Amla	South Africa	37–55
40	Martin Crowe	New Zealand	40–50
39	Mahela Jayawardene	Sri Lanka	35–45
38	Andy Flower	Zimbabwe	35–55
37	Inzamam-ul-Haq	Pakistan	33–39
36	Clive Lloyd	West Indies	29–41
35	Graeme Pollock	South Africa	35–55
34	Matthew Hayden	Australia	33–37
33	Virender Sehwag	India	33–37
32	Kane Williamson	New Zealand	30–37
31	Steve Waugh	Australia	27–37
30	Shivnarine Chanderpaul	West Indies	27–37
29	Alastair Cook	England	27–32
28	Gordon Greenidge	West Indies	26–35
27	Graeme Smith	South Africa	26–35

26	Geoffrey Boycott	England	26–32
25	Virat Kohli	India	22–32
24	AB de Villiers	South Africa	22–32
23	Javed Miandad	Pakistan	22–32
22	Younis Khan	Pakistan	21–25
21	Allan Border	Australia	20–26
20	Greg Chappell	Australia	19–25
19	Ricky Ponting	Australia	17–23
18	George Headley	West Indies	14–37
17	Ken Barrington	England	5–18
16	W.G. Grace	England	8–37
15	Rahul Dravid	India	12–20
14	Joe Root	England	10–18
13	Herbert Sutcliffe	England	8–25
12	Kumar Sangakkara	Sri Lanka	8–14
11	Wally Hammond	England	4–14
10	Jacques Kallis	South Africa	4–12
9	Garfield Sobers	West Indies	5–12
8	Viv Richards	West Indies	7–13
7	Sunil Gavaskar	India	5–10
6	Steve Smith	Australia	4–7
5	Brian Lara	West Indies	5–11
4	Len Hutton	England	4–7
3	Jack Hobbs	England	1–3
2	Sachin Tendulkar	India	1–2
1	Don Bradman	Australia	1

BIBLIOGRAPHY

Arthur, M., *Taking the Mickey* (Jonathan Ball Publishers SA, 2010)

Bracewell, P. J., Farinaz, F., Jowett, C. A., Forbes, D. G. R. and Meyer, D. H., 'Was Bradman Denied His Prime?,' *Journal of Quantitative Analysis in Sports* 5(4) (October 2009), pages 1–26.

Cricket Archive, www.cricketarchive.com

Crickether, https://crickether.com

CricViz, 'Our Database', https://cricviz.com/our-database

Desai, A., 'The Role of Age in Red Ball Batting Performance', *Boundary Line* (18 January, 2023), https://medium.com/boundary-line/the-role -of-age-in-red-ball-batting-performance-377d7d89afe4

Dexter, T., *From Bradman to Boycott: The Master Batsmen* (Queen Anne Press, 1981)

Felix, N., *Felix on the Bat* (Eyre and Spottiswoode, 1962)

Ferriday, P. and Wilson, D., *Masterly Batting: 100 Great Test Centuries* (Von Krumm Publishing, 2013)

Gollapudi, N., 'This is Virat', *The Cricket Monthly* (3 June, 2015), www .thecricketmonthly.com/story/877745/this-is-virat

Hall, K. G., director, *That's Cricket*. Australasian Gazette, 1931. 3 min 08. www.nfsa.gov.au/collection/curated/asset/96624-thats-cricket-don -bradman

Harvey, N., *My World of Cricket* (Hodder & Stoughton, 1963)

Jayaraman, S., 'Couch Talk 130 - Gordon Greenidge', *The Cricket Couch* (6 August, 2014), www.thecricketcouch.com/couch-talk/transcript-couch-talk-with-gordon-greenidge

Jones, D., *One Day Magic* (Swan Publishing, 1991)

Kimber, J., 'Sri Lanka's Brothers in Arms', *ESPNcricinfo* (14 June, 2014), www.espncricinfo.com/story/jarrod-kimber-sri-lanka-s-brothers-in -arms-752527

Kimber, J. and Chiwanza, C. W., 'Heinrich Klaasen's World', *Cricket8* (27 March, 2024), https://cricket8.in/heinrich-klaasens-world

MacDonald, R., 'The Two Eyed Stance', *London Daily Mail* (9 January, 1924), https://trove.nla.gov.au/newspaper/article/136622646

Miller, A., 'The Advent of the Finisher', *The Cricket Monthly* (3 September, 2023), www.thecricketmonthly.com/story/1377642/20 -greatest-odis-no--14---australia-vs-west-indies--hobart--1996

Monga, S., 'When I Really Wanted Things to Go Well, I Tried to Control the Outcome Through OCD', *The Cricket Monthly* (22 November, 2018), www.thecricketmonthly.com/story/1164565/-when-i-really-wanted -things-to-go-well--i-tried-to-control-the-outcome-through-ocd

Mukherjee, A., 'The Pre-Root Leftie Route: When Gavaskar Batted Left-handed in a Ranji Trophy Match', *Wisden* (6 December, 2022), www .wisden.com/series/england-in-pakistan-2022-23/cricket-news/joe -root-sunil-gavaskar-batted-left-handed-ranji-trophy

Old Ebor, 'The Extinction of the Sticky Wicket: The Confusing History of Pitch Covering' (17 May, 2022), https://oldebor.wordpress.com /2022/05/17/the-extinction-of-the-sticky-wicket-the-confusing -history-of-pitch-covering

Old Ebor, '"The Most Perfect Batsman I'd Ever Seen": How Good was Wally Hammond?' (8 March, 2022), https://oldebor.wordpress.com /2022/03/08/the-most-perfect-batsman-id-ever-seen-how-good-was -wally-hammond

Pandey, D., 'Footwork, Judging the Length are the Key to Playing Spin: Sunil Gavaskar, *The Indian Express* (18 December, 2020), https:// indianexpress.com/article/sports/cricket/footwork-judging-the -length-key-to-playing-spin-sunil-gavaskar

Perry, R., *Bradman's Best: The World's Greatest Cricketer Selects His All-time Best Team* (Corgi, 2015)

Perry, S., 'Australia Need to Look Beyond "Hardness" and Aggression to Fix Batting Woes', *The Guardian* (22 November, 2016), www .theguardian.com/sport/2016/nov/23/australia-need-to-look-beyond -hardness-and-aggression-to-fix-batting-woes

Pietersen, K., *KP: The Autobiography* (Sphere, 2014)

Ponting, R., *At The Close of Play* (HarperSport, 2014)

Pycroft, J., *The Cricket Tutor* (Leopold Classic Library, 2015)

Ramprakash, R., 'Bairstow is a Proper Batter but Coaching Him is Tricky Because he is so Instinctive', *The Guardian* (5 March, 2024), www.theguardian.com/sport/2024/mar/05/jonny-bairstow-batter -england-100-caps-india-cricket

Ranjitsinhji, K. S., *The Jubilee Book of Cricket* (William Blackwood & Sons, 1898)

Samiuddin, O., 'Is Saeed Anwar Criminally Underrated?' *ESPNcricinfo* (23 April, 2020), www.espncricinfo.com/story/come-to-think-of-it-is-saeed-anwar-criminally-underrated-1221202

Sangakkara, K., 'Kumar Sangakkara Underachieved in his International Career: Kshema Sangakkara', *The Indian Express* (25 August, 2015), https://indianexpress.com/article/sports/cricket/did-kumar-sangakkara-achieve-his-true-potential-i-dont-believe-so-kshema-sangakkara

Sawai, A. 'When He Batted Left-handed', *Open* (13 August, 2010), https://openthemagazine.com/sports/when-he-batted-left-handed

Stabroek News, 'Former WI Cricketer Lawrence Rowe Apologises' (21 June, 2011), www.stabroeknews.com/2011/06/21/news/guyana/former-wi-cricketer-lawrence-rowe-apologises

Tendulkar, S., *Playing It My Way: My Autobiography* (Hodder, 2015)

The Cricketer, 'A Dilemma as Old as T20 Cricket: Running for Running's Sake and the Last Ball of the Innings...' (14 March, 2020), www.thecricketer.com/topics/features/a_dilemma_as_old_as_t20_cricket_running_for_runnings_sake_and_the_last_ball_of_the_innings.html

The MCC, *The M.C.C. Cricket Coaching Book* (The Naldrett Press, 1952)

Warne, S., *No Spin: My Autobiography* (Ebury Press, 2018)

Wigmore, T., 'Nervous 90s? How About Calling Them Selfish Instead?' *The Cricket Monthly* (21 July, 2017), www.thecricketmonthly.com/story/1109585/nervous-90s--how-about-calling-them-selfish-instead

Wilson, D., 'The Curious Case of Don and the Sticky Wicket', CricketWeb.net (30 September, 2009), www.cricketweb.net/the-curious-case-of-the-don-and-the-sticky-wicket

Woolmer, B., *Bob Woolmer's Art and Science of Cricket* (Struik Publishers, 2008)

YouTube, 'Kevin Peterson's Batting Masterclass: Best Batting Tips, Techniques and Tutorials', [video] (uploaded 1 March, 2021), https://www.youtube.com/watch?v=5INjpGd5LMw

YouTube, '"Never Heard More Crap in my Life!" Haddin hits back at Atherton column | Willow Talk', [video] (uploaded 15 February, 2024), https://www.youtube.com/watch?v=fUKqBoPszHA

YouTube, '"The Best Cover-drive in the World" – Mithali Raj', [video] (uploaded 8 November, 2018), https://www.youtube.com/watch?v=h2oZCErdTTo

YouTube, 'Virat Kohli: The Complete Batsman | Batting Masterclass with Kohli & Nasser Hussain', [video] (uploaded 28 January, 2021 [filmed in 2017]), https://www.youtube.com/watch?v=m8u-18Qos7I

YouTube, 'Virat Kohli V Sachin Tendulkar, Who Makes the Ultimate XI? | Bumble & Kimber', [video] (uploaded 16 May, 2024), https://www.youtube.com/watch?v=ATD-laXNGfM

IMAGE CREDITS

Introduction: E. Dean/Topical Press Agency/Getty Images
Chapter 1: William Vanderson/Fox Photos/Hulton Archive/Getty Images
Chapter 2: Hulton Archive/Getty Images
Chapter 3: MARCO LONGARI/AFP via Getty Images
Chapter 4: Patrick Eagar/Popperfoto via Getty Images
Chapter 5: Fairfax Media via Getty Images via Getty Images
Chapter 6: Mark Leech/Getty Images
Chapter 7: Mike Hewitt/Getty Images
Chapter 8: Adrian Murrell/ Allsport/Hulton Archive/Getty Images
Chapter 9: Picture Post/Hulton Archive/Getty Images
Chapter 10: Evening Standard/Hulton Archive/Getty Images
Chapter 11: Fox Photos/Getty Images
Chapter 12: Adrian Murrell/Getty Images
Chapter 13: Mark Leech/Offside via Getty Images
Chapter 14: Fox Photos/Hulton Archive/Getty Images
Chapter 15: Harry Todd/Fox Photos/Getty Images

ACKNOWLEDGEMENTS

I am a slogger with infrequent bouts of good batting (three hundreds, a lot of 50s, mostly lazily giving away 20-somethings). My father Peter was my cricket coach, and even though he couldn't bat at all (a number 11, one 50), he was very good at teaching me the basics at Campbellfield Cricket Club, in North West Melbourne. From there, I travelled 15 minutes up Sydney Road to play at Coburg, where I learned about batting from Stephen Mott and Glenn Edwards. They changed my backlift, got my front foot out of the way and taught me to sweep. I still bat with their methods (if not their talent) today.

I have been talking about batting for a long time and this book sums up all those conversations. Some are with players who became friends like Martin Crowe, Jeremy Coney, Matt Prior, Gareth Batty, Iain O'Brien and Brad Hodge. But some are also with my former third's captain Russell House, friend Simon Spehr and former podcast partner Andy Zaltzman.

There are also people who helped more directly. The original idea came from hearing a discussion on the *Thinking Basketball* podcast. From there, it was the people of Bloomsbury who brought it to life, big thanks to Matthew and Caroline. I had huge help from my main researcher Shayan Ahmad Khan, who maybe got more obsessed with batting than I did. Abhishek Mukherjee was always there to tell me Clem Hill should be in the top 50. Subhankar Bhattacharya and Varun Alvakonda for their help with designs and stats. Nilesh Jain helped again with his incredible proofreading skills. Various others helped along the way like Patrick Noone, Osman Samiuddin, Tim Wigmore and Neil Fairbairn.

ACKNOWLEDGEMENTS

But the most important people were those who agreed to interviews: David 'Bumble' Lloyd, Ross Taylor, Ian Chappell, Kumar Sangakkara, Ian Bishop, Mark Butcher, Bryan Stott, Nasser Hussain, Chris Rogers, Barry Richards, Brian Lara, AB de Villiers, Mark Waugh, Jimmy Adams, and Suzie Bates. This is a collection of heroes, communicators and professors of batting. It was an honour talking to all of them.

There were also two standouts. I thought there was no chance Rahul Dravid would be able to chat, as he was India's coach when I was writing this book. But he still made a couple of hours to talk with me, even though it was only a few weeks before India headed to the US and West Indies to win a World Cup. I was also lucky enough to speak to Bob 'Knocker' White. He sadly passed away afterwards, but he did tell me the story where he turned up to play in Kent. He walked out to bat at the start of the day on his own because the rest of his team were stuck in traffic, and so the innings was declared by the umpires. A red inker, rest in runs, Knocker.

And finally, my family. Ezekiel learned to love cricket and batting while I was writing this book. Zachariah gave me advice on the cover. Clem told me all the time she wants to play cricket when she is older. And my wife Miriam, who once asked me to teach her batting but decided for the sake of our relationship that it would be better if we stopped.

INDEX

Rowe, Lawrence   16–17, 17–18
running   104–15

Samaraweera, Thilan   79, 89–91
Sangakkara, Kumar   245
    average   175
    on Aravinda de Silva   195–9,
        215
    on Matthew Hayden   153,
        155–6
    on Jacques Kallis   185
    keeper batters   187
    motivation   194, 208–9,
        215–18
    and peak   161–2
    shooting in Lahore   90–1
    and spin   79, 87–8
    technique   69–70
Sciver-Brunt, Nat   58–9
Sehwag, Virender   23, 24, 69,
        92, 239
    and attack   121–2, 126, 127
    and peak   158
    and running   113
Sidhu, Navjot Singh   76–8
Simpson, Bob   105, 107–8,
        160–1, 233
Smith, Graeme   40, 75, 158,
        201–2, 214–15, 240, 241
Smith, Steve   11, 36–7, 58–9, 70,
        72–4, 227, 247
Sobers, Garfield   42, 44, 120–1,
        184–5, 196, 246
spin   8, 76–103
Steyn, Dale   41, 44, 122
Stokes, Ben   1, 73, 139–41, 224

Strauss, Andrew   155
Sutcliffe, Herbert   107, 169, 244

Taurasi, Diana   47–8
Taylor, Claire   52–3
Taylor, Mark   153–4, 154–5
Taylor, Ross   23–5, 28
Taylor, Stafanie   60, 61
technique   66–75
Tendulkar, Arjun   xii, 185
Tendulkar, Sachin   xii, 91, 250–2
    and fast bowling   34
    Machiavellian plays   227–8,
        229
    motivation   206, 209
    technique   69, 71–2
Thomson, Jeff   45–6, 68, 128
Trott, Jonathan   186, 200
Trueman, Fred   29
Trumper, Victor   3–4, 70,
        131–4, 228–9, 237

Walcott, Clyde   169, 187–8,
        235–6
Walsh, Courtney   149, 151
Warne, Shane   23, 87, 117
    on Saeed Anwar   13
    and attack   142
    and Daryll Cullinan   172–3
    and Navjot Singh Sidhu   77
    and Sachin Tendulkar   228
Warner, David   109, 123–7, 168,
        232–3
Waugh, Mark   33–4, 42
    batting order   183
    on Mark Butcher   152